T0301385

Poverty and Entrepreneurship in Developed Economies

Poverty and Entrepreneurship in Developed Economies

Michael H. Morris

James W. Walter Eminent Scholar Chair, University of Florida, USA

Susana C. Santos

Assistant Professor, Rowan University, USA

Xaver Neumeyer

Assistant Professor, University of North Carolina at Wilmington, USA

Cheltenham, UK • Northampton, MA, USA

Published by
Edward Elgar Publishing Limited
The Lypiatts
15 Lansdown Road
Cheltenham
Glos GL50 2JA
UK

Edward Elgar Publishing, Inc.
William Pratt House
9 Dewey Court
Northampton
Massachusetts 01060
USA

A catalogue record for this book
is available from the British Library

Library of Congress Control Number: 2018945846

This book is available electronically in the **Elgar**online
Business subject collection
DOI 10.4337/9781788111546

ISBN 978 1 78811 153 9 (cased)
ISBN 978 1 78811 154 6 (eBook)

Typeset by Servis Filmsetting Ltd, Stockport, Cheshire
Printed and bound by CPI Group (UK) Ltd, Croydon CR0 4YY

Contents

Figures

Tables

Boxes

About the authors

Dr. Michael H. Morris holds the James W. Walter Eminent Scholar Chair at the University of Florida, and was formerly the Malone Mitchell Chair in Entrepreneurship at Oklahoma State University. A pioneer in curricular innovation and experiential learning, he has built top-ranked entrepreneurship programs at four universities. His entrepreneurial outreach efforts have facilitated the development of hundreds of ventures, including extensive work with low-income and disadvantaged entrepreneurs across the United States and in South Africa. Dr. Morris has published 12 books and over 180 scholarly research publications. He is co-editor of the Prentice-Hall Entrepreneurship Series and a Past President of the United States Association for Small Business and Entrepreneurship. A former Fulbright Scholar, he was selected as one of the top 20 entrepreneurship professors in the United States by *Fortune Small Business*. Dr. Morris has been awarded the Edwin & Gloria Appel Prize for contributions to entrepreneurship, the Leavey Award from the Freedoms Foundation for impacting private enterprise education, and the Dedication to Entrepreneurship Award from the Academy of Management. He received his Ph.D. from Virginia Tech.

Dr. Susana C. Santos is an Assistant Professor of Entrepreneurship at Rowan University. She received her Ph.D. from ISCTE-IUL, Instituto Universitário de Lisboa, Portugal and completed her post-doctoral program at the University of Florida. Her main research interests are focused on the cognitive and psychosocial processes of entrepreneurship at individual and team level. Other streams of research include entrepreneurship education, entrepreneurial ecosystems and poverty and entrepreneurship in developed countries. Susana has published in several journals such as *Small Business Economics, Journal of Small Business Management, Journal of Business Research, Creativity and Management Journal, International Entrepreneurship and Management Journal, Journal of Cleaner Production, Journal of Career Assessment*, and *International Journal of Entrepreneurial Behavior and Research*, among others. Susana received the Excellence in the Entrepreneurship Classroom Award at the Experiential Classroom XVI in 2015.

Dr. Xaver Neumeyer is Assistant Professor of Entrepreneurship at the University of North Carolina at Wilmington. He received his Ph.D. in mechanical engineering from Northwestern University in 2014 and his M.Sc. in Mechanical and Aerospace Engineering from the Illinois Institute of Technology in 2006. He also completed a Post-doctoral Bridge Program at the University of Florida. His research interests include entrepreneurial ecosystems (formation, interaction effects, and measurement), as well as how these ecosystems shape or are shaped by entrepreneurs. Xaver has published in several journals such as *Small Business Economics, Journal of Small Business Management, International Entrepreneurship and Management Journal*, and *Journal of Cleaner Production*, among others.

Preface: Making more than a dent in poverty

Developed economies have produced impressive levels of income, wealth, and overall quality of life for their citizens, not only in comparison to most developing countries, but also relative to historical standards. Yet, a sizeable proportion of the populations of these countries remain in poverty. Despite many billions of dollars of expenditures since the 1964 launch of the "War on Poverty" in the United States, the poverty rate remains close to 14 percent – largely where it was 50 years ago. In the European Union, 23.5 percent of the population are at risk of poverty or social exclusion (Eurostat Newsrelease, 2017). And the disparity between rich and poor continues to grow, suggesting a problem in both absolute and relative levels of poverty.

While some might argue there will always be poor people, their sheer numbers, and the corresponding cost both to those who must live in poverty conditions and the larger society, is simply unacceptable. Poverty is not just about a lack of income or wealth, it is a complex and multidimensional phenomenon. It affects and is affected by an array of issues, including housing, education, health, transportation, family relationships, personal safety, job opportunities, career prospects, and psychological and emotional well-being. The barriers that it imposes become all the more formidable as societies become more technology-centric, labor-intensive jobs disappear, and economies continue to transform.

So what can be done? Perhaps we just need to spend more money on housing, food, education, and other support programs. Maybe the need is to spend the money differently, with a more integrated (and perhaps creative) approach that reflects unique needs of poor people in differing circumstances. There are those who would simply let the poor fend for themselves, believing they just have to apply themselves, work hard, and persevere and things will work out. Others staunchly argue for forced income redistribution from the haves to the have-nots, so as to guarantee some sort of living wage. Without getting into the political discussions that surround such diverse positions, this book proposes another possibility: entrepreneurship.

In these chapters, we explore venture creation as a pathway out of poverty. While considerable attention has been devoted to entrepreneurship as a solution to poverty in developing countries (e.g., Amorós and Cristi, 2011; Bruton, Ketchen and Ireland, 2013; McMullen, 2011; Webb et al., 2013), its role within developed economies has received much less focus. Yet, we believe its potential is as great or greater in developed economies, where infrastructure exists, market opportunities can be significant, and entrepreneurship is an established vehicle for achieving economic success.

Entrepreneurship is ultimately about empowerment and transformation. It is about creating one's own future, job, income, wealth, identity, sense of purpose, and ability to give back. It transforms markets, industries, communities, families and individual entrepreneurs. In the final analysis, entrepreneurship involves a mindset, a way of approaching life and the world. It is a willingness to pursue opportunity regardless of the few resources a poor person owns or controls (Stevenson, 1983).

In these pages, we will argue that entrepreneurship is a natural inclination of the poor. As Muhammad Yunus (2005) has concluded, "the poor themselves can create a poverty-free world. All we have to do is to free them from the chains that we have put around them." As we shall see in these pages, these chains are powerful, but they can be broken. Entrepreneurship is not something that is new among the poor. There have always been people who start ventures out of conditions of poverty. In fact, it is amazing how many successful ventures have been created by the poor given the complex burdens that come with poverty and the inherent difficulties in starting a business. The question becomes, what might be possible if the poor had more help?

Entrepreneurship has never been a major policy focus when it comes to poverty. There are relatively few people who believe, or have suggested, that it could fundamentally change the overall poverty landscape. However, this is our position in this book. The challenge is to level the playing field when it comes to venture creation by the poor. It is unlikely the field could ever be completely levelled, as the poor will always have a greater struggle than those with higher income, better education, more extensive networks, fewer health problems, safer surroundings, and more exposure to entrepreneurial ventures, mentors, and role models. But to paraphrase Steve Jobs, we can do much more than simply make a dent in the poverty universe.

In the chapters to come, we first lay out the nature and extent of the poverty problem in developed economies, followed by a discussion of the nature of entrepreneurship and venture creation, and this is followed by an exploration of the challenges and opportunities in connecting the two. We introduce the SPODER framework as a simple model for understanding what is required for the low-income individual to successfully pursue the entrepreneurial path, and the kinds of issues that must be navigated during the entrepreneurial journey. What is known about types of entrepreneurs and types of ventures are then applied to the entrepreneurial efforts of the poor, with insights on why the poor disproportionately create survival and marginal lifestyle-type ventures. The critical role of opportunity recognition is examined, together with ways to expand the opportunity horizons of those in poverty. We next dedicate chapters to exploring the challenges of literacy, technology, and community infrastructure (including entrepreneurial ecosystems) as each relates to a person in poverty when trying to launch a business. Attention is devoted to financing needs and options when one has little income, lacks collateral, and may have no credit history or a low credit score. The central roles of leveraging, bootstrapping, and guerrilla skills in obtaining or accessing resources are then investigated. The tendency of the ventures created by the poor to fall into the "commodity trap," and how this can be overcome, are both reviewed, and ways to improve the underlying profit models of these ventures are identified. Finally, we look at the need for a holistic approach to developing both public policy and community-based initiatives that facilitate low-income entrepreneurs as they prepare for, launch, and grow successful ventures.

The reality is that entrepreneurship in its many forms offers promise to everyone in poverty. This is a promise of self-empowerment enabled by community support for a sector of society that is incredibly rich in entrepreneurial potential. It is a promise not being realized in our most prosperous nations. Our hope is that this book fosters a richer dialog among academics, government officials, policy-makers, economic development professionals, bankers and the financial community, leaders of non-profit organizations, and others committed to moving beyond status quo solutions – committed to finding ways to help people create their own entrepreneurial pathways out of poverty.

Michael H. Morris
Susana C. Santos
Xaver Neumeyer

REFERENCES

Amorós, J.E. and O. Cristi (2011), "Poverty and entrepreneurship in developing countries," in M. Minniti (ed.), *The Dynamics of Entrepreneurship: Evidence from Global Entrepreneurship Monitor Data*, Oxford Scholarship Online, pp. 209–30.
Bruton, G.D., D.J. Ketchen Jr. and R.D. Ireland (2013), "Entrepreneurship as a solution to poverty," *Journal of Business Venturing*, **28**(6), 683–9.
Eurostat Newsrelease (2017), 'Downward trend in the share of persons at risk

of poverty or social exclusion in the EU', October 16, accessed June 6, 2018 at http://ec.europa.eu/eurostat/documents/2995521/8314163/3-16102017-BP-EN.pd f/d31fadc6-a284-47f3-ae1c-8212a581b0c1.

McMullen, J.S. (2011), "Delineating the domain of development entrepreneurship: A market-based approach to facilitating inclusive economic growth," *Entrepreneurship Theory and Practice*, **35**(1), 185–93.

Stevenson, H.H. (1983), *A Perspective on Entrepreneurship* (Vol. 13), Cambridge, MA: Harvard Business School Press.

Webb, J.W., G.D. Bruton, L. Tihanyi and R.D. Ireland (2013), "Research on entrepreneurship in the informal economy: Framing a research agenda," *Journal of Business Venturing*, **28**(5), 598–614.

Yunus, M. (2005), "Eliminating poverty through market-based social entrepreneurship," *Global Urban Development Magazine*, **1**(1), accessed June 6, 2018 at http://www.globalurban.org/Issue1PIMag05/Yunus%20article.htm.

1.   Understanding poverty

Poverty does not belong in civilized human society. Its proper place is in a museum. That's where it will be.
(Muhammad Yunus)

A NATION OF CONTRASTS

Like most Western democracies, the United States is a rich nation. Measured by gross domestic product (GDP), overall wealth, standards of living, asset ownership, and a number of other indicators, America is pretty well off. According to the US Census Bureau (2016), median income is about $56000. Approximately 63 percent of families own homes (and close to 12 percent own a second one), the typical household owns 1.8 cars, 64 percent own a full set of working appliances, and 35 percent take a family vacation each year at least 50 miles or more away from home (American Automobile Association, 2016). The Better Life Index developed by the Organisation for Economic Co-operation and Development, which considers 11 dimensions of well-being, places the US seventh among developed nations (OECD, 2016). The US performs better than all countries on the housing, income, and wealth dimensions, and better than most on health, jobs, education and skills, social connections, personal security, subjective well-being, environmental quality, and civic engagement.

Unfortunately, data such as this only tell part of the story. When considering how a society is doing, we tend to think in terms of averages, such as median income, or GDP per capita. Yet, if we consider the distribution of income or wealth, a striking and troubling picture emerges. One might imagine a small group of wealthy people at the top, a very large middle class, and then a moderately sized group at the bottom. The reality is quite different. As Figure 1.1 makes clear, the distribution is highly skewed, with the top quintile of households accounting for 51.1 percent of income and the bottom two quintiles accounting for 11.3 percent (US Census Bureau, 2015 and 2016). Over 43 million Americans, or about 14 percent of the population, live in poverty, and many more experience low income in absolute terms.

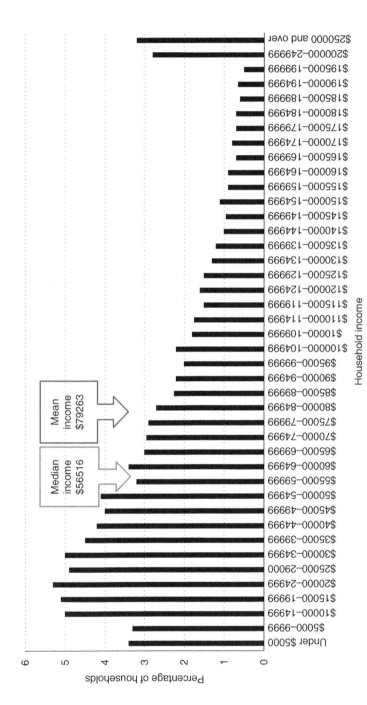

Source: US Census Bureau (2015, 2016).

Figure 1.1 Distribution of household income, US, 2015

WHAT IS POVERTY?

Poverty is not a characteristic of a person, but rather, of their situation. It can be defined in absolute or relative terms. Absolute poverty measures poverty in relation to the amount of money necessary to meet basic needs such as food, clothing, and shelter. The individual or family struggles simply to survive and faces a severely limited set of choices. In the USA, the poverty level is designated by the federal government based on the size of a household. So, as of 2017, the federal government designated a family of four that earns less than $24600 as living in poverty. Clearly, this number only paints part of the picture, as the real costs and abilities to meet a family's needs depend upon geographic location and a host of personal circumstances that define a family's needs (e.g., severe illnesses or disabilities, people outside the household one is trying to care for).

Alternatively, relative poverty considers the bigger picture within a society. While absolute poverty is concerned with meeting basic survival requirements, it does not consider a person's quality of life or how they compare to the way most people live. Recognition of the importance of non-economic needs for a person's well-being led to the creation of the concept of relative poverty. Here, a person is thought to be poor if they do not have the income to maintain the average standard of living in a society. Hence in Britain, a household that does not earn at least 60 percent of the median household income is deemed to be in poverty. As income levels increase in a country, the relative poverty level also increases, which means relative poverty will always be there.

Another perspective is provided by the Human Poverty Index, a multi-dimensional indicator created by the United Nations to assess levels of deprivation in different countries. The HPI considers not only the percentage of the population living below the poverty line (in this case 50 percent of the median household disposable income), but also how long people live (the probability at birth of not living past age 60) and knowledge, as reflected in the percentage of adults lacking functional literacy skills. The data demonstrate significant variations among developed countries, with nations such as Ireland, Italy, Spain, Great Britain, the United States, and Australia demonstrating markedly poorer scores on the combined indicator.

A distinction can also be drawn between generational and situational poverty. Where an individual is part of a family that has experienced ongoing poverty for two generations or more, it is termed generational poverty. Situational poverty occurs when circumstances such as divorce, health problems, loss of a job, bankruptcy, being a victim of serious crime, or some other sort of life crisis leave a person destitute or without sufficient resources to cover necessities. Generational poverty is argued to have its own culture, hidden rules, and belief systems (Payne, DeVol and Smith, 2001).

What becomes evident from this discussion is that poverty is both simple and complex. It is simple in the sense that it indicates a person or family does not have enough in the way of financial resources to meet basic needs. It does not take much to understand that someone cannot afford to pay for rent, transportation, health insurance, child care, or their children's education. At the same time, poverty is complex because it involves direct and indirect interactions among an array of factors that are not just economic in nature. We will explore these factors in further detail, as they have important implications for entrepreneurial behavior.

WHO ARE THE POOR?

Who are these people? One out of every seven citizens in the United States, or 44 million people, lives in poverty. Just under half of them are in deep poverty, defined as living on half or less the official poverty income level. About 10 percent have been labeled the "underclass" based on being permanently poor, welfare dependent, socially isolated, without training or skills, and largely unaffected by economic conditions or social programs (Gans, 1995). Almost 13 percent of US households will experience hunger and food insecurity at some point during a given year.

These numbers break down in some interesting ways (see also Table 1.1). Of those in poverty, 42 percent are White, 28 percent Hispanic, and 23 percent Black (Proctor, Semega and Kollar, 2016). However, Whites constitute a much bigger percentage of the total population. Again, the distribution is skewed, with disproportionate numbers of Hispanics and Blacks experiencing poverty. Women make up 56 percent, and those between the ages of 20 and 40 years old account for 35 percent (and those under 18 represent 33 percent) of the impoverished. Families headed by a single mother tend to be the poorest (if about 10 percent of all families are in poverty, the figure is over 28 percent of those headed by a single mother) (Institute for Research on Poverty, 2017). The poverty rate among children is 19.7 percent, and for those with disabilities it is just under 30 percent. Among adults, 28 percent of those in poverty do not have a high school diploma and 35 percent finished high school but went no further with their education. Just over 16 percent have a disability. Most are native born (83 percent) and live in metropolitan statistical areas (82 percent), while the largest amount of persistent poverty is in non-metro areas (Proctor et al., 2016; US Department of Agriculture, 2018). The poor also tend to

Table 1.1 Percentages of different groups that live in poverty

Group	Percentage in Poverty
Adults having a college degree or higher	4.5
Adults with no high school diploma	31.0
Foreign-born non-citizens	21.0
Hispanic Americans	21.0
Asian Americans	11.4
Black Americans	24.0
White Americans	9.1
Single moms	28.2
Single dads	15.0
Seniors	9.0
All children	20.0
Non-working adults	31.8
Full-time working adults	2.0
Part-time working adults	15.5
Adults with disabilities	28.5
People living in metropolitan statistical areas	13.0
People living outside metropolitan statistical areas	16.7

Source: Adapted from Federal Safety Net (2016).

be concentrated in regions, counties, and individual neighborhoods. One study shows that those in high-poverty neighborhoods have, on average, only $800 in accumulated wealth (Pew Charitable Trusts, 2016).

It appears, then, that poverty disproportionately affects certain groups and regions, but that its impact is also pervasive. The poor are both old and young, men and women, immigrants and long-term citizens, less and more educated, based in urban and rural communities, and from all racial groups. For many of these individuals, poverty is not a temporary thing. It persists over years and sometimes over generations. Among the poor at a given point in time, close to one-fourth are still in poverty three years later (US Census Bureau, 2011). Even for those who technically move out of poverty, more than half do not achieve incomes that are much above the poverty level. A multi-year study by Pew Charitable Trusts (2013) found that 70 percent of those born into low-income families will never move into the middle class.

Another indicator is the receipt of welfare benefits. While most families who turn to the welfare system are on it for a relatively short period of time, over half the recipients at any given point in time will be on welfare for ten or more years. Keeping in mind the high number of single women who head households and live in poverty, the average number of years a woman receives Aid to Families with Dependent Children benefits is 12 (Acton Institute, 2010). And a large number of poor people tend to move back and forth over time, entering, leaving and then re-entering the welfare system. We see similar patterns in other developed countries. Persistent poverty is experienced by 7.3 percent of the population in Britain and close to 12 percent in Germany.

THE COMPLEXITIES OF POVERTY

Poverty is not just about an inability to afford necessities. It often involves the complex interplay between a number of variables. Consider just a few of these. Those in poverty tend to be less educated and have access to lower-quality educational resources. They experience more crime, have higher teen birth rates, endure more serious health challenges, and have more difficulty finding and getting jobs. They frequently come from single-parent households. They tend to suffer more in economic downturns, must deal with more discrimination, are less socially integrated into society, and have personal networks that offer them less access to opportunity.

Consider how any two of these variables affect and are affected by one another. If a person has low income and yet must also endure more crime, and then the crime results in physical injury and so loss of work time, or it results in theft of one's limited resources, the person with little is left with even less. They certainly cannot afford expensive security systems, making them even more vulnerable to crime. Alternatively, the desperate need for money might find the person tempted to pursue better-paying criminal activities. As another example, consider the interplay between needs and debt. Those who are poor often must rely upon higher-cost forms of credit to pay their bills, such as payday loans, automobile title loans, rent-to-own schemes, tax refund loans, and the pawning of goods. Yet paying the relatively higher interest or related costs of such credit means they have even less ability to pay for things over time. Or how about teen birth rates? While these rates are generally falling in developed countries, they continue to be high among teens coming from poor families. Poverty, not promiscuity, is also seen as a driver (and consequence) of teen births (Kearney and Levine, 2012). In fact, two-thirds of young unmarried mothers in the US are poor (National Conference of State Legislatures, 2018). Having a baby at 15 years old can impact whether and how well they finish school, how much they are able to work, and the kinds of jobs they find. The costs of raising the child further add to their economic pressures, and they struggle to provide for its basic needs.

This complex interplay of variables can result in what has been termed the "cycle of poverty" when applied to families (and the "poverty trap" when applied to communities or countries). Payne (2005) has distinguished situational from generational poverty. The former finds particular incidents or sets of developments in life pushing an individual or family into poverty. Examples might include loss of a job, conviction for a crime, bankruptcy, a serious health problem, theft, or being a victim of violence. The latter involves a cycle that passes from generation to generation, where family members find it extremely difficult if not impossible to escape from poor circumstances over three or more generations. Corak (2006) notes that almost half of the children born to low-income parents in the United States become low-income adults, while the number approximates 40 percent in Britain, and 34 percent in Canada.

Ironically, then, while many factors can contribute to poverty (from lack of education and overwhelming debt to discrimination, single parenthood, addictions and a criminal record), one of the biggest causes is simply being born into a poor family. An example of such a cycle is illustrated in Figure 1.2. Here, we see how the environmental constraints that come with poverty can be self-reinforcing, such that poverty can result in an array of physical, psychological, and behavioral challenges or problems over time, which affect one's development of skills and capabilities, and limit one's economic opportunities or ability to get ahead, impacting one's economic choices and decisions, and perhaps one's affective state, keeping one in poverty. While not all of the developments in Figure 1.2 necessarily come into play with a given household, it is likely that many of them do.

The evidence suggests that long-term poverty tends to have a cumulative impact on the individual (Lynch, Kaplan and Shema, 1997; Wagmiller and Adelman, 2009). Children experiencing long-term poverty tend to have lower cognitive abilities and perform worse in school, while suffering from poorer physical and mental health (Blair et al., 2013; Korenman and Miller, 1997; Smith, Brooks-Gunn and Klebanov, 1997). They subsequently achieve lower job status and earnings in adulthood (Hauser and Sweeney, 1997) and even if they achieve higher income, the effects of poverty persist. As the Richmond Vale Academy (2017) concludes, "Poverty places people at a disadvantage that is not only environmental, but also physical and psychological. It affects people's health, how they interact with each other and how they react to external stimuli. It even affects how and why they prioritize certain things, and their academic performance."

Some believe that persistent poverty can also result in a type of "learned helplessness." Here, as they experience the kinds of factors illustrated in Figure 1.2 over a number of years, people come to believe they do not have control over their lives, and thus that success is beyond their control

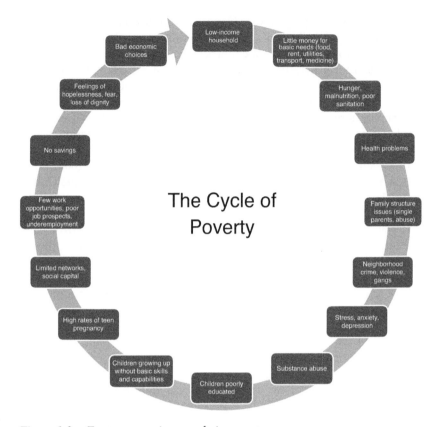

Figure 1.2   Factors trapping people in poverty

(Rabow, Berkman and Kessler, 1983). Such a sense of helplessness can give rise to living only in the moment, irresponsible spending, not saving even if one could, and not responding to incentives when they are offered. The bottom line is that the person loses hope.

Others speak of a culture of poverty. For instance, Payne (2005) concludes that generational poverty has its own distinct culture and beliefs. This notion derives from the work of Lewis (1959) and has produced considerable controversy over the years. Here it is argued that poverty is perpetuated by a set of values and norms that derive from one's lack of material goods and the experiences of those around oneself. Wilson (2012) describes this as basing decisions on a shared understanding of how the world works. While it is doubtful there is one monolithic culture of poverty, it seems likely that a given poverty setting can give rise to shared values, perceptions, and outlooks, and that these can differ meaningfully from those held by those not in poverty. Yet, such a culture need not be deterministic, such that any outcomes based on these values or perceptions are predetermined.

Less clear is any standard specification of the relevant values or norms that constitute a culture of poverty. The empirical evidence here is mixed and limited. There are some misguided stereotypes that have been discounted by the evidence, such as the notions that the poor do not value hard work, education, or marriage (Gorski, 2008; Kohut and Dimock, 2013; Trail and Karney, 2012). They may, at the same time, be less likely than those with high incomes to believe that hard work offers any guarantee of success. Importantly, as Kohut and Dimock (2013, p. 3) conclude based on an extensive values study, "among poor Americans specifically, there is little evidence that they feel sorry for themselves, or see themselves as economically doomed or morally adrift."

But what sort of (potentially negative) values might a continued experience of poverty tend to reinforce? According to some observers, they could include moral cynicism, or a belief that rules and laws were made to be broken or ignored; or acceptance of disorder, whether it relates to graffiti or the conduct of public meetings (Sampson, 2012). Another value might be one's time orientation, and specifically living in the moment versus planning for the future (Payne, 2005). At the individual level, the sense of being marginalized and not belonging, feeling dependent and not in control of one's destiny, or believing that one is unworthy might be prevalent (Blacksher, 2002).

Whether or not such values become commonly held among the poor, they certainly can exist and may make the journey out of poverty a greater challenge. The challenge is greater to the extent that such values are in conflict with those critical for economic success (and in our case, critical for success through entrepreneurship). Yet, there is little evidence that values associated with living in poverty inherently suggest that the poor will not pursue opportunity if it is available.

WHY POVERTY MATTERS FOR COMMUNITIES AND NATIONS

Why should we care about poverty? Left to their own devices, some will find their way out of poverty and some will not. But the impacts on society of ignoring poverty are significant, and they exist at multiple levels (Box 1.1).

Clearly, absent any intervention, some of the poor will die from starvation, severe health problems, exposure to the elements, or abuse from

BOX 1.1 TEN REASONS FOR REDUCING POVERTY

Among the many economic, social, psychological, political, and ethical reasons for addressing poverty, ten pragmatic considerations include the following:

Poverty affects more people than we think. Forty-four million Americans (14 percent) live below the poverty line, and almost one-third of the population cycles in and out of poverty. A much larger group (100 million) are classified as low income and struggle to get by.

Poverty among children is particularly harmful to society. One in five children live below the poverty line and half of all children will be on food stamps before age 20. Poverty can lead to lower cognitive development and educational attainment, and higher rates of incarceration and reliance on public benefits. These children end up with lower lifetime earnings.

Poverty increases health risks. Poor children are likely to have lower birth weights, experience higher rates of food insecurity, and as adults experience higher rates of illness, disease, disabilities, including chronic problems with hypertension and elevated cholesterol. Those in poverty have significantly shorter life expectancies.

Poverty weakens families. The pressure placed on the family from an inability to pay bills or meet needs can result in psychological distress, depression, more hostile family relations, and withdrawal, which in turn can lead to job losses, poor parenting, and high rates of divorce.

Poverty traps people and decreases mobility. People born to poverty are more likely to be poor as adults, undermining the American Dream. Only 6 percent of children born to poor parents eventually become high-income earners.

Poverty costs our economy billions of dollars. All citizens are impacted by poverty, as money that could be used for infrastructure or economic growth supports the poor and externalities created by poverty, such as crime. Child poverty alone is estimated to cost over $500 billion annually in lost productivity and increased health care and criminal justice costs.

Poverty weakens the middle class. The strength of the economy is tied to a stable middle class with strong purchasing power and valuable workforce contributions. As more people slip from the middle class into poverty, consumer spending, saving rates and tax revenues fall. There are downward effects on human capital development and productivity, and more underemployment.

Poverty weakens communities. Long-term, concentrated poverty leads to an increasing income and wealth gap. Children in neighborhoods that experience a 10 percent decline in poverty experience a $7000 increase in family income as adults compared to those in neighborhoods where there is no reduction. Generations of individuals become trapped in economically isolated communities with declining infrastructure, high crime, and limited opportunity.

Poverty lowers the competitiveness of the nation. Poverty dramatically harms long-term human capital development, a critical component of the nation's global competitiveness. Those who grow up in poverty underperform in school, have limited access to higher education, and are less likely to be prepared for high-skill jobs of the future.

Poverty weakens a democracy. Disparities in income, wealth, and access to opportunity are becoming greater, resulting in a system of unequal voices where millions of low-income citizens do not fully exercise their rights. Values of the poor are under-represented in policy prescriptions, which can heighten inequities and conflicts with ideals of equal representation and political equality.

Source: Adapted from Brown (2011).

others, among other causes. Most will live shorter lives. Poor nutrition, housing, and living conditions produce health problems that not only undermine the productivity of those afflicted, with a cost to society, but can also drive up health care costs, particular for medical services for those who have no insurance and cannot afford to pay. Alcohol and substance abuse among the poor further exacerbate a host of other problems, from health problems, spousal and child abuse, divorce, and single-parent households, to job loss and criminal activity.

Poverty also places huge pressure on, and can weaken, the family unit. Children are especially affected, with detrimental impacts on their cognitive development, school performance, self-esteem, socialization abilities, and employment prospects. A critical result is the lower lifetime earnings of children born into poverty. A major study by Holzer et al. (2008) found that the total cost of childhood poverty in the United States was about $500 billion annually.

Crime rates tend to be consistently higher in low-income communities. Criminal activity heightens the stress experienced by poor families, while also undermining their ability to escape from poverty. The cost to society in terms of loss of life, property loss, law enforcement, the judicial process, and prison systems is enormous.

Beyond this, at a community level or neighborhood level, pervasive poverty can result in a hopeless, downward spiral where less money is spent (or remains) within the community, property values and tax revenues tumble, infrastructure declines, businesses leave, opportunities become fewer, and any sort of safety net disappears. The evidence suggests that momentum is everything. Where there is a sense of progress and new possibility, it fosters optimism that feeds on itself, with community members becoming more engaged, trying new things, pursuing more opportunity, and attracting more resources from outside the community (Morris et al., 2011).

If we consider society as a whole, the reduction of poverty offers potentially dramatic benefits. In a fascinating study on the economics of poverty, Duncan, Kalil and Ziol-Guest (2008) demonstrate how investments in specific initiatives targeting children could increase the aggregate lifetime earnings of the poor by up to $36 billion, reduce government spending by up to $500 million, and increase tax revenues by up to $20 000 per child assisted.

Beyond this, the global competitiveness of a nation is harmed to the extent that large numbers of people live in poverty. Those who grow up poor tend to underperform in school, are often unable to pursue higher education, and are less likely to develop the kinds of skills required as the economy evolves. As such, poverty dramatically harms long-term human capital development, lowers productivity, and results in higher underemployment within the labor force. Moreover, the economy is dependent upon a strong middle class. Movement of people from the middle class into or towards poverty leads to a decline in consumer spending, saving rates, investment, and tax revenues.

As disparities in income, wealth, and access to opportunity become greater, the fabric of society is threatened. There is a greater sense of the haves and have nots, leading to more social strife and conflict. Core institutions are questioned. Tensions can result in protests, riots, and destruction of property – and in low-income communities, such properties frequently are not redeveloped, further exacerbating the problem.

ESCAPE FROM POVERTY

The unemployment rate is high among the poor, representing about 37 percent of those eligible to work (Gould, Davis and Kimball, 2015). Yet, this also indicates that almost two-thirds are working, and about 44 percent work full-time. Many tend to move into and out of employment. Unfortunately, the jobs at which they work tend to be among the lowest-paying occupations, with the lowest skill requirements. Jobs themselves tend to be unstable. Leading areas of employment include food service, cleaning and housekeeping, retail sales clerks, laborers, production workers, nursing/personal care aids, groundskeepers/landscaping, child care workers, office secretaries/assistants, and transportation/truck drivers.

Three key problems that hinder a worker's ability to earn an income above the poverty level are low pay rates, periods of unemployment, and involuntary part-time employment. It appears that 85 percent of the working poor who usually worked full-time experience at least one of these problems (US Bureau of Labor Statistics, 2015). Health problems are often a contributor. Unaffordable child care is another major issue among the working poor, especially given the large number of single-parent households.

Yet, poverty does not have to be forever. There are dynamics involved in terms of people moving into and out of poverty over time. Large numbers of people are able to escape poverty in a given year, and the rate at which they do so is relatively stable. Shorter-term or situational poverty is usually driven by some triggering event, such as job loss, reduction in or loss of a source of income, divorce, changes in family structure, or a health crisis in one's family. A study by Stevens (2012b) found that 56 percent exit from poverty within just one year, but the longer one is in poverty the lower the likelihood of exiting. She found the average time in poverty to be 2.8 years. These rates also vary by subgroup, with minorities and female-headed households generally experiencing lower exit rates. There is also a disturbing tendency for the exit to be temporary, with 36 percent of those who escape subsequently returning to poverty within four years.

Research suggests that exit is more likely where the individual is able to stay in a job for at least 30 weeks of the year, maintain his or her level of real wages, and reside in a stable or improving local economy (particularly in terms of the unemployment rate) (Stevens, 2012a). Arguably, the area receiving the greatest attention as a contributor to moving out of poverty is education. Graduating from high school is clearly important, but so too are exposure to quality pre-school programs and access to post-secondary education and skills training (Abner et al., 2015). Waiting until marriage to have children in also an important factor, especially when combined with effective parenting. Transportation is another issue. In areas with long commute times, the availability of dependable public transport (or other forms of transportation) can meaningfully impact the rate at which individuals move up the economic ladder (Chetty and Hendren, 2015). Conversely, limited research on the impact of social psychological variables such as the individual's locus of control or level of personal initiative has not produced significant results in terms of explaining the movement of people out of poverty (Caputo, 1997).

SOLUTIONS TO POVERTY

While many would argue that it has not received enough attention, the reality is that poverty has been a focus of public policy for many decades. In the US, the so-called "War on Poverty" was launched by President Lyndon Johnson in 1964, and in the first few years produced a meaningful decline (about 30 percent) in poverty. Subsequently there has been relatively little change (although the gap between rich and poor has increased). Today, the government spends over $1 trillion annually in cash, food, housing, and medical care to low-income Americans. At the federal level, spending per person is over $13 000. Total spending has increased almost every year for over half a century, and has more than tripled since 1980 on a per person basis (Chetty and Hendren, 2015).

There are conflicting views regarding how successful these efforts have been. The poverty rate has hovered at around 14 percent of the population, with variations above and below, for 50 years. President Ronald Reagan famously noted how it appeared that, in the war on poverty, poverty had won. On the one side, using a more comprehensive measure of poverty, Haskins (2014) concludes that government spending focused on low-income households cuts the poverty rate by about half, and was a major factor in holding down the poverty rate during the great recession of 2008–10 (see also Fox et al., 2015). In a cross-national study involving the US and other developed countries, Smeeding, Rainwater and Burtless (2000) found a significant correlation between social spending and reduction in poverty, but suggest effectiveness is tied to the design of properly targeted assistance programs (e.g., programs that provide child care assistance to single mothers). On the other side, critics argue that the impact of government spending in actually reducing poverty (as opposed to helping the poor survive) has been nominal, and may actually serve to increase dependency and reduce the desire to work (Cato Institute, 2017; Muhlhausen, 2013; Tanner, 2003). The answer is likely somewhere in between and varies by subsector. For instance, poverty among the elderly has been significantly reduced, while there has been a negligible decline among children.

Poverty assistance programs take a number of forms. Chief among these are:

- Earned Income Tax Credits: federal and state programs that reduce tax liabilities and provide a wage supplement work like a negative income tax for low-income people;
- Temporary Assistance for Needy Families: cash disbursements for up to five years with the aim of transitioning someone from welfare to work;
- Child Tax Credit: helps offset the cost of raising children;
- Head Start: provides early childhood education, health, nutrition, and parent involvement services;
- Supplemental Nutrition Assistance Program: known as food stamps, provides a monthly supplement for purchasing nutritious food;

- Women, Infants, and Children (WIC): helps eligible pregnant women, new mothers, babies and young children eat well, learn about nutrition, and stay healthy;
- child nutrition programs: provide breakfast, lunch, and after-school assistance;
- housing assistance: provides rental housing for low-income households, the elderly, and those with disabilities;
- Medicaid: a federal health insurance program for low-income and needy individuals;
- Supplemental Security Income: pays cash to low-income people over 65 years of age and those under 65 if blind or disabled;
- Pell Grants: grants for students from low-income household to attend college and trade schools;
- job training: a variety of programs through the Department of Labor that provide training, displacement, and employment services targeting low-income citizens;
- Child Care: block grant program to states and local agencies who provide child care for low-income families.

Increasingly, many of the key programs and proposals that address poverty reduction focus on employment – creating more jobs for the poor, better equipping them for these jobs, and incentivizing them to pursue jobs (e.g., Abner et al., 2015). And a wide range of new proposals continue to appear. These include: stronger work requirements tied to housing and food stamp programs; payments that subsidize jobs; a higher minimum wage; more programs to reduce teen pregnancy, support family planning, and encourage proper parenting; skill and apprenticeship programs in high schools attended by low-income individuals; changes to mandatory sentencing laws for non-violent offenses; extending the earned income tax credit to single adults; more support for preschool programs; various approaches to reducing the stigmas attached to programs such as food stamps; and simply spending more on particular programs, among others. The general trend appears to be towards programs that target particular problems and groups, a greater focus on evidence-based program design, and better tracking of program outcomes.

WHY ENTREPRENEURSHIP?

Missing from most of these discussions is the potential for poor people to create their own jobs, and how this can be supported. Our purpose in this book is to explore entrepreneurship as an alternative (although certainly not the exclusive) path out of poverty. While far too many discussions of entrepreneurship focus on high-tech, high-growth start-ups, the vast majority of new ventures do not involve leading-edge, complex technologies, are not funded by venture capital, do not seek to achieve exponential growth, and never go public. As we shall discuss in Chapter 4, most are simple lifestyle and survival ventures. Yet they provide a living, and potentially a very good living, for those who launch these ventures.

Entrepreneurship is inherently democratic. One's age, gender, race, ethnicity, creed, sexual orientation, or disability status do not matter. And as we shall argue in the chapters ahead, neither should one's poverty status matter. The issue is to make entrepreneurship an option for the poor, and to demonstrate how those in adverse circumstances can successfully pursue the entrepreneurial path.

Three of the great myths in entrepreneurship become important here. The first myth is that only certain people can be entrepreneurs. The inference is that entrepreneurship is somehow in one's DNA, that entrepreneurs are born. This is simply not supported based on over 50 years of research on the entrepreneurial persona. In fact, there is no evidence to support the idea that entrepreneurship is only for a few genetically predestined people. It is not tied to a specific set of personality traits that indicate, should you not have them, that you have no business starting a venture. The second myth concerns resource requirements – that it takes a lot of money to start a business. An advantage of the twenty-first century and the technology revolution is that it is easier than ever to start a venture, and one can do so with very little in the way of one's own resources. The third myth concerns risk and failure. Wildly speculative numbers are thrown around concerning new venture failure – with some suggesting that over 95 percent of new ventures fail. In reality, failure rates are much lower, vary by industry or business type, and go down significantly if one can achieve certain thresholds. More importantly, the associated risks can be mitigated. The reality, then, is that anyone can start a business, that resources can be leveraged when one does not have much money, and that risks can be managed to minimize the likelihood and costs of failure.

Ultimately, entrepreneurship is about empowerment and transformation. Through venture creation, people are empowered to create their own jobs, futures, income, wealth, and contributions to the community and society. They discover and act on opportunity in the environment, and they do so regardless of resources under their control. As they do so, they transform themselves, families, markets, and communities. These are the themes of this book.

In the chapters ahead, we approach entrepreneurship as a process and as a journey. The nature of this process, and what one can expect in terms of the journey, are examined from the vantage point of a person in adverse circumstances. The kinds of ventures created by entrepreneurs, and their underlying implications for someone in poverty, are explored. We look at a typical low-income start-up, identify the kinds of liabilities these ventures confront, and investigate how these liabilities can be overcome. The available infrastructure within and beyond low-income communities available to support entrepreneurial activity is assessed, as are the challenges of literacy rates, technological literacy, and limited educational backgrounds. Creative approaches to bootstrapping, leveraging resources, and engaging in guerrilla behaviors when one has no resources are introduced. Attention is devoted to common mistakes in terms of economics and financial decision-making, and how they can be better addressed by the low-income entrepreneur. Finally, we identify priorities in terms of how those involved with economic development and public policy can do more to support low-income entrepreneurship.

REFERENCES

Abner, L., S. Butler and S. Danziger et al. (2015), *Opportunity, Responsibility, and Security: A Consensus Plan for Reducing Poverty and Restoring the American Dream*, American Enterprise Institute for Public Policy and The Brookings Institution, accessed June 6, 2018 at http://www. brookings.edu/~/media/research/files/reports/2015/12/aei-brookings-poverty-report/full-report.pdf.

Acton Institute (2010), "Welfare: Separating fact from the rhetoric," July 20, accessed June 6, 2018 at https://acton.org/pub/religion-liberty/volume-5-number-5/welfare-separating-fact-rhetoric.

American Automobile Association (2016), "AAA: More than one-third of Americans will take a family vacation this year," *Newsroom*, April 21, accessed June 6, 2018 at http://newsroom.aaa.com/2016/04/aaa-one-third-americans-will-take-family-vacation-year/.

Blacksher, E. (2002), "On being poor and feeling poor: Low socioeconomic status and the moral self," *Theoretical Medicine and Bioethics*, **23**(6), 455–70.

Blair, C., D. Berry and R. Mills-Koonce et al. (2013), "Cumulative effects of early poverty on cortisol in young children: Moderation by autonomic nervous system activity," *Psychoneuroendocrinology*, **38**(11), 2666–75.

Brown, D. (2011), "Ten reasons why cutting poverty is good for our nation: A hand up creates a stronger and more vibrant middle class," *Center for American Progress Action Fund*, December 6, accessed June 9, 2018 at https://www.americanprogressaction.org/issues/poverty/news/2011/12/06/10771/10-reasons-why-cutting-poverty-is-good-for-our-nation.

Caputo, R. (1997), "Escaping poverty & becoming self-sufficient," *Journal of Sociology and Social Welfare*, **26**(3), 5–23.

Cato Institute (2017), *Cato Handbook for Policymakers*, 8th edition, Washington, DC: Cato Institute.

Chetty, R. and N. Hendren (2015), "The impacts of neighborhoods on intergenerational mobility: Childhood exposure effects and county-level estimates," *NBER Working Paper No. 23001*.

Corak, M. (2006), "Do poor children become poor adults? Lessons from a cross-country comparison of generational earnings mobility," in J. Creedy and G. Kalb (eds), *Dynamics of Inequality and Poverty, Vol. 13*, Bingley: Emerald Group Publishing Limited, pp. 143–88.

Duncan, G.J., A. Kalil and K. Ziol-Guest (2008), "Economic costs of early childhood poverty," paper at the Population Association of America Annual Meeting, New Orleans.

Federal Safety Net (2016), "US poverty statistics," accessed June 6, 2018 at http://federalsafetynet.com/us-poverty-statistics.html.

Fox, L., C. Wimer and I. Garfinkel et al. (2015), "Waging war on poverty: Poverty trends using a historical supplemental poverty measure," *Journal of Policy Analysis and Management*, **34**(3), 567–92.

Gans, H. (1995), *The War Against the Poor: The Underclass and Antipoverty Policy*, New York: Basic Books.

Gorski, P. (2008), "The myth of the culture of poverty," *Educational Leadership*, **65**(7), 32–6.

Gould, E., A. Davis and W. Kimball (2015), *Broad-based Wage Growth is a Key Tool in the Fight Against Poverty*, Economic Policy Institute, accessed June 6, 2018 at http://www.epi.org/publication/broad-based-wage-growth-is-a-key-tool-in-thefight-against-poverty.

Haskins, R. (2014), "Poverty and opportunity: Begin with facts," *Brookings*, January 28, accessed June 12, 2018 at http://www.brookings.edu/research/testimony/2014/01/28-poverty-opportunity-beginwith-facts-haskins.

Hauser, R.M. and M.M. Sweeney (1997), "Does poverty in adolescence affect the life chances of high school graduates?," in G.J. Duncan and J. Brooks-Gunn (eds), *Consequences of Growing Up Poor*, New York: Russell Sage Foundation, pp. 541–95.

Holzer, H.J., D. Whitmore Schanzenbach, G.J. Duncan and J. Ludwig (2008), "The economic costs of childhood poverty in the United States," *Journal of Children and Poverty*, **14**(1), 41–61.

Institute for Research on Poverty (2017), *Who is Poor?*, Madison, WI: University of Wisconsin, accessed June 6, 2018 at https://www.irp.wisc.edu/resources/who-is-poor/.

Kearney, M.S. and P.B. Levine (2012), "Why is the teen birth rate in the United States so high and why does it matter?," *The Journal of Economic Perspectives*, **26**(2), 141–66.

Kohut, A. and M. Dimock (2013), "US poor express strong values, not self-pity," *Bloomberg View*, May 9, accessed June 6, 2018 at https://www.bloomberg.com/view/articles/2013-05-09/u-s-poor-express-strong-values-not-self-pity.

Korenman, S. and J.E. Miller (1997), "Effects of long-term poverty on physical health of children in the National Longitudinal Survey of Youth," in G.J. Duncan and J. Brooks-Gunn (eds), *Consequences of Growing Up Poor*, New York: Russell Sage Foundation, pp. 70–99.

Lewis, O. (1959), *Five Families: Mexican Case Studies in the Culture of Poverty*, New York: New American Library.

Lynch, J.W., G.A. Kaplan and S.J. Shema (1997), "Cumulative impact of sustained economic hardship on physical, cognitive, psychological, and social functioning," *New England Journal of Medicine*, **337**(26), 1889–95.

Morris, M., M. Schindehutte, V. Edmonds and C. Watters (2011), "Inner city engagement and the university: Mutuality, emergence and transformation," *Entrepreneurship & Regional Development*, **23**(5–6), 287–315.

Muhlhausen, D.B. (2013), *Do Federal Social Programs Work?*, Santa Barbara, CA: ABC-CLIO.

National Conference of State Legislatures (2018), "Teen pregnancy prevention," March 12, accessed June 6, 2018 at http://www.ncsl.org/research/health/teen-pregnancy-prevention.aspx.

OECD (2016), "United States," *OECD Better Life Index*, accessed June 6, 2018 at http://www.oecdbetterlifeindex.org/countries/united-states/.

Payne, R.K. (2005), *A Framework for Understanding Poverty*, Highlands, TX: Aha! Process, Inc.

Payne, R.K., P. DeVol and T.D. Smith (2001), *Bridges Out of Poverty: Strategies for Professionals*, Highlands, TX: Aha! Process, Inc.

Pew Charitable Trusts (2013), "Faces of economic mobility," September 17, accessed June 6, 2018 at http://www.pewtrusts.org/en/multimedia/data-visualizations/2013/faces-of-economic-mobility.

Pew Charitable Trusts (2016), *Neighborhood Poverty and Household Financial Security*, accessed June 6, 2018 at http://www.pewtrusts.org/~/media/assets/2016/01/chartbook--neighborhood-poverty-and-household-financial-security_v3.pdf.

Proctor, B., J.L. Semega and M.A. Kollar (2016), *Income and Poverty in the United States: 2015*, US Census Bureau, Report No. P60-256, accessed June 6, 2018 at https://www.census.gov/library/publications/2016/demo/p60-256.html.

Rabow, J., S.L. Berkman and R. Kessler (1983), "The culture of poverty and learned helplessness: A social psychological perspective," *Sociological Inquiry*, **53**, 419–34.

Richmond Vale Academy (2017), "Effects of poverty on behavior and academic performance," accessed June 6, 2018 at http://richmondvale.org/effects-of-poverty-on-behavior-and-academic-performance/.

Sampson, R.J. (2012), *Great American City: Chicago and the Enduring Neighborhood Effect*, Chicago, IL: University of Chicago Press.

Smeeding, T.M., L. Rainwater and G. Burtless (2000), "United States poverty in a cross-national context," *LIS Working Paper Series No. 244*.

Smith, J.R., J. Brooks-Gunn and P.K. Klebanov (1997), "The consequences of living in poverty for young children's cognitive and verbal ability and early school achievement," in G.J. Duncan and J. Brooks-Gunn (eds), *Consequences of Growing Up Poor*, New York: Russell Sage Foundation, pp. 132–89.

Stevens, A.H. (2012a), "Poverty transitions," in P. Jefferson (ed.), *Oxford Handbook of the Economics of Poverty*, Oxford: Oxford University Press.

Stevens, A.H. (2012b), *Transitions Into and Out of Poverty in the United States*, Davis, CA: Center for Poverty Research, University of California.

Tanner, M.D. (2003), *The Poverty of Welfare: Helping Others in Civil Society*, Washington, DC: Cato Institute.

Trail, T.E. and B.R. Karney (2012), "What's (not) wrong with low-income marriages," *Journal of Marriage and Family*, **74**(3), 413–27.

US Bureau of Labor Statistics (2015), *A Profile of the Working Poor 2013*, BLS Report No. 1055, Washington, DC: US Bureau of Labor Statistics, accessed June 6, 2018 at https://digitalcommons.ilr.cornell.edu/key_workplace/1651/.

US Census Bureau (2011), "Census Bureau survey shows poverty is primarily a temporary condition," *Newsroom*, March 6, Washington, DC: US Census

Bureau, accessed June 6, 2018 at https://www.census.gov/newsroom/releases/archives/poverty/cb11-49.html.

US Census Bureau (2015), *Annual Social and Economic Supplement of the Current Population Survey*, Washington, DC: United States Census Bureau.

US Census Bureau (2016), *Annual Social and Economic Supplement of the Current Population Survey*, Washington, DC: US Census Bureau.

US Department of Agriculture (2018), "Rural poverty and well-being," *USDA, Economic Research Series*, accessed June 14, 2018 at https://www.ers.usda.gov/topics/rural-economy-population/rural-poverty-well-being/.

Wagmiller, R.L. and R.M. Adelman (2009), *Childhood and Intergenerational Poverty: The Long-term Consequences of Growing Up Poor*, Columbia University Academic Commons, accessed June 6, 2018 at https://doi.org/10.7916/D8MP5C0Z.

Wilson, W.J. (2012), *The Truly Disadvantaged: The Inner City, the Underclass, and Public Policy*, Chicago, IL: University of Chicago Press.

2. The nature of entrepreneurship

> Human beings are not born to work for anybody else. For millions of years
> that we were on the planet, we never worked for anybody. We are go-getters.
> We are farmers. We are hunters. We lived in caves and we found our own food,
> we didn't send job applications. So this is our tradition.
>
> (Muhammad Yunus)

WHAT IS ENTREPRENEURSHIP?

Entrepreneurship is about new possibilities – it is about acting on a dream, and concerns what is possible with hard work and imagination. The work of an entrepreneur is to create new ventures, make them sustainable and grow them. While there are many formal definitions of entrepreneurship, let us consider two that are especially useful when thinking about those in poverty.

The first of these is more descriptive, and approaches entrepreneurship as "the process of creating value by bringing together unique resource combinations to exploit an opportunity" (Stevenson and Jarrillo-Mossi, 1986). Most important in this definition is the idea that entrepreneurship is a process, one that can be learned and managed. This is an empowering notion. It reinforces the idea that anyone can be an entrepreneur. Second, value must be created – one is solving a problem, addressing a need, removing "pain" in the marketplace. Third, entrepreneurship is accomplished by putting resources together in a different way than before, even if only slightly differently. There is some level of uniqueness to one's approach. One is innovating, either with a product or service, the experience that is being created, the processes used to produce and deliver the product or service, or the underlying business model. Last, entrepreneurship is opportunity-driven behavior, which brings us to our second definition.

This definition is more concise. It approaches entrepreneurship as "the pursuit of opportunity without regard to resources controlled" (Stevenson, Roberts and Grousbeck, 1998). This is an action-centered perspective. One sees a possibility and does what is necessary to capitalize upon it. The individual is not held back, and does not compromise their vision or dream, based on the fact that they have little to no resources. This, of course, raises an important question: how does one pursue opportunity when one does not have the necessary resources? The answer lies with the entrepreneurial mindset, a topic to which we now turn.

ENTREPRENEURSHIP AS A MINDSET

The most critical element for success in venture creation is not one's existing knowledge or skill level in accounting, marketing, finance or operations – it is the development of an entrepreneurial mindset. Here we are referring to the individual's overall approach to opportunity recognition, problem-solving, resource constraints, and the creation of something new. But what exactly is the entrepreneurial mindset? McGrath and MacMillan (2000) describe it as an ongoing focus on recognizing opportunities and pursuing the most attractive ones with passion and discipline while leveraging the resources of those around them. Ireland, Covin and Kuratko (2009) stress the ability to rapidly sense opportunity, act upon it, and mobilize resources, even under uncertain conditions. In Figure 2.1, we propose a conceptualization of the entrepreneurial mindset that approaches it as a way of both thinking (Haynie et al., 2010) and acting (McGrath and MacMillan, 2000). As such, the approach in Figure 2.1 includes attitudinal and behavioral components.

The mindset concerns how individuals see themselves and the world around them. From an attitudinal perspective, the person who starts a venture tends to believe they are able to effect change in their environment – that they are not victims of their surroundings. They tend to be optimistic, and recognize that, even in dire circumstances, the world is filled with opportunities. The term "healthy dissatisfaction" is used to capture a belief that anything can be improved, done better, or enhanced in some way. Individuals embrace change and new approaches, and appreciate that trying new things involves failure and learning. They have a passion for what they do.

With regard to behavior, the mindset includes an action orientation, where the individual is willing to pursue new, innovative approaches. They demonstrate tenacity and persevere in the face of obstacles. The entrepreneur is able to continually adapt to these obstacles and emerging opportunities. They are not big risk-takers, but instead are adept at mitigating and managing risks. They understand the importance of leveraging resources, creatively finding ways to bootstrap, using other people's resources, and recognizing things as resources that others do not. They appreciate the need to act in guerrilla ways, employing clever, low-cost and often unusual tactics to accomplish tasks. As they are so critical to the person in poverty,

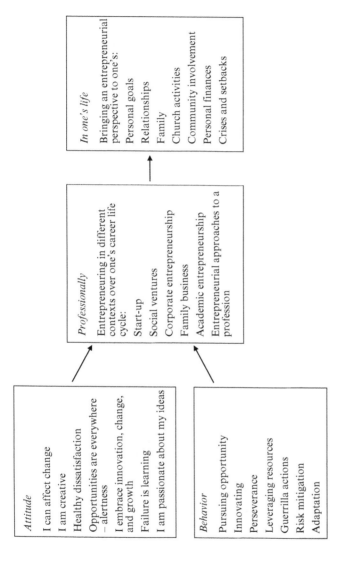

Attitude

I can affect change
I am creative
Healthy dissatisfaction
Opportunities are everywhere – alertness
I embrace innovation, change, and growth
Failure is learning
I am passionate about my ideas

Behavior

Pursuing opportunity
Innovating
Perseverance
Leveraging resources
Guerrilla actions
Risk mitigation
Adaptation

Professionally

Entrepreneuring in different contexts over one's career life cycle:
Start-up
Social ventures
Corporate entrepreneurship
Family business
Academic entrepreneurship
Entrepreneurial approaches to a profession

In one's life

Bringing an entrepreneurial perspective to one's:
Personal goals
Relationships
Family
Church activities
Community involvement
Personal finances
Crises and setbacks

Figure 2.1   Capturing the entrepreneurial mindset

we will explore these last three elements (risk mitigation, resource leveraging, and guerrilla behavior) in more detail in Chapter 10.

Again, anyone can be an entrepreneur, including those in poverty. This mindset is something that can be developed and nurtured among the poor. It is enhanced with practice – by doing entrepreneurial things all the time – and arguably it declines with lack of practice. Adverse circumstances can be a key incentive for thinking and acting in entrepreneurial ways. The individual is forced to adapt and rely on their ingenuity just to survive. He or she may work two low-paying jobs, sell things on eBay and Amazon, rent out rooms in their home, market homemade cakes at farmers' markets or community events, drive for Uber, tutor neighborhood kids, collect and sell coupons, and pursue any number of other money-generating activities. In the process, the individual can become more entrepreneurially alert (see Chapter 5), recognize new opportunities as they emerge, and continually discover novel ways to bootstrap and leverage resources (see Chapter 10). At the same time, the poor can be especially vulnerable when a major setback occurs, as they may have little to no safety net and quickly find available options becoming more limited or disappearing altogether. When a child is arrested and needs legal assistance, or a family member develops a major illness and there is no insurance, or a car is lost because an accident occurs and there is no ability to replace it, it can be more difficult to see entrepreneurial possibilities. And when these setbacks seem to continually happen, such as with those experiencing generational or long-term poverty, the development of an entrepreneurial mindset can be undermined and replaced with pessimism, a sense that one has less control over events, and a lack of future focus.

ENTREPRENEURSHIP AS A PROCESS

One of the most critical developments in the research on entrepreneurship over the past 50 years is the recognition that entrepreneurship is a process. The process perspective is the dominant view among scholars today (McMullen and Dimov, 2013; Shane, 2003). In essence, it approaches entrepreneurship as a logical set of steps that unfold over time and can be ongoing. This is critical, as it allows for the fact that these steps can be managed and the process can be learned. Further, the process can be applied by anyone and in a wide variety of contexts (e.g., in start-up, social or non-profit, corporate contexts).

While there are different conceptualizations of the entrepreneurial process, Figure 2.2 provides a concise picture of the key stages involved. The process begins with identifying an opportunity. Opportunities derive from

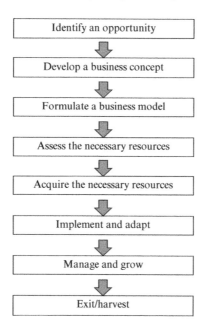

Figure 2.2 Entrepreneurship as a process

forces in the external environment creating a gap or opening for something new. This gap or opening represents an unmet need. The external environment has many subcomponents, including the customer, competitor, social, regulatory, economic, financial, technological, supplier, labor, and ecological environments confronting the entrepreneur. Developments in one or more of these subcomponents creates the opening, and the entrepreneur who recognizes the opportunity then develops a solution for addressing this need. The solution takes the form of a business concept.

The business concept is a novel approach for creating and capturing value. The entrepreneur formulates a value proposition around a new or different product, service or process. Based on this concept, a business model is designed. In essence, the entrepreneur is now envisioning the core elements of a functioning business through which the new product, service or process will be provided. The business model captures the essence of how the firm will create value, for whom, what the firm's core capabilities will be, how it will be differentiated from competitors, how profit will be made, and the intended growth model for the business.

The next two stages concern resources. First the entrepreneur must determine the nature and types of resources necessary to launch the business. These could include money, people, intellectual property, facilities and equipment, and key relationships (e.g., with suppliers, distributors, key customers, important influencers, and sources of money), among others. Once these critical resources have been identified, the entrepreneur must find ways to acquire them. While some resources may be purchased, a central aspect of entrepreneurial behavior finds the individual leveraging the resources of others. Sample leveraging approaches include sharing, borrowing, bartering, leasing, outsourcing, and giving up equity to get resources.

Implementation of the venture means setting up operations, launching marketing and sales efforts, putting accounting systems in place and otherwise executing the business model. Early on, the entrepreneur is making lots of adjustments and adapting to conditions as he or she addresses the realities of finding and dealing with customers, competitors, suppliers, regulators and other stakeholders. Many assumptions made before the launch prove to be wrong and the entrepreneur may have to change directions or pivot in terms of key decisions (e.g., product features, price points, target audiences, distribution approaches). And a number of unanticipated obstacles arise that must be overcome.

While a number of new ventures will fail in the first two years, those that make the appropriate adjustments get to the point where they have a sustainable business model. The entrepreneur must become a manager, putting in systems and structures, learning how to delegate, professionalizing operations, and otherwise directing the extent to which the venture grows, and how fast.

The final stage involves harvesting the venture. Often termed the "exit strategy" the entrepreneur decides when and how he or she will leave the venture, and what will subsequently happen to the business. Examples of exit strategies include simply shutting the business down, selling it or merging it with another company, passing it on to an heir or other party, or taking it public.

For those in poverty, the entrepreneurial process has a number of unique aspects. For instance, the kinds of opportunities available to them or identifiable by them can be limited by a number of factors, as we shall explore in Chapter 6. With regard to the business concept and business model, economically disadvantaged entrepreneurs tend to create survival types of businesses that are difficult to differentiate from the ample competition that they typically face. We shall examine aspects of the types of businesses created by low-income entrepreneurs in Chapter 5. The severe resource constraints faced by these firms require that the entrepreneur become adept at leveraging, bootstrapping, and use of guerrilla techniques, areas investigated in Chapter 10. The entrepreneur can suffer from other limitations, such as those related to literacy levels, as we shall consider in Chapter 6. Additional unique aspects of the process will be addressed throughout the remainder of this book.

The process as presented in Figure 2.2 appears to be a fairly straightforward, linear set of steps or stages. Yet, in reality, venture creation tends to be anything but linear. The entrepreneur gets to a particular stage and encounters obstacles and new information that require adjustments to a previous stage. Aspects of different stages are pursued in tandem, and ongoing adjustments are made to decisions from earlier stages. Let us explore this reality in more detail.

NAVIGATING THE EXPERIENCE: ENTREPRENEURSHIP AS A JOURNEY

What is it actually like to create a venture? What is the nature of the experience? It is important to approach entrepreneurship as a journey – but one where the path is not well marked, there are lots of twists and turns, and the ultimate course taken depends on key decisions made by the entrepreneur along the way (Morris et al., 2012). Although every entrepreneur's experience is unique, there do tend to be some common characteristics.

To use a different metaphor, entrepreneurship is like being an actor in an unscripted play. The founder of a business is constructing reality as he or she goes. It is an experience filled with uncertainty and ambiguity, particularly early on. The days are long and tend to be filled with highs and lows surrounding extended periods of hard work and little result.

While a business plan is helpful on this journey, it only serves to capture the entrepreneur's intentions and expectations, and to help organize things at the outset. As the venture experience unfolds, many of the entrepreneur's assumptions prove to be wrong (e.g., costs are higher, the market smaller, customers more demanding, logistics more complex) and a host of unexpected developments occur (every bank rejects a loan request, the first employee starts a competing business, damage from a water pipe breaking destroys all the inventory). These developments suggest that the entrepreneurial journey is an unpredictable, often chaotic one, where the entrepreneur controls much less than one might imagine. They also make clear that entrepreneurs succeed because of tenacity, perseverance, a continued ability to learn, and constant adaptation.

Much of the entrepreneurial experience is emergent (Morris and Webb, 2015). What one starts out to create is rarely what is actually created. Three core elements are emerging: the opportunity, the business concept, and the entrepreneur. The opportunity concerns the need that is being addressed, the target market that ends up generating most of the firm's revenue, and the market niche the firm seeks to fill. As the entrepreneur interacts with the marketplace, experimenting and making mistakes, the real opportunity, if there is one, starts to emerge and become clearer. The cleaning company that thought the opportunity was in cleaning private residences finds it is actually in serving medical facilities. This assumes, of course, that the entrepreneur is learning and adjusting. Changes are made as well to the business approach to serving that market. Products or services can be modified or new ones introduced, while the pricing approach, customer service, distribution methods, and a host of other implementation variables are altered to achieve a better fit with market requirements. Finally, we see emergence with the business founder as this person learns to be an entrepreneur.

It is this last point that is especially important when considering venture creation by those in poverty. Many people ask themselves whether they have what it takes to launch a venture. But there is no single set of characteristics or traits that one must absolutely have in order to start a business. And entrepreneurs are not born – they do not have some sort of genetic predisposition to start ventures. Much of what is required is learned. It certainly helps to have passion, a strong work ethic, and to be well-organized. Further, one must be open to change, and have the ability to learn and adapt. The entrepreneur is learning how to make sense of developments as they occur, to tolerate ambiguity, and to manage when surrounded by uncertainty. He or she is also learning the many different roles that have to be played as a venture unfolds (e.g., salesperson, money manager, service provider, supervisor, record keeper, delegator, planner, organizer, innovator, etc.).

In the end, just as the entrepreneur creates a venture, over time the venture is creating the entrepreneur. By being immersed in the experience, one is being formed into an entrepreneur. Every entrepreneur is different based on how they process and respond to the pressures, resource constraints, misdirection and mistakes, unanticipated problems, threats, lack of clarity and emergent opportunities that occur during the journey.

COMPETENCIES AND THE ENTREPRENEUR

In trying to understand what it takes to be successful at venture creation, scholars increasingly focus on the development of particular competencies or skills (Morris et al., 2013; Sánchez, 2013; Santos, Caetano and Curral, 2013). A competency refers to the knowledge, skills, attitudes, values and behaviors that people need to successfully perform a particular activity or task, in this case launching and managing a successful enterprise (Brophy and Kiely, 2002; Rankin, 2004).

BOX 2.1   CRITICAL COMPETENCIES FOR STARTING AND
GROWING A VENTURE

General managerial competencies	*Specific entrepreneurial competencies*
Organizing	Opportunity recognition
Team building and staffing	Opportunity assessment
Communicating and social abilities	Risk management/mitigation
Budgeting	Conveying a compelling vision
Delegation	Tenacity/perseverance
Cash management	Creative problem-solving/imaginativeness
Controlling	Resource leveraging and bootstrapping
Motivating	Guerrilla skills
Planning	Value innovation
Directing and supervising	Maintaining focus yet adapting
Operating (producing)	Resilience
Assessing	Self-efficacy
Selling	Building and using networks
Pricing	

These competencies can be divided into two groups, managerial and entrepreneurial, as illustrated in Box 2.1. Managerial competencies involve skills that managers in any company must have, including someone trying to manage a start-up. So the entrepreneur must understand how to sell, how to manage cash flow, how to hire and supervise people, and how to ensure the quality of what is being provided to customers. But there are also skills unique to the entrepreneurial journey, where one is trying to create something from virtually nothing and make it sustainable. Examples include the abilities to recognize and assess opportunities, mitigate risks, adapt, leverage resources, and be resilient.

Both the managerial and entrepreneurial competencies are learnable. Unfortunately, when it comes to the poor, educational and training opportunities in both areas are typically quite limited. This is especially the case with the entrepreneurial competencies. While some middle schools and high schools have developed entrepreneurship courses in their curricula, and community organizations sometimes offer basic training programs on starting a business, these tend to focus more on managerial competencies or the mechanics of setting up a business entity. Yet, apart from any sort of classroom training, there is evidence to suggest that competencies associated with entrepreneurship are best mastered through experiential approaches to learning (Morris and Kaplan, 2014). Learning by doing is accomplished through incubators, internships in entrepreneurial companies, pitch and business plan competitions, entrepreneurial mentoring programs, access to fablabs and makerspaces[1] or other facilities where prototypes and products can be developed, working for entrepreneurs, and participating in business simulations, among other possibilities. Clearly, this kind of infrastructure is not usually available within or accessible by those living in poorer communities.

Yet, there are exceptions. One of the most impressive efforts to address this challenge among the youth can be found with the programs of the Network for Teaching Entrepreneurship (NFTE). Offered in low-income communities and schools in countries across the globe, these programs particularly focus on development of an entrepreneurial mindset together with presentation, leadership, financial literacy, and problem-solving skills. Amy Rosen of NFTE notes that low-income high school students drop out at a rate six times higher than their high-income peers, and suggests entrepreneurship education as a vehicle to keep them in school (Rosen, 2013).

Apart from the limited availability of relevant training or experiential learning opportunities is the question of literacy. Helping those in poverty develop their skills at opportunity recognition and assessment, management of cash flow, or writing a business plan can be problematic if they lack basic math, reading and writing skills. We shall explore the issues surrounding literacy as related to entrepreneurship in more depth in Chapter 6.

ECONOMIC DEVELOPMENT, ENTREPRENEURSHIP AND REDUCTION IN POVERTY

As discussed in Chapter 1, poverty is complex and multifaceted. Addressing it requires solutions on many fronts, including education, housing assistance, child care, family counseling, substance abuse, health care, and prisoner rehabilitation, among others. Arguably, the greatest priority in its alleviation is economic development (Alexiou, 2009; Leigh and Blakely, 2016). It is a critical factor in revitalizing cities, sustaining rural communities, and forging a path out of the cycle of poverty. Governments are spending large amounts of money on economic development initiatives, ranging from attempts to get major corporations to relocate or build plants in their communities, to providing incentives to existing companies for job creation, investing in sizeable construction and infrastructure development projects, and developing new education and social support programs.

Underemphasized in many of these efforts is the vital role of entrepreneurship. Sustainable economic development does not occur without entrepreneurship. The more entrepreneurship there is, the more economic development occurs. In most developed countries, entrepreneurial ventures are responsible for 70 percent or more of the new jobs created (Baptista, Escária and Madruga, 2008; Birch, 1987). Higher levels of entrepreneurship are directly associated with increases in GDP, societal wealth, and quality of life (Acs, Audretsch and Strom, 2009; Lazear, 2005; Thurik and Wennekers, 2004).

At the same time, the emergence of relatively free markets across the globe has produced an entrepreneurial revolution, with rates of start-up activity at unprecedented levels in many countries. This is true for both new for-profit enterprises and non-profits. In many places, it is easier than ever to start a venture, as costs of entry and exit have fallen and the potential has become much greater to leverage resources and do considerably more with much less in terms of one's own resources.

It is interesting to note the impact of this revolution at the so-called base of the pyramid, or among the poorest people in some of the most undeveloped contexts. The fostering of microenterprise activity has produced impressive results in a number of developing economies, producing income and community development, and contributing to improvements on a number of dimensions of quality of life (Dalglish and Tonelli, 2016; Hall et al., 2012; Servon, 1999).

All this points to the potential of entrepreneurship as a key part of the solution to poverty in developed countries. Fostering venture creation not only creates jobs for founders and others living in poor communities, but also helps to stabilize these communities both economically and socially. Empirical evidence from the United States supports a relationship between average rates of entrepreneurship in a given state and rates of poverty. One study concluded that each percentage point increase in entrepreneurship corresponds to a 2 percent decrease in the poverty rate (Rugalo, 2014).

In this chapter, we have explored the fundamental nature of entrepreneurship, approaching it as both a process and a personal journey. A central theme has been conceptualizing aspects of entrepreneurship in ways that make it relevant for those in poverty. Yet, while entrepreneurship may hold significant potential, the ability (of societies, communities, economic development experts, and others) to dramatically increase levels of start-up activity by those in poverty is not well developed. More fundamentally, entrepreneurship among the poor is generally not well understood.

In the chapters that follow, we delve into the challenges confronting those in poverty when attempting to start ventures, their associated needs, and possible approaches for addressing these issues.

NOTE

1. These terms are often used interchangeably. A fablab (fabrication lab) is a facility where people can manufacture things on a small scale. It usually contains digitized equipment, machines and tools that allow for cutting and shaping different materials and producing prototypes or small numbers of finished products. A makerspace is similar in that it is a collaborative work space, often inside a school, library or existing public or private building where people can make things, learn, experiment, and share. It has a range of equipment and tools, such as 3D printers, laser cutters, soldering irons, and sewing machines – but also more basic items such as art supplies. Some serve as business incubators.

REFERENCES

Acs, Z.J., D.B. Andretsch and R.J. Strom (eds) (2009), *Entrepreneurship, Growth, and Public Policy*, Cambridge, UK: Cambridge University Press.

Alexiou, C. (2009), "Government spending and economic growth: Econometric evidence from the South Eastern Europe (SEE)," *Journal of Economic and Social Research*, 11(1), 1–16.

Baptista, R., V. Escária and P. Madruga (2008), "Entrepreneurship, regional development and job creation: The case of Portugal," *Small Business Economics*, 30(1), 49–58.

Birch, D.G. (1987), *Job Creation In America: How Our Smallest Companies Put The Most People To Work*, New York: Free Press.

Brophy, M. and T. Kiely (2002), "Competencies: A new sector", *Journal of European Industrial Training*, 26, 165–76.

Dalglish, C. and M. Tonelli (2016), *Entrepreneurship at the Bottom of the Pyramid*, Abingdon: Taylor & Francis.

Hall, J., S. Matos, L. Sheehan and B. Silvestre (2012), "Entrepreneurship and innovation at the base of the pyramid: A recipe for inclusive growth or social exclusion?," *Journal of Management Studies*, 49, 785–812.

Haynie, J.M., D.A. Shepherd, E. Mosakowski and P.C. Earley (2010), "A situated metacognitive model of the entrepreneurial mindset," *Journal of Business Venturing*, 25(2), 217–29.

Ireland, R.D., J.G. Covin and D.F. Kuratko (2009), "Conceptualizing corporate entrepreneurship strategy," *Entrepreneurship Theory Practice*, 33(1), 19–46.

Lazear, E.P. (2005), "Entrepreneurship," *Journal of Labor Economics*, 23(4), 649–80.

Leigh, N.G. and E.J. Blakely (2016), *Planning Local Economic Development: Theory and Practice*, Newbury Park, CA: Sage Publications.

McGrath, R.G. and I.C. MacMillan (2000), *The Entrepreneurial Mindset: Strategies for Continuously Creating Opportunity in an Age of Uncertainty, Vol. 284*, Boston, MA: Harvard Business Review Press.

McMullen, J.S. and D. Dimov (2013), "Time and the entrepreneurial journey: The problems and promise of studying entrepreneurship as a process," *Journal of Management Studies*, 50(8), 1481–512.

Morris, M.H. and J. Kaplan (2014), "Entrepreneurial (versus managerial) competencies as drivers of entrepreneurship education," in M.H. Morris (ed.), *Annals of Entrepreneurship Education and Pedagogy, 2014*, Cheltenham, UK and Northampton, MA, USA: Edward Elgar Publishing, pp. 134–51.

Morris, M.H. and J. Webb (2015), "Entrepreneurship as experience," in C. Shalley, M. Hitt and J. Zhou (eds), *The Oxford Handbook of Creativity, Innovation, and Entrepreneurship*, Oxford: Oxford University Press, pp. 457–75.

Morris, M.H., D.F. Kuratko, M. Schindehutte and A.J. Spivack (2012), "Framing the entrepreneurial experience," *Entrepreneurship Theory and Practice*, **36**(1), 11–40.

Morris, M.H., J.W. Webb, J. Fu and S. Singhal (2013), "A competency-based perspective on entrepreneurship education: Conceptual and empirical insights," *Journal of Small Business Management*, **51**(3), 352–69.

Rankin, N. (2004), *The New Prescription for Performance: The Eleventh Competency Benchmarking Survey. Competency and Emotional Intelligence Benchmarking Supplement 2004/2005*, London: IRS.

Rosen, A. (2013), "Financial literacy for all young Americans", *Forbes*, February 19, accessed June 6, 2018 at https://www.forbes.com/sites/amyrosen/2013/02/19/financial-literacy-for-all-young-americans/#7225f5687104.

Rugalo, S. (2014), "Entrepreneurship is a key to poverty reduction," Goldwater Institute, November 4, accessed June 12, 2018 at https://goldwaterinstitute.org/article/entrepreneurship-is-a-key-to-poverty-reduction/.

Sánchez, J.C. (2013), "The impact of an entrepreneurship education program on entrepreneurial competencies and intention," *Journal of Small Business Management*, **51**(3), 447–65.

Santos, S.C., A. Caetano and L. Curral (2013), "Psychosocial aspects of entrepreneurial potential," *Journal of Small Business and Entrepreneurship*, **26**(6), 661–85.

Servon, L.J. (1999), *Bootstrap Capital: Microenterprises and the American Poor*, Washington, DC: Brookings Institution Press.

Shane, S.A. (2003), *A General Theory of Entrepreneurship: The Individual–Opportunity Nexus*, Cheltenham, UK and Northampton, MA, USA: Edward Elgar Publishing.

Stevenson, H.H. and J. Carlos Jarrillo-Mossi (1986), "Preserving entrepreneurship as companies grow," *Journal of Business Strategy*, **7**(1), 10–23.

Stevenson, H.H., M.J. Roberts and H.I. Grousbeck (1998), *New Business Ventures and the Entrepreneur*, New York: McGraw-Hill/Irwin.

Thurik, A.R. and S. Wennekers (2004), "Entrepreneurship, small business and economic growth," *Journal of Small Business and Enterprise Development*, **11**(1), 140–49.

3. Entrepreneurship and the poor

> All people are entrepreneurs, but many don't have the opportunity to find
> that out.
> (Muhammad Yunus)

ENTREPRENEURSHIP AS A WAY OUT

Entrepreneurial activity offers a means for breaking out of the vicious cycle of poverty. The experience of poverty poses social and economic challenges that directly impact the choices people make, constraints they face, and opportunities available to them. Yet, all around the world, the poor are starting ventures, attracting resources, and building sustainable businesses (Banerjee and Duflo, 2007). In the process, millions of people have been pulled out of poverty (Abraham, 2012).

Critically, pursuit of entrepreneurship should not be seen as the exception – something that only unusual and especially gifted or lucky individuals are able to use to lift them from poverty. Our argument is that, in spite of the substantial obstacles faced by the poor, it should be the norm. Whether they are starting ventures that are part-time or full-time, formal or informal, legal or less than legal, for-profit or non-profit, entrepreneurship is accessible to all. It is a worthy path of self-empowerment, where the individual creates and then captures value, addresses needs, and can contribute to the fabric of a community.

In this chapter, we look at the patterns in entrepreneurial activity among the poor in developed economies. Characteristics of those who start businesses when coming from poverty are reviewed. Critical aspects of the poverty condition and their direct implications for entrepreneurial activity are summarized. In spite of the significant challenges, entrepreneurship is approached as a natural path for the poor. Motives for pursuing this path are then examined. Building on this foundation, a framework is introduced for increasing entrepreneurial activity among the poor. The remaining chapters of this book are structured around this framework.

PATTERNS IN LOW-INCOME ENTREPRENEURSHIP

Statistics and established facts on poverty and entrepreneurship in developed economies are surprisingly limited. National data on start-up activity itself is not that extensive, and in many cases, not especially accurate. This shortcoming explains the confusion or inconsistencies around such issues as national start-up rates for different types of ventures; demographics of those who start different types of ventures; factors that contribute to higher start-up rates; success and failure rates and their causes; temporal dynamics of ventures and their lifecycles, and a host of other questions. When poverty is factored into the equation, even less is known. The lack of data can be traced to a number of causes. First, poverty issues are usually not a priority of those responsible for collecting national, regional and local data on entrepreneurial activity. And when registering a business, the founder does not generally indicate that they are poor. Second, disagreements continue to exist over how poverty should be defined, and the types of measures that should be employed when gathering data. Third, in terms of data collection and reporting, finding poor people who have launched ventures and getting them to complete surveys or submit data can be problematic. Finally, research efforts are limited by the fact that poverty in developed countries, despite being widespread, is often hidden (see De Vos and Zaidi, 1997 for an illustration of these issues). The result is a picture that is both scant in terms of its details, and filled with mixed and sometimes conflicting findings.

Poverty itself is not a static phenomenon, and this further complicates our ability to understand its role in entrepreneurship. Although poverty rates are relatively stable (around 14 percent in the US), the total number of poor people has obviously grown with the population. Numbers of the poor in single-parent households headed by women have been on the increase. Also on the rise are numbers of people in poverty who were formerly in the lower middle class. Historically concentrated in rural areas, poverty in the US evolved to be more prevalent in metropolitan-core areas, but nowadays there are more poor people living in the suburbs (Brown and Hirschl, 1995). Data from 2014 revealed that American cities had roughly 13 million poor people, while the suburban poor totaled almost 17 million (Allard, 2017). It is likely that the poor can increasingly be found virtually anywhere within developed countries and regions.

Entrepreneurship and Poverty in the United States

To what extent do the poor start ventures? The research to date has produced mixed results. Based on data from the Kauffman Foundation,

Slivinski (2015) determined that 380 of every 100 000 low-income Americans are entrepreneurs, indicating an average entrepreneurship rate of 0.38 percent. When compared to a national rate of 0.30 percent (Fairlie, 2010), we find that a larger proportion of the low-income population are entrepreneurs than the proportion for the general population (Slivinski, 2015). Other research notes that minorities are more heavily represented among the poor, and they have demonstrated higher start-up rates in recent decades than society at large (Barr, 2008; Edelman et al., 2010). Further, data from the Panel Study of Entrepreneurial Dynamics suggests that, while the poor represent 14 percent of the population, about 17 percent of nascent entrepreneurs (people actively involved in trying to start a business) live in low-income households (Edmiston, 2008).

These findings are countered by studies that consider only low-income neighborhoods or communities (keeping in mind that the poor can reside and operate ventures outside of low-income neighborhoods). The Center for an Urban Future (Laney, 2013) conducted research in the five boroughs of New York City, and found that the postal codes with the lowest rates of self-employment were those with the lowest median family incomes. Further, these neighborhoods have higher percentages of native-born Americans than the average for the city. Another perspective on low-income neighborhoods is provided by the US Small Business Administration. Entrepreneurial activity in these areas was assessed using data from the American Community Survey (focusing on labor market patterns) and County Business Patterns (focusing on business activity) (Kugler et al., 2017). The authors note that two out of every nine workers reside in low-income areas, when only two out of every 11 self-employed workers reside in these areas. Finally, research on Appalachia, one of the poorest regions in America, found lower firm birth rates when compared to the US as a whole (Acs and Kallas, 2008).

Does entrepreneurship actually impact poverty rates? Here the evidence is clearer. Slivinski (2015) calculated the low-income entrepreneurship rate in each state by taking the number of low-income entrepreneurs divided by the number of total low-income respondents in the population (Table 3.1). The results indicated that Colorado has the highest rate of low-income entrepreneurship (0.75 percent) and Mississippi has the lowest rate (0.10 percent). It is interesting to note that six of the top 15 states ranked by low-income entrepreneurship rate are home to Hispanic and Latino populations twice the size of the national average. Perhaps the most important finding, however, concerns the relationship between a state's rate of entrepreneurship and the change in the state's poverty rate (between 2001 and 2007). Those states with the highest rates of entrepreneurship demonstrated the largest reductions in poverty, while lower rates of

Table 3.1   Low-income entrepreneurship rate by state

State	Rate (%)	State	Rate (%)
Colorado	0.75	South Dakota	0.40
Vermont	0.72	Arizona	0.36
New Mexico	0.70	Ohio	0.34
Arkansas	0.62	North Carolina	0.33
Maryland	0.56	Virginia	0.33
New Jersey	0.54	Michigan	0.33
Washington	0.54	Wyoming	0.33
Florida	0.50	Delaware	0.32
Idaho	0.48	Georgia	0.31
Nevada	0.45	Montana	0.30
California	0.44	Massachusetts	0.30
Texas	0.44	Rhode Island	0.30
Indiana	0.44	Nebraska	0.28
Minnesota	0.44	Alabama	0.28
Oklahoma	0.44	Tennessee	0.27
Maine	0.43	Connecticut	0.27
Alaska	0.42	West Virginia	0.27
New York	0.42	Louisiana	0.23
Oregon	0.42	Missouri	0.22
Iowa	0.41	South Carolina	0.19
Illinois	0.41	Kansas	0.19
Hawaii	0.41	Pennsylvania	0.19
New Hampshire	0.41	Kentucky	0.18
North Dakota	0.40	Wisconsin	0.18
Utah	0.40	Mississippi	0.10

Note: Low-income entrepreneurs defined as individuals involved in entrepreneurial activities who were within the bottom two income quintiles in each state.

Source: Adapted from Slivinski (2015).

entrepreneurship corresponded to increases in poverty (Slivinski, 2012, 2015). More specifically, for every percentage point increase in the rate of entrepreneurship, there is a 2 percent decline in the poverty rate.

Separately, the Self-Employment Learning Project of the Aspen Institute followed over 405 individuals running microbusinesses for five years (from 1991 to 1997), of which 133 were poor at the time of the study (i.e., households less than 150 percent of the poverty level) (Clark et al., 1999). They found that 72 percent of poor microentrepreneurs increased their household income over five years (the average increase was $8484), enough to move 53 percent of these entrepreneurs out of poverty. Because of these household family gains, poor microentrepreneurs were able to diminish their dependence on public assistance programs by 61 percent on average.

It is also possible to shed some light on what these entrepreneurs look like. Relying on the annual report on income and poverty from the US Census Bureau (e.g., Semega, Fontenot and Kollar, 2017) and the Kauffman Index of Entrepreneurial Activity (Fairlie et al., 2015), Slivinski (2015) created a demographic picture of low-income entrepreneurs (i.e., those in the bottom two income quintiles in each state). Although males (45 percent) represent a smaller portion of the low-income population than females (55 percent), Slivinski (2015) concludes that males constitute a higher proportion of low-income entrepreneurs (67 percent versus 33 percent). With regard to race, the largest group of low-income entrepreneurs appears to be White (59 percent), followed by Hispanic/Latinos (24 percent) and African American (10 percent). As Hispanics/Latinos make up 17 percent of the population, they are disproportionately likely to start a business. Immigrants make up a large percentage of low-income entrepreneurs, and Hispanics generally compose about 90 percent of immigrant entrepreneurs. Half of the low-income entrepreneur population falls within the age range of 30 to 49 years old, 22 percent are between 20 and 29 years old, 22 percent are between 50 and 59 years old, and 6 percent are over 60. Low-income entrepreneurs generally achieve lower education levels than the general population, with 23 percent of the general population holding a bachelor's degree, compared to 11 percent of low-income entrepreneurs.

Kugler et al. (2017) found entrepreneurs in low-income areas to be younger, less educated, and disproportionally female (in contrast to the Slivinski finding above), Black and Hispanic. They were less likely to be married and less likely to speak English. Their businesses had fewer employees. Entrepreneurs in low-income areas who had incorporated their businesses generated higher average incomes than those who did not.[1]

Most low-income entrepreneurial activity results in survival types of ventures, as we will discuss in Chapter 4. A study involving 1000 microbusiness owners[2] in the United States found that half of them could survive just one month or less (i.e., 55 percent could cover just one month or less of business expenses using current savings), 30 percent had no savings, and 15 percent would be unable to cover a $1000 emergency business expense (McKay, 2014). These figures support the argument that the low-income condition of the individual is frequently mimicked in the marginal income type of business that they create.

The majority of self-employed workers in low-income areas own businesses in five sectors: construction (15.2 percent), professional services (14 percent), other services (12 percent), trade (10.9 percent), and health care (8.9 percent). The least represented industries are food and accommodation services (2.9 percent), arts, entertainment and recreation (2.5 percent), education (1.5 percent), information (1.1 percent), mining and extraction (0.4 percent), and manufacturing (0 percent). The majority of these business are operated from home and are not incorporated (Kugler et al., 2017).

Additional Insights from Other Developed Countries

In Europe, as reflected in the European Commission's Entrepreneurship 2020 Action Plan, entrepreneurship is considered an important vehicle for economic development and poverty alleviation. Other developed countries, such as Australia and Canada, have also identified entrepreneurship as a solution to poverty (Blyth, 2015; Kendall, 2001). Despite such recognition, even less data are available on poverty and its relationship to entrepreneurial activity in these developed economies.

The limited research suggests extensive poverty among entrepreneurs in Europe. Studies of the 28 European Union (EU) countries indicate that self-employed individuals are more at risk of in-work poverty[3] than regularly employed individuals (Crettaz, 2011; Herman, 2014), especially those running businesses that do not have employees (Spasova et al., 2017). This finding is in line with previous research that found high in-work poverty rates among the self-employed (Halleröd, Ekbrand and Bengtsson, 2015). Table 3.2 illustrates these rates for the various EU countries and how they differ for the employed, the self-employed and the self-employed who have employees. The likelihood of the self-employed being in poverty actually rose in most European countries between 2007 and 2014 (Eurofound, 2017).

A different perspective can be found in the work of Amórós and Cristi (2011). Building on an established body of research demonstrating that rates of start-up are higher in less developed countries, they explore how start-up activity affects poverty in both developed and developing economies. Using data from 29 developed and 37 developing countries, their findings indicate that higher levels of entrepreneurship are associated with greater reductions in poverty in *both* developed and developing countries – with a higher relative impact in developing countries.

Yet another perspective has examined informal sector entrepreneurship in a developed economy. As noted in Chapter 4, the poor frequently launch unregistered and unlicensed businesses, as well as ventures engaged in illegal or illicit activities. Williams (2007) attempts to measure informal sector activity using a stratified sample of households representative of localities across England. He finds that 5.3 percent of adults in the sample

Table 3.2   At risk of poverty rates for workers and the self-employed in EU countries

Country	Employee	Self-employed With Employees	(a)	Self-employed Without Employees	(b)	(c)
Austria	6.3	7.1		17.1	***	**
Belgium	3.7	12.9	**	13.9	***	
Bulgaria	8.8	1.5	***	18.1	**	***
Cyprus	7.8	2.7	**	9.0		*
Czech Republic	2.9	5.0		7.5	***	
Germany	8.6	14.3	*	23.7	***	**
Denmark	3.9	–		–		
Estonia	9.9	25.4	***	35.4	***	(*)
Greece	8.5	12.2		23.6	***	***
Spain	10.1	19.1	***	26.6	***	**
Finland	2.2	6.7	**	15.8	***	***
France	6.4	16.5		21.0	***	
Croatia	4.8	12.4	*	15.3	***	
Hungary	6.3	2.2	***	9.2		**
Ireland	3.6	9.3	*	14.7	***	(*)
Italy	8.5	14.8	***	21.6	***	**
Lithuania	7.6	9.7		16.2	**	
Luxembourg	10.1	23.7	*	24.0	**	
Latvia	7.2	7.8		23.1	***	***
Netherlands	4.3	12.8	*	11.1	***	
Norway	3.8	–		12.7	***	
Poland	7.2	6.5		27.4	***	***
Portugal	7.9	33.6	***	30.0	***	
Romania	6.4	15.3		57.2	***	***
Sweden	6.6	14.0	**	23.4	***	*
Slovenia	4.4	15.3	***	25.4	***	**
Slovakia	4.3	17.2	**	12.7	***	
United Kingdom	7.1	17.7	**	20.1	***	

Note: $***p < 0.001$; $** p < 0.01$; $* p < 0.05$; $(*) p < 0.10$: significance levels of t-test differences in poverty rates between (a) those who are employees and those who are self-employed with employees; (b) employees and those self-employed without employees; (c) those self-employed with employees and those self-employed without employees; – data unavailable.

Source: Adapted from Horemans and Marx (2017).

were early-stage entrepreneurs engaged in informal activities, while 4.5 percent ran established informal businesses. He refers to a hidden enterprise culture that is an asset to be harnessed. This conclusion is reinforced by the work of Cristi, Amorós and Couyoumdjian (2011) who provide empirical evidence regarding the positive impact of informal sector entrepreneurship on poverty reduction and economic development.

CONDITIONS OF POVERTY: IMPLICATIONS FOR ENTREPRENEURSHIP

How poverty is experienced may differ significantly from person to person – even among individuals within the same family – but there are commonalities in what is experienced. Let us consider some of the most critical aspects of the poverty experience, with a particular focus on conditions that can impact entrepreneurial behavior.

The most salient aspect is a severe lack of resources, such that priorities must be set and choices made between addressing one necessity (the utility bill in the winter season) and taking care of others (feeding the family, paying for transportation, seeing the doctor). Ongoing pressing financial needs create a very short-term orientation (Wilson, 1996). They undermine the ability to learn how to save, while late payments and defaults compromise the building of a good credit history and strong credit score.

Time is another scarce resource. When work can be found, it is typically labor-intensive and often part-time employment with no benefits. The individual may be working two jobs, taking long commutes, and rushing home to take care of children and other family members. The result is not just a lack of time to plan or consider new possibilities, but constant fatigue and even physical exhaustion (Tirado, 2015).

Schools attended by the poor are frequently substandard and lack critical skills training, and few other mechanisms exist for developing skills (e.g., local jobs training programs, enlisting in the military). High school drop-out rates are high (about 16 percent higher than the average) among the poor. Hernandez (2011) found substandard reading and writing skills combined with conditions of poverty contribute to these drop-out rates. Literacy is a multi-faceted problem that encompasses not only difficulties in reading, comprehension and communication, but also math literacy, financial literacy, and technological literacy (see also Chapter 6).

Inadequate housing conditions and a poor diet, coupled with unaffordable medical care, can result in poor health and chronic medical conditions for potential entrepreneurs and their family members (e.g., Morland et al., 2002). Unable to afford the expenses that go with owning a car, public transportation must often be relied upon. Crime rates are typically high, as are property insurance rates. The presence of gangs can contribute to crime while also imposing strong social pressures on young people. Taken together, these factors can discourage community engagement.

People in poor neighborhoods tend to be segregated from much of the rest of society (Wilson, 2012). This segregation, combined with lack of resources, a substandard education, literacy challenges, lack of transportation, and many of the other conditions described here, places real limits on the nature and reach of their social networks. Further, when growing up in low-income communities, the individual learns rules, norms, and values that enable them to survive and that differ from those of the middle or wealthy classes. Payne, DeVol and Smith (2009) discuss rules related to everything from money and possessions to language, time, destiny, and worldviews. In addition, the person in poverty is less likely to have entrepreneurial role models (particularly in the formal sector) and mentors, or exposure to the operations of small enterprises. In noting that poverty is disproportionately experienced by African Americans, Fairlie and Robb (2007) provide evidence that Black business owners are much less likely than others to have had a self-employed family member, and associate this with poor venture performance.

Some of the more important implications of these poverty conditions for the starting of a venture are summarized in Table 3.3. Let us further consider which of them have the greatest implications for (1) the rate of venture start-up; (2) what actually gets started; and (3) the subsequent performance of these ventures.

A lower tendency to pursue venture creation is traceable to many of the conditions we have described, but especially the severe resource constraints and perceived inability to obtain resources (e.g., from savings, access to banks or private investors). Chapters 9 and 10 elaborate on these issues. Other key contributors include a lack of time and energy, lack of transportation (i.e., mobility to meet clients, suppliers, and be immersed in the local ecosystem), and the presence of gangs and negative social influences. Just as important, though, is recognizing entrepreneurship as a possibility, and encouragement from others to become an entrepreneur. Here, key drivers might include not having entrepreneurial role models, mentors or entrepreneurs in the family, and a general state of low self-efficacy.

What about the kinds of ventures that get started? Beyond the dearth of resources, the businesses of the poor are strongly impacted when entrepreneurs have weaker educational backgrounds, literacy problems, and lack relevant skills. The venture opportunities (i.e., industries entered and markets pursued) receiving attention are restricted by segregation and limited social networks, few entrepreneurial role models, and limited opportunity

Table 3.3   Poverty conditions and their implications for entrepreneurship

Poverty Condition	Implications for Entrepreneurship
Lack of financial resources and an inability to save	No money to start venture; entrepreneur limited to more labor-intensive ventures with limited growth prospects; reduced capacity to expand or grow; customers often also lack buying power
Lower-quality schooling, limited education, lack of skills training	Narrow skills set can limit venture types pursued and constrain the opportunity horizon
Poor literacy (including reading and writing but also financial and technical literacy)	Difficulties in pricing, managing cash flow, understanding contracts, marketing, preparing tenders, bookkeeping, complying with regulations, filing taxes, using technology, using social media and online tools, etc.
Preoccupation with immediate needs and crises	Lack of planning for the future, reduced cognitive resources to focus on the business, divided attention with individual and family problems
Lack of time from working multiple jobs, child care, etc.	Need to start the business while keeping other part-time jobs, and slowly making transition to full-time business owner – may compromise on some key tasks requiring attention
Physical exhaustion from working multiple jobs, child care, etc.	Reduced cognitive bandwidth; lack of energy to dedicate to the business
Health problems from poor diet, poor environment, unaffordable health care	Ill-health limits time and depth or quality of attention the entrepreneur can give the business
Lack of transportation	Reduced mobility to meet potential and current clients, suppliers and others, attend networking events, and get immersed in local ecosystem
Prevalence of crime	Higher vulnerability to robberies, theft, defaulting clients; subject to distrust by suppliers, bankers and partners; increased costs of doing business

Table 3.3   (continued)

Poverty Condition	Implications for Entrepreneurship
Social pressures from gangs and other negative influences	Tendency to engage in the informal economy, pursue illicit strategies
Segregation and limited social network	Limited access to key people, critical resources, diversified markets; limited opportunity horizon
Lack of understanding of hidden rules of other income classes	Limited access and ability to successfully interact with customers, suppliers, investors, regulators, distributors, gatekeepers and others who come from different economic classes and backgrounds
Lack of entrepreneurial role models	Lack of inspiration to guide one's efforts; lack of appreciation for values and behaviors required to succeed in small business; possible lowering of self-efficacy; lower social capital
Lack of entrepreneurial mentors, support network	Limited guidance and direction on business decisions; no reinforcement and encouragement
Lack of exposure to operations of small businesses	Reduced knowledge of pricing, marketing, bookkeeping, accounting, operations, inventory, etc.; unrealistically low expectations regarding time and cost requirements

horizons. Such factors can lead the poor to create survival or marginal lifestyle ventures (see Chapter 4). All too often, these entrepreneurs find themselves selling a "commodity" type of product or service, where there is little perceived difference among providers (see Chapter 11). They must operate in highly competitive markets, sell to customers with low buying power, and compete on the basis of price. These conditions generally result in small margins on every product or service sold.

Beyond this, entrepreneurship can be incredibly time consuming, particularly in the early days. Lack of time and money can force the poor to hold onto part- or full-time jobs and make a slower transition to becoming a full-time business owner, again limiting the types of ventures that emerge. Hence, they often create ventures that reflect their personal circumstances and that can inhibit their abilities to overcome these circumstances.

Last, let us turn to the issue of performance. The fact that many of these businesses perform marginally or actually lose money (Fairlie and Robb, 2007) is due to more than just the types of ventures being launched. If we consider the requirements of managing daily operations, procurement, pricing, marketing, bookkeeping, social media, cash flows, online tools, informatics, administrative paperwork, tax preparation, regulatory compliance and other basic responsibilities, additional factors contribute to anemic performance and small returns. Chief among these are a short-term orientation and weaker planning skills, literacy problems (including financial literacy), and a substandard education. Other key contributors include a limited understanding of the hidden rules of others (e.g., suppliers, financiers, distributors, customers, etc.) who come from middle- and upper-income classes, little previous exposure to the internal operations of a small business, and the absence of mentors and an entrepreneurial support network. Also important here are factors beyond the limitations of the entrepreneur, such as high crime rates (which affect both the business and the willingness of others, such as suppliers and bankers, to do business with the entrepreneur) and the limited buying power (and high credit risk) of the kinds of customers targeted by many of these ventures.

Growth of the business then becomes an even more problematic undertaking (Gartner and Bhat, 2000). Lack of cash flow and the inability to save make it impossible to invest in growth. While there may also be some fear of growth, as we shall discuss in Chapter 11, the vehicles for growth (e.g., adding employees, buying additional machinery, expanding the product/service line, integrating technology and otherwise making small and time-lagged investments) are beyond the reach of the operating entrepreneur.

THE NATURAL INSTINCT TOWARDS ENTREPRENEURSHIP

It may seem, based on this discussion, that the outlook for entrepreneurship among the poor is fairly bleak. Such a negative conclusion is reflected in an aggregate assessment of entrepreneurship within low-income communities conducted by Acs and Kallas (2008). They conclude that the supply side in these communities is characterized by low-quality human capital, limited financial capital, poor infrastructure, and limited leadership; the demand side includes little export demand, weak backward linkages and few tradable goods. Yet, while the conditions may be highly adverse, the potential for entrepreneurship remains quite promising.

The numbers presented earlier in this chapter suggest that, on balance, considerable entrepreneurial activity occurs among the poor. The start-up numbers are especially impressive when compared to entrepreneurs coming from the middle and upper economic classes – people operating in far more favorable circumstances. What is striking is not the slightly lower percentage of start-ups among the poor (at least in some studies, but actually higher in others) compared to the rates for these other groups, but the fact that the gap is not a lot larger. More remarkable is the fact that these numbers do not consider the large numbers of start-ups not captured in official databases or the available research. Although some of these missed ventures are formally registered entities, many are unregistered and operate in the informal economy providing legitimate goods and services. Still others engage in activities that are illicit or criminal. Regardless of the nature of their businesses, there is a sizeable hidden economy in most poor communities. Banerjee and Duflo (2011), in an 18-country study, report that 44 percent of the extremely poor in urban areas operate a business.

Hence, in spite of all the challenges, large numbers of those in poverty do start ventures, and many create sustainable businesses that enable them to climb out of poverty and afford them a decent lifestyle (Shirk and Wadia, 2004). Moreover, as highlighted in Table 3.4, some are able to build highly successful enterprises that generate tremendous wealth. It is our conviction that entrepreneurship is a natural path for someone in poverty, certainly more natural than working for someone else at low wages, with few (or no) benefits, limited opportunity for advancement or personal development, and the potential to be fired at will. To create something of value, benefit directly from the fruits of one's labors, take control of one's future, hire others who are poor, and make a contribution to one's community is a more innate tendency.

The indomitable spirit of the individual cannot be underestimated. Neither should we undervalue the significant inventory of underutilized resources to be found in poor communities (Edmiston, 2008). In addition, perhaps because of its deplorable nature, aspects of surviving in poverty can help prepare one for entrepreneurship. Living in vulnerable conditions where people must continually adapt, find creative ways to survive, make the most of limited resources, and rely on non-conventional approaches to addressing basic needs can serve as a vehicle for nurturing the development of entrepreneurial competencies. So too can dissatisfaction with the status quo and a propensity for breaking rules. Daymond John, founder of the hip hop apparel company FUBU (among other ventures), and star of the popular television program *Shark Tank*, reinforces this point in a book

Table 3.4   Prominent entrepreneurs who grew up in poverty

Founder/Co-founder	Business	Industry
Robert L. Johnson	BET Network, RLJ Companies	Media, television
Madam C.J. Walker	Walker Manufacturing Co.	Haircare products
Amancio Ortega	Inditex Group Zara	Retail clothing chains
Cordia Harrington	Tennessee Bun Company	Buns and baked goods
Daymond John	FUBU	Urban apparel
Chris Gardner	Gardner Rich LLC	Stock brokerage firm
Do Won Chang	Forever 21	Clothing retail store
Tyler Perry	Tyler Perry Studios	Movie and television production
Howard Schultz	Starbucks	Tea and coffee, retail bakeries
Jan Koum	WhatsApp	Communications/social media
John Paul DeJoria	Paul Mitchell, Patron Spirits	Hair products, alcoholic beverages
Kenny Troutt	Excel Communications	Telecommunications
Manny Khoshbin	Khoshbin Company	Real estate
Oprah Winfrey	Harpo Productions	Multimedia production
Ingvar Kamprad	IKEA	Furniture
Roman Abramovich	Millhouse LLC	Private investments
Leonardo Del Vecchio	Luxottica Group	Glasses and lenses
Michelle Mone	MJM Ltd./Ultimo	Lingerie
Sheldon Adelson	Las Vegas Sands, Comdex	Casinos, resort hotels
Beto Perez	Zumba Fitness	Exercise, music, clothing, books
Jay-Z	Roc-A-Fella Records, Roc Nation, Rocawear	Music recording labels, entertainment, fashion

titled *The Power of Broke* (John and Poisner, 2016). Building on his own poverty experience, he provides a series of case examples of people who took advantage of the fact that they have nothing, were committed and hungry for success, stayed laser-focused, and had to scrape and scramble. Such individuals have a greater need to succeed, and tend to be more fully invested emotionally and personally. He concludes (2016, p. 11), "Broke, on its own, is just broke. If you let broke beat you down, if you let it break you, you'll never find a way to thrive or even survive. You'll never lift yourself up. . . But if you look broke in the face, if you define it, own it, make it a part of who you are and how you go about your business, well, then you've got something."

MOTIVES OF LOW-INCOME ENTREPRENEURS

Entrepreneurial action requires motivation. Living in poverty and chronically disadvantaged communities can produce apathy, inaction, and a negative impact on emotional and mental well-being. The psychological burden and cognitive load on the poor can be significant enough that they suffer from reduced mental "bandwidth" with which to perform everyday tasks and engage in activities that might help them escape from poverty – such as completing more schooling or searching for better jobs (Mani et al., 2013). The question becomes one of understanding the motives that offset such forces and enable the individual to pursue venture creation.

Motivation is an inducement or incentive to act, usually in satisfying some need. The motivational process has three components: (1) direction – which actions the individual will work upon; (2) effort – how hard the individual will work upon those actions; and (3) persistence – how long the individual will work upon those actions (Pritchard and Ashwood, 2007). The underlying needs exist at different levels, with individuals in poverty conditions especially concerned with basic physiological and safety needs. However, having a need is not enough to trigger the motivation to perform a task, as the individual also requires physical, mental and emotional resources. The energy and resources available determine the direction, effort and persistence of the individual's actions (ibid.). As such, individuals in adverse conditions must deal with a double-edged sword: they have several needs to trigger the motivation process, but often have a deficit of resources (tangible and intangible) and energy (cognitive, affective and social) to dedicate to the task.

Extensive research has explored the central role of motivated human action in successfully navigating the entrepreneurial process (e.g., Shane, Locke and Collins, 2003; Hessels, van Gelderen and Thurik, 2008; Miller et al., 2012). Entrepreneurial motivation is an expressed, focused and directed effort towards opportunity recognition, assembly of resources and acting dynamically through business life stages (Jayawarna, Rouse and Kitching, 2011). In a start-up context, we can distinguish general (e.g., need for achievement, desire for independence) and task-specific (i.e., achieving a certain sales goal) motives (Shane et al., 2003). Further, the motives to start and run a venture can differ from those related to pursuing meaningful growth of the business (Baum and Locke, 2004).

Again, with the poor, addressing basic needs is paramount. Limited employment options and the need to pay for food, housing, and other foundational needs can lead to the launch of a business. The poor see in entrepreneurship a possible avenue to financially supporting themselves and their families. For some, taking on the risks of a venture can be a better option than staying where they are and doing nothing. This is traditionally referred to as necessity driven, as opposed to opportunity driven entrepreneurship (see Chapter 4). Empirical studies using country-level data have found that necessity-motivated entrepreneurship is prevalent in low-income and developing countries (e.g., Singer et al., 2015). In developed countries, the necessity- versus opportunity-driven distinction can be more nuanced, especially when it comes to the poor. Certainly, limited opportunities and basic needs push people to engage in activities that evolve into ventures, but the poor often have some sort of opportunity, or sense of unmet need, in mind as well (see Chapter 5). There is less tendency to create ventures that one would quickly give up should the right job come along. At the same time, once created, the low-income entrepreneur is generally forced to take money out of the venture to support family needs, leaving less for reinvestment and growth.

Beyond pure necessity, a key motive for entrepreneurship can be realizing a more productive use of one's resources. For many poor people, there is a sense that their skills, capabilities, and other personal resources are being underutilized. Even where other work is available, they perceive that self-employment can generate a better return on their labors than working for others, both in financial and non-financial terms (e.g., Brice and Nelson, 2008; Edmiston, 2008). Their own potential and what it could produce motivates them to step out from their current conditions and proactively create a venture (Dorward et al., 2009). Related here are the desires for self-realization and enhanced self-identity (Edelman et al., 2010).

Another key motive is the need for achievement (McClelland, 1965). Here, the entrepreneur is motivated by an idealized goal to be achieved, or a unique image of the future. He or she has a vision of a venture that would enable a better future, including what the business would look like, where it could go, and how to get there. This picture may not be highly detailed, but there is an image that contributes to the intention to pursue a course of action. Accomplishing this vision in spite of any obstacles or resistance is what drives them – not any personal recognition or the eventual financial return.

Desire for independence is also a major motivator. Conditions of poverty can lead one to aspire to be more autonomous and independent. The individual seeks to take control over the important decisions in their life, fighting against the conditions in which they are immersed. Rather than being dependent on government, institutions, charity or community support, or subject to the whims of employers who undervalue and underinvest in them, a person pursues business ownership as a source of independence and means for control. The venture allows them to determine what the priorities should be, when and how hard they work, who they work with, how resources are allocated, and what happens to the fruits of their labors.

In reality, entrepreneurship can play different roles in the lives of the poor, and these roles reflect different motives. Examples include part-time ventures to supplement family income from regular jobs, ventures that have a social purpose or that help the community, ventures that allow for self-expression (e.g., through cooking, sewing, design, music, fashion, or making something), ventures that can build wealth, and ventures that simply allow the freedom of not having to work for anyone else. The implication is that entrepreneurial motives vary for the poor just as they do for everyone else. Those in poverty demonstrate the same entrepreneurial motivations as do others, and are no less motivated.

Finally, it is important to note that motives such as achievement, independence, and a more productive return go hand in hand with the concepts of self-efficacy and locus of control. Self-efficacy reflects the extent to which someone perceives they have the ability to execute courses of action necessary to perform a given task or behavior (Bandura, 1997). In entrepreneurship, it indicates an ability to perform the tasks and cope with the contingencies surrounding the launch of a venture – including persevering in the face of obstacles. Locus of control concerns the extent to which one perceives that one's own actions determine outcomes. Either external forces dictate what happens in one's life (external locus of control), or one's personal efforts, persistence and hard work explain outcomes (internal locus of control). Entrepreneurs demonstrate a higher self-efficacy and a stronger internal locus of control. Not surprisingly, higher self-efficacy tends to be associated with an internal locus of control (Judge et al., 2002).

Research findings suggest that poverty conditions can result in lower self-efficacy (Quane and Rankin, 1998; Wilson, 1996). Boardman and Robert (2000) report that both individual and neighborhood socio-economic status contribute to low self-efficacy, such that living in a better neighborhood can lead to higher self-efficacy for a person with low socio-economic status. Chen, Greene and Crick (1998) note, in considering disadvantaged populations, that there are those who shun entrepreneurial activities not because they actually lack necessary skills but because they believe they do. Similarly, lower socio-economic status has been associated with a stronger external locus of control (Rotter, 1966). Accordingly, the motivation to start a business is undermined when those in poverty evidence low self-efficacy and an external locus of control. These linkages highlight the significance of our earlier discussion regarding the importance of entrepreneurial role models, exposure to small business operations, and a community infrastructure that supports and reinforces entrepreneurial actions – factors that contribute to higher self-efficacy and an internal locus of control (Chen et al., 1998).

A MODEL FOR ENHANCING ENTREPRENEURSHIP AMONG THE POOR

In this chapter, we have emphasized that entrepreneurial activity is common among the poor. Yet, the fact that start-up rates may be lower in poor communities suggests there is significant room for improvement. These are communities that are rich both in opportunity and talent, but they also represent environments that pose unique challenges when it comes to entrepreneurial activity. The question becomes one of determining how the amount of start-up activity by the poor can be increased, and ways in which the ventures that are created can become more successful. Our focus in the chapters to come is to explore the issues that surround this two-part question. The approach is built around what we will call the SPODER framework, as illustrated in Figure 3.1.

The framework begins with development of a supportive infrastructure (S). Low-income neighborhoods generally lack an entrepreneurial

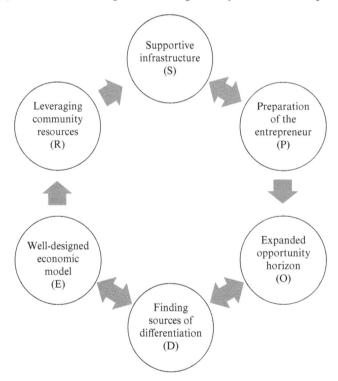

Figure 3.1   SPODER: A framework for fostering low-income entrepreneurship

ecosystem, and the poor struggle to tap into whatever ecosystems exist within the larger community or region (see Chapter 8). Importantly, the infrastructure must reflect the unique conditions and needs of the poor, as outlined earlier in this chapter. Key infrastructure elements include education/training mechanisms, availability of finance, incubators/accelerators, a supportive business community, vehicles for social networking/connecting, small business support organizations, small business service providers, entrepreneurial role models, and entrepreneurial mentors, among others. We then focus on the low-income individual and their preparation (P) for the entrepreneurial journey. Gaps and shortcomings in the individual's background must be addressed as he or she learns to master business and entrepreneurial competencies (see Chapters 6, 7 and 13). Thus, it is critical to prepare individuals in low-income conditions to become entrepreneurs, providing them with the knowledge, tactics and tools needed to think and act more entrepreneurially. Next, entrepreneurship is opportunity-driven behavior, and our focus becomes the opportunity horizon (O) of the entrepreneur. Here the priority is to continually extend this horizon, enabling the low-income individual to recognize more attractive and higher-potential possibilities both as the basis for launching the venture, but also to enable ongoing growth and expansion of the business (see Chapter 5). Based on the market opportunity, a business is then conceptualized. All too often, the value proposition on which the business is based is not sufficiently unique. When this happens, customers see the business as a commodity. It becomes difficult for the entrepreneur to achieve sustainable differentiation (D) from competitors. The key is strategic thinking, as opposed to reactive or tactical management, as sources of differentiation exist for virtually any business (see Chapter 11). Then, the business designed by the low-income entrepreneur must be developed around a viable economic model (E). This typically means not trying to compete with high unit costs, relatively small volumes, and low prices and margins. Rather, the entrepreneur must find innovative ways to capture revenue, price on a value basis, achieve cost economies while keeping overhead low, and reach higher potential market segments (see Chapter 12). Finally, the low-income entrepreneur must continually acquire resources (R), which includes not only money, but a wide range of other tangible and intangible resources (see Chapters 9 and 10). The key concept here is resource leveraging, which means finding creative ways to borrow, share, rent, outsource, barter, partner and otherwise tap into resources not owned by the entrepreneur, including community resources. It involves recognizing things as resources that others do not, taking advantage of one's surroundings, and using resources in non-conventional ways.

The model in Figure 3.1 is presented as a circle. This shape reflects the fact that a cycle is involved, one that is ongoing as the venture interfaces with the infrastructure to gain new inputs, and the entrepreneur continually learns and improves, new market opportunities are discovered, enhanced sources of differentiation are identified, the economic model is refined, and additional resources are leveraged to enable venture growth.

NOTES

1. Incorporated self-employment refers to people who work for themselves in corporate entities; unincorporated self-employment refers to people who work for themselves in other legal entities.
2. Annual revenues ranging from less than $30 000 to $2 million.
3. In-work poverty risk defined as "Individuals who are classified as 'employed' (distinguishing between 'wage and salary employment plus self-employment' and 'wage and salary employment' only) and who are at risk of poverty. [This] [i]ndicator needs to be analysed according to personal, job and household characteristics, and also in comparison with the poverty risk faced by the unemployed and the inactive" (European Commission, 2009, p. 11). People are considered at risk of poverty when their annual equivalized household disposable income is below 60 percent of the national median (Dennis and Guio, 2003).

REFERENCES

Abraham, R. (2012), "Doing business at the base of the pyramid: The reality of emerging markets," *The Journal of Field Actions: Field Actions Science Reports, Special Issue 4: Fighting Poverty, Between Market and Gift*.

Acs, Z.J. and K. Kallas (2008), "State of literature on small- to medium-sized enterprises and entrepreneurship in low-income communities," in G. Yago, J.R. Barth and B. Zeidman (eds), *Entrepreneurship in Emerging Domestic Markets*, New York: Springer.

Allard, S.W. (2017), *Places in Need: The Changing Geography*, New York: Russell Sage Foundation.

Amorós, J.E. and O. Cristi (2011), "Poverty, human development and entrepreneurship," in M. Minniti (ed.), *The Dynamics of Entrepreneurship: Theory and Evidence*, Oxford: Oxford University Press.

Bandura, A. (1997), *Self-Efficacy: The Exercise of Control*, New York: Freeman and Co.

Banerjee, A.V. and E. Duflo (2007), "The economic lives of the poor," *Journal of Economic Perspectives*, **21**(1), 141–67.

Banerjee, A.V. and E. Duflo (2011), *Poor Economics: A Radical Rethinking of the Way to Fight Global Poverty*, New York: Public Affairs Books.

Barr, M. (2008), "Policies to expand minority entrepreneurship," in G. Yago, J.R. Barth and B. Zeidman (eds), *Entrepreneurship in Emerging Domestic Markets*, New York: Springer, pp. 141–50.

Baum, J.R. and E.A. Locke (2004), "The relationship of entrepreneurial traits, skills, and motivation to subsequent venture growth," *Journal of Applied Psychology*, **89**(4), 587–98.

Blyth, A. (2015), "Entrepreneurship as a solution to poverty," *Sydney Morning Herald*, September 25.

Boardman, J.D. and S.A. Robert (2000), "Neighborhood socioeconomic status and perceptions of self-efficacy," *Sociological Perspectives*, **43**(1), 117–36.

Brice, J.J. and M. Nelson (2008), "The impact of occupational preferences on the intent to pursue an entrepreneurial career," *Academy of Entrepreneurship Journal*, **14**(1/2), 13–36.

Brown, D.L. and T.A. Hirschl (1995), "Household poverty in rural and metropolitan-core areas of the United States," *Rural Sociology*, **60**(1), 44–66.

Chen, C.C., P.G. Greene and A. Crick (1998), "Does entrepreneurial self-efficacy distinguish entrepreneurs from managers?," *Journal of Business Venturing*, **13**(4), 295–316.

Clark, P., A. Blair and L. Zandiniapour et al. (1999), "Microenterprise and the poor: Findings from the Self-Employment Learning Project five year survey of micro-entrepreneurs," *Microenterprise*, January 1, accessed June 7, 2018 at https://www.aspeninstitute.org/publications/microenterprise-poor-findings-self-employment-learning-project-five-year-survey-microentrepreneurs/.

Crettaz, E. (2011), *Fighting Working Poverty in Postindustrial Economies: Causes, Trade-Offs and Policy Solutions*, Cheltenham, UK and Northampton, MA, USA: Edward Elgar Publishing.

Cristi, O., J.E. Amorós and J.P. Couyoumdjian (2011), "Does it make sense to go against shadow entrepreneurs?," in *Proceedings of the 7th European Conference on Innovation and Entrepreneurship*, Reading: Academic Publishing International.

Dennis, I. and A.C. Guio (2003), *Poverty and Social Exclusion in the EU After Laeken – Part 1*, Eurostat, Statistics in Focus Theme 3-8/2003.

De Vos, K. and M.A. Zaidi (1997), "Equivalence scale sensitivity of poverty statistics for the member states of the European Union," *Review of Income and Wealth*, **43**(3), 319–33.

Dorward, A., S. Anderson and Y.N. Bernal et al. (2009), "Hanging in, stepping up and stepping out: Livelihood aspirations and strategies of the poor," *Development in Practice*, **19**(2), 240–47.

Edelman, L.F., C.G. Brush, T.S. Manolova and P.G. Greene (2010), "Start-up motivations and growth intentions of minority nascent entrepreneurs," *Journal of Small Business Management*, **48**(2), 174–96.

Edmiston, K.D. (2008), "Entrepreneurship in low and moderate income communities," in G. Yago, J.R. Barth and B. Zeidman (eds), *Entrepreneurship in Emerging Domestic Markets: Barriers and Innovation*, New York: Springer.

Eurofound (2017), *In-Work Poverty in the EU*, Luxembourg: Publications Office of the European Union.

European Commission (2009), *Portfolio of Indicators for the Monitoring of the European Strategy for Social Protection and Social Exclusion – 2009 Update*.

Fairlie, R.W. (2010), *Kauffman Index of Entrepreneurial Activity: 1996–2009 Report*, accessed June 7, 2018 at https://www.entrepreneurship.org/articles/2010/05/kauffman-index-of-entrepreneurial-activity-1996-2009-report.

Fairlie, R.W. and A. Robb (2007), "Families, human capital, and small business: Evidence from the Characteristics of Business Owners Survey," *ILR Review*, **60**(2), 225–45.

Fairlie, R.W., A. Morelix, E.J. Reedy and J. Russell (2015), *2015 Kauffman Index:*

Startup Activity, National Trends, accessed June 7, 2018 at https://www.kauff man.org/kauffman-index/reporting/~/media/f2095874896d43a097c2b3a226b933 f5.ashx.

Gartner, W. and S. Bhat (2000), "Environmental and ownership characteristics of small businesses and their impact on development," *Journal of Small Business Management*, **38**(3), 14–27.

Halleröd, B., H. Ekbrand and M. Bengtsson (2015), "In-work poverty and labour market trajectories: Poverty risks among the working population in 22 European countries," *Journal of European Social Policy*, **25**(5), 473–88.

Herman, E. (2014), "Working poverty in the European Union and its main determinants: An empirical analysis," *Engineering Economics*, **25**(4), 427–36.

Hernandez, D.J. (2011), "Double jeopardy: How third-grade reading skills and poverty influence high school graduation," *ERIC*, April, Baltimore, MD: Annie E. Casey Foundation.

Hessels, J., M. van Gelderen and R. Thurik (2008), "Entrepreneurial aspirations, motivations, and their drivers," *Small Business Economics*, **31**(3), 323–39.

Horemans, J. and I. Marx (2017), "Poverty and material deprivation among the self-employed in Europe," *IZA DP No. 11007*, IZA Institute of Labor Economics.

Jayawarna, D., J. Rouse and J. Kitching (2011), "Entrepreneur motivations and life course," *International Small Business Journal*, **31**(1), 34–56.

John, D. and D. Poisner (2016), *The Power of Broke*, New York: Currency Publishing.

Judge, T.A., A. Erez, J.E. Bono and C.J. Thoresen (2002), "Are measures of self-esteem, neuroticism, locus of control, and generalized self-efficacy indicators of a common core construct?," *Journal of Personality and Social Psychology*, **83**(3), 693–710.

Kendall, J. (2001), "Circles of disadvantage: Aboriginal poverty and underdevelopment in Canada," *American Review of Canadian Studies*, **31**(1–2), 43–59.

Kugler, M., M. Michaelides, N. Nanda and C. Agdayani (2017), *Entrepreneurship in Low-Income Areas*, US Small Business Administration Office of Advocacy, accessed June 7, 2018 at https://www.sba.gov/advocacy/entrepreneurship-low-income-areas.

Laney, K. (2013), *Launching Low-Income Entrepreneurs*, New York: Center for an Urban Future.

Mani, A., S. Mullainathan, E. Shafir and J. Zhao (2013), "Poverty impedes cognitive function," *Science*, **341**(6149), 976–80.

McClelland, D.C. (1965), "Need achievement and entrepreneurship: A longitudinal study," *Journal of Personality and Social Psychology*, **1**(4), 389–92.

McKay, K.L. (2014), "Achieving financial security through entrepreneurship: Policies to support financially vulnerable microbusiness owners," *Federal Policy Proposal*, Corporation for Enterprise Development, August 2014, accessed June 7, 2018 at https://prosperitynow.org/files/PDFs/financial_capability_plan ning_guide/Entrepreneurship_policy_proposal.pdf.

Miller, T.L., M.G. Grimes, J.S. McMullen and T.J. Vogus (2012), "Venturing for others with heart and head: How compassion encourages social entrepreneurship," *Academy of Management Review*, **37**(4), 616–40.

Morland, K., S. Wing, A. Diez Roux and C. Poole (2002), "Neighborhood characteristics associated with the location of food stores and food service places," *American Journal of Preventive Medicine*, **22**(1), 23–9.

Payne, R.K., P. DeVol and T.D. Smith (2009), "Bridges out of poverty," in *Strategies for Professionals and Communities*, New York: Aha! Process Inc.

Pritchard, R.D. and E.L. Ashwood (2007), *Managing Motivation: A Manager's Guide to Diagnosing and Improving Motivation*, New York: LEA/Psychology Press.
Quane, J.M. and B.H. Rankin (1998), "Neighborhood poverty, family characteristics, and commitment to mainstream goals," *Journal of Family Issues*, **19**(6), 769–94.
Rotter, J. (1966), "Generalized expectancies for internal versus external control of reinforcement," *Psychological Monographs*, **80**(1), 1–28.
Semega, J.J., K.R. Fontenot and M.A. Kollar (2017), *Income and Poverty in the United States: 2016*, Report No. P60-259, US Census Bureau, accessed June 7, 2018 at https://www.census.gov/library/publications/2017/demo/p60-259.html.
Shane, S., E. Locke and C.J. Collins (2003), "Entrepreneurial motivation," *Human Resources Management Review*, **13**(2), 257–79.
Shirk, M. and A.S. Wadia (2004), *Kitchen Table Entrepreneurs: How Eleven Women Escaped Poverty to Become Their Own Bosses*, Boulder, CO: Westview Press.
Singer, S., J.E. Amorós, D. Moska and Global Entrepreneurship Research Association (2015), *Global Entrepreneurship Monitor 2014 Global Report*, Babson Park, MA: Babson College.
Slivinski, S. (2012), "Increasing entrepreneurship is a key to lowering poverty rates," *Policy Report No. 254*, Goldwater Institute, accessed June 7, 2018 at http://www.realclearmarkets.com/docs/2012/11/PR254%20Increasing%20Entrepreneurship.pdf.
Slivinski, S. (2015), *Policy Report No. 252: Bootstraps Tangled in Red Tape: How State Occupational Licensing Hinders Low-Income Entrepreneurship*, Goldwater Institute, accessed June 7, 2018 at https://goldwaterinstitute.org/article/bootstraps-tangled-in-red-tape/.
Spasova, S., D. Bouget, D. Ghailani and B. Vanhercke (2017), *Access to Social Protection for People Working on Non-Standard Contracts and as Self-Employed in Europe: A Study of National Policies*, Brussels: European Social Policy Network, European Commission.
Tirado, L. (2015), *Hand to Mouth: Living in Bootstrap America*, New York: Penguin.
Williams, C.C. (2007), "The nature of entrepreneurship in the informal sector: Evidence from England," *Journal of Developmental Entrepreneurship*, **12**(02), 239–54.
Wilson, W.J. (1996), *When Work Disappears*, New York: Vintage Books.
Wilson, W.J. (2012), *The Truly Disadvantaged: The Inner City, the Underclass, and Public Policy*, Chicago, IL: University of Chicago Press.

4. Types of entrepreneurs and types of ventures

> The poor are very creative. They know how to earn a living and how to change their lives.
> (Muhammad Yunus)

FINDING PATTERNS IN DIVERSITY

Think of any five people you know who have started a venture. Consider the businesses that each of them managed to build. In all likelihood, these individuals are more different than they are similar, and their ventures look nothing like each other. The path each entrepreneur follows is idiosyncratic, determined by where they started, their motives, how they interpret and respond to ongoing developments, chance events, their goals and priorities and how they change with time, their willingness to take risks, and a host of other situational and personal factors. As a result, it can be difficult to generalize about entrepreneurs or their ventures, which suggests a pretty messy landscape when exploring entrepreneurship and the poor. It is a landscape to which we need to bring more order.

In this chapter we consider two big questions in entrepreneurship: (1) Who is the entrepreneur? (2) What do they actually create? The first of these two questions considers what we know about the characteristics, traits and motives of successful entrepreneurs. While there is significant diversity among these individuals, we consider patterns in terms of general types or categories of entrepreneurs that tend to emerge. With the second question, we examine patterns in the types of ventures created by entrepreneurs, identifying four distinct types and their associated characteristics. In addressing both questions, we draw implications for a person in poverty, including the unique challenges that they confront, and what is required to overcome these challenges.

CHARACTERISTICS AND VALUES OF ENTREPRENEURS COMPARED TO THE POOR

In Chapter 2, it was argued that virtually anyone can start a business. Among the population of entrepreneurs one will find a wide mix of ages, races, genders, religions, sexual orientations, income groups, and educational backgrounds. But are there certain characteristics that entrepreneurs have in common, and do the poor tend to share these characteristics? A significant amount of research has attempted to address the question "Who is the entrepreneur?," with scholars trying to identify various traits and characteristics associated with those who launch ventures. The findings have been mixed at best, with surprisingly little in the way of consistent results (Bird, 1989; Morris, 1998). Entrepreneurs tend to be optimistic, calculated risk takers, motivated more by achievement (making a go of the venture, satisfying customers, creating jobs) than attaining wealth, with a strong work ethic, and tolerant of ambiguity. They have an internal locus of control, or sense that they can influence or change the environments in which they operate, and value their independence. Beyond this, the people who start ventures are more different than they are alike.

These kinds of characteristics reflect the nature of the entrepreneurial task, where the entrepreneur is facing difficult odds, trying to affect change, dealing with uncertainty and ambiguity, unable to endure significant losses, and largely alone. People develop such characteristics as a function of their upbringing, surroundings, and experiences. The research provides no indication that the poor inherently score lower on these characteristics, and there is nothing about being poor to suggest an individual could not develop these characteristics. Again, poverty is a circumstance, not an endemic characteristic of a person.

Another relevant variable is self-efficacy, or one's belief in their own ability to succeed in specific situations or accomplish a particular task (Bandura, 1977), such as starting and running a business. Self-efficacy combined with personal goals can enhance motivation, increase intentions, and result in higher achievement in terms of desired results (including venture performance) (Baum and Locke, 2004). It plays a significant role in how the individual approaches tasks and challenges. For instance, higher entrepreneurial self-efficacy has been associated with the ability to engage in improvisational behaviors that positively impact venture performance (Hmieleski and Corbett, 2008).

When we consider the poor, there is evidence that low socio-economic status of both the individual and his or her surrounding community (i.e., percentage of families in the neighborhood in poverty, the neighborhood unemployment rate) are associated with lower general self-efficacy and career self-efficacy (Ali, McWhirter and Chronister, 2005; Berkman, 2015; Boardman and Robert, 2000). Unfortunately, we know less about entrepreneurial self-efficacy and the poor. At the same time, there is evidence that entrepreneurial self-efficacy can be elevated through training and education (Alvarez, DeNoble and Jung, 2006; Zhao, Seiber and Hills, 2005), which reinforces the importance of integrating entrepreneurship into the curriculum of schools attended by those in poverty and developing more community-based training programs centered on entrepreneurship and the poor.

What about values? Do the poor have values that are inconsistent with entrepreneurial behavior (see Morris and Schindehutte, 2005)? Gans (1995) discusses the unfair tendency to blame the poor for society's problems and stereotype them as shiftless or lazy, irresponsible, morally inferior, culturally deprived, promiscuous, and failing to behave in mainstream ways. While such stereotypes result in discrimination and segregation, closing doors to those in poverty, there is, in fact, no evidence to support such stereotypes.

More critically, people suffering from poverty do not have different values when it comes to a wide range of key economic and social variables. For example, Gorski (2008) concludes that poor people do not have a weaker work ethic or place any less importance on education relative to others. Kohut and Dimock (2013) report little difference in feelings of efficacy, individualism, and personal empowerment when comparing lower- to higher-income groups. They note that the poor believe in the importance of business success for the country's future, and are not more likely to resent the wealthy, particularly those who became wealthy by working hard. In addition, the poor do not differ from those with higher incomes when it comes to believing that individual effort is central to personal success, and that their children will have a better standard of living than they do.

Beyond this, those at the low end of the income scale are actually more likely than others to value living a religious life. The poor demonstrate roughly the same values toward volunteerism and a sense of community (Kohut and Dimock, 2013). Trail and Karney (2012) found that, relative to those with higher incomes, low-income individuals held more traditional values toward marriage, had similar romantic standards for marriage, and experienced similar skills-based relationship problems, while also experiencing more problems related to economic and social issues surrounding marriage (e.g., money, drinking/drug use). The Pew Research Center (2012) reports that, although the importance of marriage and family do not differ much, the poor are more likely to be supportive of single parenting and to not see children born out of wedlock as a bad thing. The same

Pew report further notes that things do not appear to be changing in the contemporary environment – lower-income and less-educated Americans value hard work, patriotism, religion, or family as much as they ever have.

So it would seem we can discard the notion that there is an inherent culture of poverty that is somehow inconsistent with entrepreneurship. In fact, the poor often demonstrate high levels of resilience, adaptability, tenacity, independence, willingness to work hard, and comfort with uncertainty, factors critical for entrepreneurship. Perhaps the bigger mistake is to treat the poor as a monolithic group. Gorski (2008) notes that differences in values and behaviors among the poor are considerable, suggesting they represent a fairly heterogeneous segment of society. Arguably, the same would seem to describe their attitudes, perceptions, beliefs, and preferences when it comes to entrepreneurship.

The reality is that entrepreneurship is a natural path for many of those in poverty (Morris, Pitt and Berthon, 1996). Perhaps to an even greater extent than those in more comfortable circumstances, people in poverty adapt to the opportunities available within their environments. Some of these opportunities are criminal in nature, such as ventures centered on the drug trade, prostitution, money laundering, car theft, gun trading, and credit card fraud. Others involve unregistered or unlicensed businesses that provide goods and services available in the traditional marketplace, but operate informally or in the underground economy. In a study of the underground economy in the inner city, Venkatesh (2006) describes a vibrant business community consisting of a wide range of "off the books" ventures ranging from organized criminal gangs and back alley car repair businesses to hustlers, street musicians, artists, and a homeless person who is not simply sleeping behind a building but actually providing a security service as a night watchman. He notes that those involved see such activity not as illicit behavior but as work, or as a business.

At the same time, while their start-up rate may be lower than that of higher-income individuals, many formal, registered businesses are launched by those in poverty. Unfortunately, of the roughly 700 000 ventures launched each year in the United States, there is strikingly little data on how many are started by those in poverty. But the limited research suggests the number is not insignificant. One study of low-income areas in the US (which made up 20 percent of all areas) concluded that 9.2 percent of all workers were self-employed (keeping in mind that not all poor people reside in low-income areas) (Kugler et al., 2017). Researchers in the United Kingdom report an average rate of self-employment of 5 percent in the country's most deprived communities (Douglas, 2017). Other data suggest that about 30 percent of ventures in the US are started by minorities (McManus, 2012), and minorities are disproportionately represented among the poor (keeping in mind that many in the minority population are not in poverty, and many of the poor who start ventures are not minorities).

TYPES OF ENTREPRENEURS

The challenge in looking for common characteristics among entrepreneurs, again, is that differences tend to outweigh the similarities. Given this heterogeneity, it may be worthwhile to consider general categories of entrepreneurs.

Perhaps the most well-known distinction between types of entrepreneurs was introduced by Smith (1967) and further developed by Smith and Miner (1983). They distinguished "craftsmen" and "opportunists" (or promoters), and suggested a continuum where the entrepreneur tends more toward one versus the other. The "craftsman" has a narrow background in terms of education and training, low social awareness and involvement, weak social skills, and a limited time orientation. They engage in little ongoing planning and are paternalistic toward employees. They tend to create a more rigid venture that does not grow very much. The "opportunist" has a broader background in terms of education and training, high social awareness and involvement, is confident in dealing with the social environment, and is future oriented. This individual tends to embrace change and create a more adaptive enterprise. They demonstrate stronger abilities to delegate and manage strategically. The venture tends to experience higher rates of growth and become more complex with time. Separately, Filley and Aldag (1978) suggest there might be a third type between these two – the entrepreneur who is more of a professional manager, has strong administrative skills, and grows the business at a steady rate.

While there are certainly exceptions, many of those who live in poverty are probably closer to the craftsman type of entrepreneur. They start ventures based on what they know, their previous work experience, and/or what they can quickly learn, and that do not require significant upfront investment (e.g., cleaning services, transport companies, restaurants, construction firms, hair salons, retail stores, various types of repair shops). Creating fairly rigid enterprises, they do not change production methods or experiment with new technologies. New products or capabilities are rarely introduced and their sales tend to derive from the immediate community. Their motives are more to make a living than to become wealthy.

Yet another distinction is drawn between those who are pushed versus pulled into entrepreneurship. Push entrepreneurs are driven by necessity. A layoff or retrenchment, inability to find a job, dissatisfaction with one's job, need to feed one's family, divorce, lack of transportation, and related personal circumstances push them into starting some sort of venture just to survive. Consider the single mother of three who cannot find work (at least nothing within a reasonable distance), or loses her job, receives no child support, and is simply out of options. She starts cutting hair out of her house, making jewelry and selling it from stalls in community markets, or cleaning houses in the hours when she can get someone to watch her children. Not surprisingly, this sort of push (or necessity) entrepreneurship increases in developed economies during economic recessions (Block et al., 2015). In a study of older entrepreneurs in Finland, Tervo (2014) found push motives stronger among women and the less educated.

Pull entrepreneurs are driven by opportunity. They see a possibility, recognize a major unmet need or pain point in the marketplace, and are motivated by the attractiveness of the business idea. This business idea usually represents a novel or innovative approach for capitalizing on the opportunity. However, it does not have to be a major technological breakthrough. For example, the entrepreneur might recognize a whole new approach to junk removal (e.g., 1-800 Got Junk) or a new way to clean houses (e.g., Merry Maids) that offers the potential for rapidly scaling a business. It is also possible that individuals could be influenced by both push and pull motives, but with a tendency for one or the other to be more prominent at a particular point in time (Williams and Williams, 2014).

Block and Wagner (2010) found that pull entrepreneurs have more room to plan their venture compared to push entrepreneurs and are in a better position to acquire the specific human and social capital necessary to discover profitable opportunities. They have higher opportunity costs and so are less likely to pursue low potential ventures. Alternatively, push entrepreneurs pursue low-cost strategies more so than differentiation strategies, which tends to limit their ability over time to adapt to changing customer preferences and marketplace developments (Block et al., 2015).

While the length of time they remain self-employed does not differ between these two types of entrepreneurs, and the evidence on any difference in their respective failure rates is mixed, pull entrepreneurs create more growth-oriented ventures and ventures that are more profitable (Amit and Muller, 1995; Block and Sandner, 2009; Dawson and Henley, 2012; Morris et al., 2006). In separate research conducted in Germany, Block and Koellinger (2009) examined satisfaction levels, finding that financial performance, independence and creativity were all associated with satisfaction for both kinds of entrepreneurs, but also that push or necessity entrepreneurs were generally less satisfied than pull entrepreneurs with their start-up.

Low-income entrepreneurs can demonstrate both push and pull motives (Williams and Williams, 2014). However, at the outset of the venture, a large proportion of them are pushed into entrepreneurship by their circumstances. They have a dream to create something, and perhaps a desire not to work for someone else, but the availability of a good, well-paying job with benefits would likely be enough to dissuade them from pursuing the venture. In fact, they often do not have the data or analytical tools necessary to properly capture the nature, size, and potential of the opportunity, or the underlying market segments that constitute the opportunity. This can lead the entrepreneur to simply assume there is a market, define the market too broadly, and approach the market in an undifferentiated manner. To the extent that they are pushed into entrepreneurship, their background, circumstances, and needs may limit their goals and aspirations for the venture.

TYPES OF VENTURES CREATED BY ENTREPRENEURS

The central focus of entrepreneurship is the act of creating a new organization (Gartner, 1990). Entrepreneurs create many different kinds of organizations, ranging from Google or Facebook to a regional financial services firm, to a local lawn care business. In an attempt to bring some clarity to our understanding of what entrepreneurs create, Morris et al. (2016) propose an integrative typology that includes four basic types of ventures: survival, lifestyle, managed growth and aggressive growth firms. As illustrated in Table 4.1, these four types are defined based on their management focus, management style, entrepreneurial orientation, technology investment, sources of financing, structure, reward emphasis, economic motives, annual growth rate and exit approach.

Survival ventures are primarily a subsistence income source for the owner. They are normally funded by personal finances and the business is principally a source of employment for the business owner. It is a hand-to-mouth existence for the entrepreneur, who often has no permanent premises and a labor-intensive operation (e.g., a handyman, street vendor, seamstress, or person selling fruit and vegetables by the side of the road). The annual growth rate is nominal, and things are managed on a day-to-day basis, with a low entrepreneurial orientation, and no technology investment. The management style is one of reacting to circumstances as they occur, and the venture often centers on a skill or trade.

Lifestyle ventures have an annual growth rate smaller than 5 percent, are focused on weekly and monthly operations, and have a simple

Table 4.1   A typology of venture types

	Survival	Lifestyle	Managed Growth	Aggressive Growth
Annual growth	Nominal	< 5%	10–15%	> 20%
Management focus	Selling	Maintain working business model	Incremental strategic growth	Scalability
Management style	Reactive	Tactical	Strategic	Strategic and proactive
Entrepreneurial orientation	Very low	Low	Moderate	High
Technology investment	None	Limited	Moderate	High
Funding	Self	Self, family & friends, banks	Self, family & friends, banks, private investors	Banks, private investors, venture capital firms, public markets
Structure	Little to none	Simple	Functional, centralized	Functional, product and market based
Economic motives	Sustain oneself	Income substitution	Wealth creation	Wealth creation
Reward emphasis	Weekly income	Salary	Salary, performance incentives, equity	Equity, capital gain
Exit strategy	Shut down	Shut down, sell, transfer	Sell, merge, transfer	Sell, merge, go public

Source: Adapted from Morris et al. (2016).

organizational structure. This type of firm is mainly centered on maintaining a working business model (e.g., for a local hardware store, restaurant, hair salon, or small accounting firm), with a tactical management style, low entrepreneurial orientation, little intellectual property, limited technology investment and financing from the founder, family and friends, and bank institutions. The business provides income substitution for the founder. Money can be periodically reinvested in the business to replace aging equipment, upgrade facilities, or occasionally add a new product or service. Success depends on the operational capabilities and basic management skills of the entrepreneur.

Managed growth ventures have an annual growth rate between 10 percent and 15 percent, where the planning time horizon is one to three years, and the firm executes incremental and controlled growth (i.e., new locations, markets, products or services). Examples might include a regional construction firm, community bank with 15 locations, chain of car dealerships, or a custom job manufacturing plant. There is a more strategic management style, with a moderate entrepreneurial orientation, a moderate technology investment, development of intangible assets, and a functional centralized organizational structure. This type of venture is primarily financed by the founder, family, friends, bank institutions and private investors. The founder has planning, strategizing, delegating and leveraging skills, is aiming to create wealth, and often offers salaries, performance incentives, and sometimes equity to employees (Morris et al., 2016).

Aggressive growth ventures have an annual growth rate exceeding 20 percent, and a planning horizon of two to five years. Sometimes labeled "gazelles," there is a focus on scalability, often based on a new technological development or significant innovation. The firm is characterized by a strategic and proactive management style, with a high entrepreneurial orientation, high technology investment, and a functional, product- and market-based structure emerging over time. This type of venture is financed by banks, private investors, venture capital firms and public markets. Key skills include planning, innovation, cash flow, management and negotiation skills. The founder aims to create wealth by growing the value of the firm's equity (Morris et al., 2016).

Examples exist of poor and even homeless people creating each of the four types, including many managed and aggressive growth ventures. Consider the success of Robert Johnson, who grew up in poverty in Mississippi with nine siblings and went on to found Black Entertainment Television (BET) and create a media conglomerate. Amancio Ortega Gaona went from humble beginnings in La Coruna, Spain where he dropped out of school to work after hearing his mother plead for credit at local stores to buy basic necessities. He created Inditex, which owns such major fashion chains as Zara, Pull & Bear and Stradivarius. Similarly, Daymond John was raised in Queens, New York by a mother who worked multiple jobs to support her seven children and sometimes had so little money they could not turn on the heat. He subsequently built the urban clothing company FUBU into a $6 billion dollar brand and became a star on the television show *Shark Tank*.

However, the poor are disproportionately represented among survival and lifestyle ventures (Fairlie and Robb, 2007). This has important implications for what it takes to succeed with the venture and the kinds of returns they can expect. These types of ventures are built more around tangible than intangible (and harder to mimic) resources, have little in the way of intellectual property (and the unique sources of value that it can produce), operate in mature industries that are highly competitive, and are quite vulnerable to environmental developments (new competitor entry, economic downturn, technological change, new industry regulation, change in customer demand, natural disaster). Based on standard routines and maintenance of the status quo, such ventures are income sources but do not produce much wealth. At the same time, despite their vulnerability, the poor are often able to sustain these kinds of ventures for relatively long periods of time with very little in the way of resources.

Morris and colleagues (2016) have demonstrated how both the entrepreneurial identity of the founder and the organizational identity of the venture differ across the four types of ventures. As such, the characteristics and unique identities of each type can make it difficult for someone in poverty to transition from one venture type to another (e.g., a lifestyle business does not tend to evolve into a managed growth business) (see also Smith and Miner, 1983). The initial resource configuration (including the entrepreneur) combined with capabilities developed to be successful at a given type of venture constrain the ability to transition to another type. When these transitions do occur, they require significant unlearning and development of a new set of skills and capabilities.

A TYPICAL LOW-INCOME START-UP

Based on this discussion, the extant literature, and our experiences in working with poverty-based entrepreneurs over many decades, we can construct a picture of the typical venture launched by the poor within developed economies. While there are exceptions, the large majority of these ventures struggle with ten fundamental challenges:

- *Lack of capital.* Little savings, few assets, lack of collateral, a poor or unestablished credit history, and a limited social network find the entrepreneur launching the business with less than is actually needed, constraining their abilities to serve customers and provide consistent quality, leaving them unable to stock sufficient inventory, and limited in their ability to generate capital for improvements, expansion, or growth.

- *Low entry barriers.* These ventures are frequently launched in industries that have very low entry barriers, suggesting that even if the entrepreneur makes money, it is easy for new competitors to come in. Because these are often older, mature industries and more saturated markets (with little growth opportunity), the new competitors end up taking sales away from the entrepreneur.
- *Difficulty in establishing legitimacy.* The low-income entrepreneur usually has no track record and struggles to achieve legitimacy and a strong negotiating position in dealing with suppliers, distributors/ retailers, and customers.
- *Labor intensity.* Most of these ventures provide either services or hand-made and self-produced products that are labor intensive. As a result, the venture centers on the entrepreneur and his or her skills and personal labor, while employing less in the way of machines and capital equipment.
- *Lack of technology.* The entrepreneur is unable to afford, and may not have the requisite knowledge and skills, to employ technologies in different areas of the business that could increase efficiencies, lower costs, and increase the volume of work that can be handled in a given time period.
- *Little differentiation and competition on a price basis.* Many of these ventures are effectively selling a commodity, where customers perceive relatively little difference among the competing firms in the market and demonstrate little loyalty. Because they will buy from whomever is cheapest, the entrepreneur is forced to keep prices reasonably low.
- *No economies in procurement, buying at retail, and low margins.* As a small operation with little to no excess cash flow, the entrepreneur is forced to buy in small quantities, raising the unit cost. They may be unable to procure from wholesalers, forcing them to buy at retail (when they are selling at retail). This combined with relatively low prices results in very low margins on most of the items being sold.
- *Cash-based operations and inconsistent separation of business and personal expenses.* To the extent that these businesses accept cash only, or a majority of their transactions are in cash, they can experience problems with theft from employees or others and difficulties with properly accounting for revenues. The added tendency for the entrepreneur to use business revenues to pay for personal expenses further undermines the ability to grow the venture.
- *No unique brand identity.* Lack of resources and difficulties in differentiating the business can find the entrepreneur struggling to build a unique brand identity and associated brand equity in the

marketplace. Instead, whatever identity is established tends to be tied to the personal reputation of the entrepreneur.

● *Difficult to scale.* With limited integration of technology and capital equipment into the business, relying on a more labor-intensive operation, with no economies in procurement and little outsourcing capability, and operating with low barriers and intensive competition, it becomes extremely difficult to scale (or even grow) the operation.

What emerges is a very difficult but certainly not hopeless picture. The key is that the entrepreneur understands these liabilities and proactively looks for ways to address them. This again raises the importance of the entrepreneurial mindset described in Chapter 2. Such a mindset can result in a range of effective solutions. Examples include creative approaches to leveraging resources that the entrepreneur does not own; finding and serving unique market niches that are less attractive to larger competitors but that allow for higher prices and margins; uncovering alternative sources of differentiation; tapping into low-cost or free technology solutions; building and using one's network relationships to accomplish business tasks; employing value-based pricing and guerrilla tactics; finding ways to standardize operations; and effectively establishing entry barriers to competitors, among other approaches. We will further explore a number of these approaches in the chapters to come.

REFERENCES

Ali, S.R., E.H. McWhirter and K.M. Chronister (2005), "Self-efficacy and vocational outcome expectations for adolescents of lower socioeconomic status: A pilot study," *Journal of Career Assessment*, **13**(1), 40–58.

Alvarez, R.D., A.F. DeNoble and D. Jung (2006), "Educational curricula and self-efficacy: Entrepreneurial orientation and new venture intentions among university students in Mexico," in C.S. Galbraith and C.H. Stiles (eds), *Developmental Entrepreneurship: Adversity, Risk, and Isolation*, Bingley: Emerald Group Publishing Limited, pp. 379–403.

Amit, R. and E. Muller (1995), "'Push' and 'pull' entrepreneurship," *Journal of Small Business and Entrepreneurship*, **12**(4), 64–80.

Bandura, A. (1977), "Self-efficacy: Toward a unifying theory of behavioral change," *Psychological Review*, **84**(2), 191–215.

Baum, J. and E. Locke (2004), "The relationship of entrepreneurial traits, skill, and motivation to subsequent venture growth," *Journal of Applied Psychology*, **89**(4), 587–98.

Berkman, E. (2015), "It's not a lack of self-control that keeps people poor," *The Conversation*, September 22, accessed June 8, 2018 at https://theconversation.com/its-not-a-lack-of-self-control-that-keeps-people-poor-47734.

Bird, B.J. (1989), *Entrepreneurial Behavior*, Glenview, IL: Scott, Foresman and Company.

Block, J. and P. Koellinger (2009), "I can't get no satisfaction – necessity entrepreneurship and procedural utility," *Kyklos*, **62**(2), 191–209.

Block, J. and P. Sandner (2009), "Necessity and opportunity entrepreneurs and their duration in self-employment: Evidence from German micro data," *Journal of Industry, Competition and Trade*, **9**(2), 117–37.

Block, J. and M. Wagner (2010), "Necessity and opportunity entrepreneurs in Germany: Characteristics and earnings differentials", *Schmalenbach Business Review*, **62**, 154–74.

Block, J.H., K. Kohn, D. Miller and K. Ullrich (2015), "Necessity entrepreneurship and competitive strategy," *Small Business Economics*, **44**(1), 37–54.

Boardman, J.D. and S.A. Robert (2000), "Neighborhood socioeconomic status and perceptions of self-efficacy," *Sociological Perspectives*, **43**(1), 117–36.

Dawson, C. and A. Henley (2012), "'Push' versus 'pull' entrepreneurship: An ambiguous distinction?," *International Journal of Entrepreneurial Behavior and Research*, **18**(6), 697–719.

Douglas, L. (2017), "Rags to riches: Why the privileged are more likely to become entrepreneurs," *The Guardian Small Business Network*, February 20, accessed June 8, 2018 at https://www.theguardian.com/small-business-network/2017/feb/20/rags-riches-privileged-entrepreneurs-business-resilience-michelle-mone.

Fairlie, R.W. and A.M. Robb (2007), "Why are black-owned businesses less successful than white-owned businesses? The role of families, inheritances, and business human capital," *Journal of Labor Economics*, **25**(2), 289–323.

Filley, A.C. and R.J. Aldag (1978), "Characteristics and measurement of an organizational typology," *Academy of Management Journal*, **21**(4), 578–91.

Gans, H. (1995), *The War Against the Poor: The Underclass and Antipoverty Policy*, New York: Basic Books.

Gartner, W.B. (1990), "What are we talking about when we talk about entrepreneurship?," *Journal of Business Venturing*, **5**(1), 15–28.

Gorski, P. (2008), "The myth of the culture poverty," *Educational Leadership*, **65**(7), 32–6.

Hmieleski, K.M. and A.C. Corbett (2008), "The contrasting interaction effects of improvisational behavior with entrepreneurial self-efficacy on new venture performance and entrepreneur work satisfaction," *Journal of Business Venturing*, **23**(4), 482–96.

Kohut, A. and M. Dimock (2013), "Resilient American values: Optimism in an era of growing inequality and economic difficulty," *Renewing America Working Paper*, accessed June 9, 2018 at https://www.cfr.org/report/resilient-american-values.

Kugler, M., M. Michaelides, N. Nanda and C. Agbayani (2017), *Entrepreneurship in Low-Income Areas*, Washington, DC: Office of Advocacy, US Small Business Administration.

McManus, M. (2012), *Minority Business Ownership: Data from the 2012 Survey of Business Owners*, Washington, DC: Office of Advocacy, US Small Business Administration.

Morris, M.H. (1998), *Entrepreneurial Intensity: Sustainable Advantages for Individuals, Organizations, and Societies*, Westport, CT: Quorum Books.

Morris, M.H. and M. Schindehutte (2005), "Entrepreneurial values and the ethnic enterprise: An examination of six subcultures," *Journal of Small Business Management*, **43**(4), 453–79.

Morris, M.H., L.F. Pitt and P. Berthon (1996), "Entrepreneurial activity in the Third World informal sector: The view from Khayelitsha," *International Journal of Entrepreneurial Behavior and Research*, **2**(1), 59–76.

Morris, M.H., N.N. Miyasaki, C.E. Watters and S.M. Coombes (2006), "The dilemma of growth: Understanding venture size choices of women entrepreneurs," *Journal of Small Business Management*, **44**(2), 221–44.

Morris, M.H., X. Neumeyer, Y. Jang and D.F. Kuratko (2016), "Distinguishing types of entrepreneurial ventures: An identity-based perspective," *Journal of Small Business Management*, accessed June 8, 2018 at https://doi.org/10.1111/jsbm.12272.

Pew Research Center (2012), *The Lost Decade of the Middle Class: Fewer, Poorer, Gloomier*, Washington, DC: Pew Research Center, accessed June 8, 2018 at http://www.pewsocialtrends.org/2012/08/22/the-lost-decade-of-the-middle-class.

Smith, N.R. (1967), *The Entrepreneur and His Firm: The Relationship Between Type of Man and Type of Company*, Bureau of Business and Economic Research, Michigan State University.

Smith, N.R. and J.B. Miner (1983), "Type of entrepreneur, type of firm, and managerial motivation: Implications for organizational life cycle theory," *Strategic Management Journal*, **4**(4), 325–40.

Tervo, H. (2014), "Who turns to entrepreneurship later in life? Push and pull in Finnish rural and urban areas," in *Proceedings of 54th European Congress of the Regional Science Association, St. Petersburg 26–29 August*, Louvain-la-Neuve: European Regional Science Association, pp. 236–49.

Trail, T.E. and B.R. Karney (2012), "What's (not) wrong with low-income marriages," *Journal of Marriage and Family*, **74**(3), 413–27.

Venkatesh, S.A. (2006), *Off the Books: The Underground Economy of the Urban Poor*, Cambridge, MA: Harvard University Press.

Williams, N. and C.C. Williams (2014), "Beyond necessity versus opportunity entrepreneurship: Some lessons from English deprived urban neighbourhoods," *International Entrepreneurship and Management Journal*, **10**(1), 23–40.

Zhao, H., C. Seibert and C. Hills (2005), "The mediating role of self-efficacy in the development of entrepreneurial intentions," *Journal of Applied Psychology*, **90**(2), 1265–72.

5. Opportunity horizons and the poor

> All they need is opportunity.
> (Muhammad Yunus)

OPPORTUNITY AS THE BEGINNING POINT

In Chapter 2, entrepreneurship was introduced as a process comprising a set of stages. It begins with the recognition of an opportunity, ostensibly one that is big enough to sustain a new venture and any competitors that follow the entrepreneur into the marketplace. This first stage produces one of the most critical questions in entrepreneurship: Why do some people, and not others, discover a particular opportunity (Shane, 2003)? As we shall see, scholarly researchers have made some progress in attempting to answer this question. Our focus in this chapter is to explore the challenges of recognizing attractive opportunities, particularly when one grows up in, and is surrounded by, poverty.

An opportunity refers to a favorable set of circumstances in the external environment creating a need or opening for a new business concept. It is a gap or hole in the marketplace. The existence of an opportunity suggests an unmet or insufficiently met customer need. It is a situation where something can be improved or done differently at a profit. Entrepreneurs look for the presence of "pain" or dissatisfaction in the marketplace that can be removed with a new product or service that is different or better than what currently exists. Most definitions of opportunity share the assumption that they bring into existence new goods, services, raw materials and organizing methods that can be sold at more than their cost of production (Eckhardt and Shane, 2003; Grégoire, Shepherd and Lambert, 2010). Opportunities vary on four critical characteristics: the potential economic value that they represent, their relative newness, their perceived desirability, and a temporal dimension (how long they last) (Baron, 2006).

We might also consider the criterion of acceptability within a given society. That is, we can distinguish so-called bona fide opportunities, or ones that are consistent with the values and laws of a society, from ones that are not. The latter often generate new ventures or selling activities, but fall within the informal economy (see Chapter 4). Webb et al. (2009)

define the informal sector in terms of "activities to recognize and exploit opportunities occurring outside formal institutional boundaries but within informal institutional boundaries" (p. 496). Lack of resources, skills, capabilities, and other constraints typical of those experiencing poverty and adverse circumstances can drive individuals to pursue opportunities in the informal economy (e.g., Pessar, 1995; Raijman, 2001).

In contemporary developed economies, entrepreneurial opportunities are abundant, perhaps more so than at any time in history. New technologies, rapid social change, heterogeneous markets, changing demographics, and highly mobile resources, among other factors, contribute to the constant emergence of new gaps or openings that can be capitalized upon by entrepreneurs. But is this abundance of opportunities the case for those experiencing poverty? Certainly if one focuses on their immediate surroundings, the opportunities can be limited, but they exist. The bigger issue is the ability to recognize opportunities that extend beyond those surroundings. The term "entrepreneurial alertness" is used to describe a person's ability to spot market imperfections, recognize patterns, and be open to an ongoing discovery process (Gaglio and Katz, 2001; Kirzner, 1979). In this chapter we argue that poverty circumstances do not limit one's alertness to opportunity, but rather, may limit the kinds of opportunities one is able to perceive, and the ability to capitalize on those opportunities.

THE NATURE OF OPPORTUNITY

The challenge for many low-income entrepreneurs is that they start with an idea for a business without a clear sense of the underlying opportunity. Hence, they start a cleaning service, or purchase a truck for the purpose of providing a moving service, and just assume that there is enough of a market opportunity to support their new venture. In fact, by focusing too much on the particular business idea, they often constrain the possible opportunities they might have been able to capitalize upon.

While they come in all shapes and sizes, there are four general categories of opportunities, each of which readily applies to someone in poverty. Perennial opportunities are those that are always there. They concern the potential to find customers who will pay to have something done cheaper, quicker, with higher quality, more reliably, or incrementally better than it is being done at present. For example, the need for transport services is ongoing in urban areas, and the entrepreneur who can move people or packages on a timelier basis or at a lower price is pursuing a perennial opportunity. Occasional opportunities occur based on situational developments, such as natural disaster, introduction of a new capability, withdrawal from the market of a key supplier, demand surge, new regulation, emergence of a new market segment, or existence of a market hole. An example is the need for generators, building materials, or tree removal services after a hurricane or tornado. Multiple-cause opportunities emerge based on a confluence of developments in the external environment. For instance, if there are more single mothers who are working full-time and are also worried about how much exercise their children are getting, the combination of these three developments may represent an opportunity for some new type of neighborhood recreational service. Multiple-effect opportunities emerge when a particular development in the external environment opens a number of new possibilities simultaneously. The launch of smartphones created new opportunities for car sharing, delivering educational courses, providing patient care, monitoring employee activities, and scheduling deliveries, among many others.

Opportunities can be big or small and attractive or unattractive. Seven factors go into delineating something as an entrepreneurial opportunity (Figure 5.1). These include: (1) identifying particular forces in the external environment that drive or create the opportunity; (2) defining a customer need and understanding associated customer perceptions; (3) specifying the boundaries on the market being served and the distinct customer segments being focused upon; (4) estimating market size (potential units or sales revenue); (5) delineating the window of time during which the opportunity can be successfully capitalized upon; (6) recognizing the strength of customer loyalties to existing products or services that could address the same need and the associated customer switching costs; and (7) determining the nature, extent, and aggressiveness of current and potential competitors.

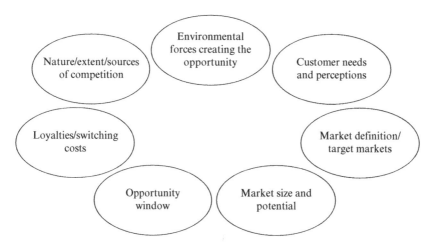

Figure 5.1   Factors that contribute to the existence of an opportunity

For the low-income entrepreneur, a significant challenge concerns actually determining the size and financial attractiveness of an opportunity. This is generally more art than science. Far too often, the actual opportunity is much smaller than the entrepreneur assumed or estimated – forcing the business to fail or quickly adapt toward a different opportunity. While they may lack access to extensive databases or sophisticated methodologies for quantifying how much of an opportunity exists, it is important that these entrepreneurs interview customers, visit and conduct research on competitors, talk to suppliers, and otherwise develop insights on the scope of the available opportunity. We will further explore guerrilla and low-cost research approaches in Chapter 10.

In practice, the opportunities pursued by low-income entrepreneurs are often smaller and/or less attractive, and center on more basic customer needs. They can be limited due to the presence of multiple competitors, a lack of barriers to entry, and a limited potential customer base made up of users who are more price sensitive. Further, even where the overall opportunity appears to be sizeable, the entrepreneur is only able to compete for a very small and often marginal piece of what might be available because of resource and capacity constraints. The key to changing such tendencies begins with rethinking how the entrepreneur recognizes and defines opportunity.

UNCOVERING OPPORTUNITIES

How does the entrepreneur uncover an opportunity? It is critical that we appreciate how, even for someone in poverty, opportunities (imperfections in factor or product markets) are everywhere – they just need to be seen. The beginning point is to understand the principal sources of opportunities. Again, opportunities derive from developments in the external environment. Consider some examples (see also Figure 5.2):

- The passing of new laws or regulations, such as the lengthening of the school day, legalization of marijuana, banning of smoking in public areas, or requirements that cars be inspected.
- Demographic changes such as the aging of the boomer population, the growth of the immigrant population, an increase in single-parent households, or the decline of the middle class.
- Technological developments such as smartphone apps, miniaturization of electronic components, 3D printing, drones, telemedicine, and touch technology that create new capabilities or possibilities.
- Social trends that capture changes in people's behaviors, habits, values, perceptions, and beliefs. For example, people eating healthier,

Figure 5.2   Sources of opportunities

a preference for home schooling, concerns about environmental degradation, or a growing tendency for students to move home after college or get married later.

- Changes in supplier and labor markets, such as the employee desire for flex time or to work remotely, the ability to outsource key activities, the availability of third-party logistics companies, and the emergence of new supply or distribution channels.
- Underserved or poorly served markets, perhaps due to the remote locations of customers, weak infrastructure, supply shortages, poor economic conditions, lack of competition, or high crime rates.
- Unexpected occurrences, including natural disasters (e.g., flood, drought), war, a prolonged labor strike, pandemic disease, among many other possibilities.

Entrepreneurs are engaged in pattern recognition, using mental tools to recognize meaningful patterns from developments in the external environment, and structural alignment, where they make comparisons in order to detect common and contrasting aspects between events (Baron and Ensley, 2006; Grégoire, Barr and Shepherd, 2010; Santos et al., 2015). While sometimes uncovered through a process of deliberate search, they are often stumbled upon in the course of everyday life. The entrepreneur observes these sorts of patterns, developments or cues and begins to ask such questions as "What problems or needs does this change produce?"; "What does this change enable me to do that previously might not have been possible?"; and "How can I make money from this change?" It is through the process of addressing these kinds of questions that the entrepreneur is able to identify a potential market opportunity.

If opportunities derive from developments in the external environment, then the environment surrounding those in poverty plays a critical role in determining what kinds of opportunities they are able to discern or recognize. The key, then, is to understand the critical aspects of the context within which the individual might launch a business, and how this context affects the tendency to recognize promising opportunities.

OPPORTUNITY ALERTNESS AND THE POOR

The concept of entrepreneurial alertness refers to the ability of a person to notice opportunities overlooked by others (Kirzner, 1979). When individuals are more alert, they demonstrate a better ability to uncover and clarify gaps and cues in the environment, as if they have an "antenna" that continually recognizes stimuli that represent opportunities (Tang, Kacmar and Busenitz, 2012). Alertness is built upon a person's interpretation framework (which is reflective of their perceptual and cognitive processing skills and the mental schemas they rely upon), stock of knowledge, and everyday life experiences (Lee et al., 1999; Shepherd and DeTienne, 2005; Yu, 2001). Further, there is a greater tendency for opportunities to be recognized in areas of stronger interest, passion or vocation (Cardon et al., 2009; Chen, Yao and Kotha, 2009). People's attention is directed to things that they are on the lookout for and, accordingly, are able to perceive more clearly (Minniti, 2004).

The implication is that opportunity recognition is an idiosyncratic process. The poor are no different than others in that some are more entrepreneurially alert and some are less so. Different individuals exposed to the same information may recognize (or fail to recognize) different business opportunities, even when they have similar backgrounds and come from similar contexts. Further, alertness is a variable that can change over time, such that levels of alertness can be increased among the poor. It is impacted by personal traits that may be less amenable to change, but also by motivational incentives (e.g., inability to find a job or to support one's family), by the information one is able to obtain from the environment in which one finds oneself, and by entrepreneurially related experience (people become more alert based on starting things) (Gaglio and Katz, 2001; Minniti, 2004). Yu (2001, p. 52) argues that self-competition, or "intertemporal competition between future and past selves stemming from the desire of the present self to test self-ability" is the most important consideration in enhancing alertness.

Particular factors might make someone in poverty less entrepreneurially alert. While pure necessity can promote alertness, the presence of urgent or overwhelming problems (hunger, illness, emotional strain, violence) can so preoccupy the individual that they have less cognitive room to be alert. Similarly, individuals may develop fairly fixed interpretation frameworks in order to ensure basic survival in a challenging poverty context. Information that derives from new events or novel developments is made to fit the person's existing interpretation framework, and anything that disrupts or challenges this framework is ignored or viewed as a deviance or obstacle (Yu, 2001). Modifying one's framework, interpreting things in different ways, and uncovering new ways of seeing how things fit together can seem quite risky. They may therefore have less motivation to search for information that refutes existing assumptions or the status quo. Further, the nature of new informational inputs available to the poor could produce opportunities of such limited potential, or which require resources that seem so far beyond the reach of the individual, that they become less motivated over time to recognize new possibilities.

THE ENTREPRENEUR'S OPPORTUNITY HORIZON

Assuming some level of alertness then, a related issue concerns the kinds of opportunities that are identified by those in poverty. As noted in Chapter 4, the poor launch ventures of all types, including high-growth ventures, but they disproportionately start survival and lifestyle ventures. Various factors account for this tendency, but a key one concerns the entrepreneur's opportunity horizon, or the range of possibilities they are able to perceive (Morris, Schindehutte and LaForge, 2002). As Berkman (2015) notes, poverty restricts a person's vision of what might be possible.

When thinking about starting a business, we tend to consider the things we know. The realm of possibilities tends to be limited to (1) the needs we become familiar with in our daily lives as a mother, student, military veteran, victim, shopper, person with a health ailment or disability, owner of a pet, hobbyist, and so forth; (2) skills we possess and work experiences we have had; and (3) things we directly observe in our surroundings, particularly our fairly immediate environs. While other factors may come into play, we are most influenced by what we are familiar with. The person in poverty may be alert to opportunities, but the range of opportunities that they are able to recognize at any point in time is delimited by this horizon. Quite simply if a person has never been exposed to a computer, it is difficult for them to perceive opportunities related to computer equipment, software, networks, or services.

This suggests that the environment, circumstances or context in which the individual is embedded can impose boundaries on their opportunity horizon (Morris et al., 2002). One's context can limit the information content to which one is exposed while imposing rules and norms regarding how things are done, how one gets ahead, and what is appropriate (Baumol, 1990; Welter, 2011). It provides information while serving as a lens through which information is processed.

Opportunity horizons of the poor can be characterized in terms of two dimensions: breadth and depth. Breadth refers to the range of different opportunity arenas within which the entrepreneur is able to perceive or recognize possibilities. While one may see opportunities in personal care, cleaning, transport, or construction, one may be unable to recognize opportunities related to genetic engineering of crops or design of underwater drones. Depth concerns a number of possibilities that are apparent within the specific opportunity arenas apparent to the entrepreneur. So within plumbing, one may see the opportunity to provide plumbing services to households who have a specific problem, but not perceive the need for selling plumbing service contracts that provide preventative maintenance and repair at a fixed annual rate. A nurse may see opportunities to build a business around home health care visits, but not see the possibility of providing patient assistance via telemedicine.

The opportunity horizon for each individual is unique. Consider an individual living in a low-income neighborhood, with high unemployment rates and low earnings for individuals with low levels of education. The neighborhood might be characterized by segregation, inequality, crime, gangs, violence, inadequate housing, lower-quality schools, limited job opportunities, disorder, a lack of exposure to technology, and lots of families who struggle just to get by. The individual may have lived all their life in this kind of neighborhood, exposed to in-group socialization (i.e., establishing social ties and interacting with others from that same inner circle) (Harding, 2009). For many, moving out of such neighborhoods would seem to be a myth – one study found that 70 percent of the families living in such high-poverty neighborhoods in 1972 were found to be still living in similar neighborhoods 40 years later (Sharkey, 2013). This sort of environment can limit the kinds of demographic, social, technological, competitive, regulatory or other developments of which one is aware or to which one is exposed. Thus, the opportunity horizon of such an individual is inevitably constrained, often to very small and short-lived pockets of disequilibrium in the marketplace.

But opportunity horizons do not have to be static and predetermined. They can be flexible, dynamic, and elastic. Opportunity horizons can be enhanced where the individual is exposed to new sources or types of information, influences, and experiences. For example, as a teenager from such a context pursues an internship out of the neighborhood, joins the military and travels abroad, takes on a hobby that leads them to pursue whole new sources of information and expertise, is able to attend college, engages in or expands their social network by connecting with people in different social and economic milieus, they can be stimulated by a different reality and their opportunity horizon expands. The social context is particularly important for expanding the individual's opportunity horizon (Aldrich and Zimmer, 1986).

Similarly, the institutional context matters. The culture, values, societal norms and attitudes of the neighborhood can serve to highlight opportunities in the informal economy, including technically illegal, anti-social or socially incongruent activities (De Soto, 1989). Lack of support from formal institutions coupled with severe resource constraints can make the identification and exploitation of opportunities in the informal economy especially attractive (Webb et al., 2013).

Figure 5.3 represents a conceptualization of the opportunity horizon for someone in poverty. Here, three levels of boundaries can serve to expand or contract the opportunity horizon. At the core level, the opportunity horizon of someone in poverty can be expanded by exposure to new knowledge, information, education, personal experiences, and self-observation of other realities. Second-level factors include out-group socialization, peers and leaders, connections with different neighborhoods and communities, and role models. At a more macro level, institutional support, government support and requirements, empowering programs, and active civic participation are examples of strategies and devices to promote the expansion of opportunity horizons among the poor. It is at this third level where entrepreneurship intervention programs directed at the poor fit in.

Alvarez and Barney (2014) provide a related argument regarding limits to the kinds of opportunities those in poverty are most likely to recognize. They distinguish self-employment, discovery and creation opportunities (see also Yu, 2001 and his discussion of ordinary versus extraordinary discovery). In essence, a self-employment opportunity involves replication

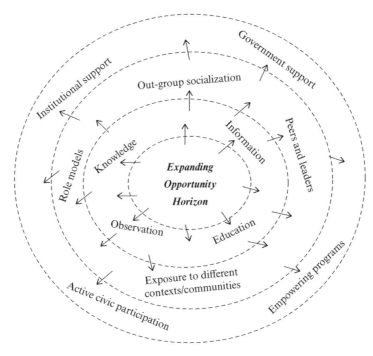

Figure 5.3   Elements impacting opportunity horizons of the poor

of existing business concepts to fill some unmet demand. They are not scalable and have limited potential. Discovery opportunities are formed by exogenous shocks to an industry or market (e.g., significant regulatory, social, or demographic change), where being early in seeing the potential of these developments and creating barriers to entry are critical for scalability and success. Creation opportunities find the entrepreneur actually initiating change in the environment that opens up new possibilities, generally by developing new knowledge or technology. New needs are created or needs that previously could not be addressed are now addressed. The result is new behaviors and routines on the part of both the entrepreneur (and other members of the value chain) and the users. The authors argue that those living in conditions of abject poverty will be more likely to recognize and exploit self-employment opportunities than discovery or creation opportunities This likelihood is due to the lower levels of human, social, and financial capital and more limited infrastructure necessary to support self-employment opportunities. However, the authors acknowledge that all three are possible when the challenges of the capital constraints and infrastructure can be overcome.

EMERGENCE AND THE CORRIDOR PRINCIPLE

More often than not, the opportunity one initially recognizes is not the opportunity that ultimately results in a successful venture (Morris and Webb, 2015). That is, the opportunity the entrepreneur has in mind at the outset often proves to not really exist or to be too small. However, by starting the venture, interacting with market forces, learning from what does not work, and experimenting with alternative approaches, the entrepreneur is able to discover where the real opportunity lies. This tendency suggests that opportunities tend to emerge. Related to the emergent nature of opportunities is the so-called corridor principle (Ronstadt, 1988), which suggests that the act of starting allows the entrepreneur to see other possibilities that would not have been apparent had the venture not been launched.

Emergence and the corridor principle often work against the poor when they start ventures. Severely under-resourced, highly vulnerable to unexpected developments, and facing ongoing pressures to support themselves and their families, they are not able to engage the marketplace in sufficient depth or to experiment (and make mistakes) in the kinds of ways that allow for the discovery of alternative opportunities that have real potential. Or, if they are able to recognize the higher potential opportunity, they are unable to capitalize on it.

Consider an example. An entrepreneur starts a cleaning business and initially perceives that the opportunity lies with the residential market. While some inroads are made with this market, it proves to be too crowded or insufficiently profitable. Yet, based on new information that becomes available because the entrepreneur is interacting with stakeholders in the marketplace, they are able to determine that the real opportunity may lie with cleaning medical offices or warehouses or government buildings. By the time these alternative opportunities start to become apparent, the entrepreneur does not have the resources or time to validate them through experimentation. Alternatively, at the outset they configure their very limited resources in ways that can work against the ability of the firm to adapt in ways that would enable it to pivot and satisfactorily serve the medical office niche. That is, the initial resource configuration creates a path dependency where future decision options are delimited by past resource commitments.

FROM OPPORTUNITIES TO VENTURES: THE ISSUE OF FIT

A central theme of this chapter is that opportunities drive the entrepreneurial process. Unfortunately, many low-income entrepreneurs are more focused on establishing the business itself while assuming there must be an opportunity out there, or they operate from a "build it and they will come" mentality. Alternatively, they may have a generic sense of some need they are satisfying, but a less clear understanding of unique aspects of that need, distinct market segments or niches with different requirements and buying behaviors, or of particular gaps with regard to competitor offerings or capabilities. Even when reasonably well-identified and understood, the opportunities they identify often involve fairly well-established markets where the entrepreneur is offering modest modifications from that available through existing competitors, and where it is quite difficult to establish any sort of entry barriers or sustainable advantage. As we have seen, some of this is due to their opportunity horizons, and how the range of possibilities that they can envision is limited by the context. Yet there are clearly exceptions, such as the creation of retail giant Zara by Amancio Ortega who was raised in extreme poverty in Northern Spain, or the building of Starbucks by Howard Schultz who grew up in low-income housing, or the launch of WhatsApp by Jan Koum after immigrating to the US as a child with his mother and rising out of poverty (Hess, 2017; Olson, 2014; O'Shea, 2012).

Once recognized, the venture created by the entrepreneur must fit the opportunity. This fit is reflected in everything from the products offered and the pricing approach to operating hours, customer service, marketing methods, web presence, logistics and staffing. This fit can be difficult to achieve for the low-income entrepreneur based on a weak understanding of the opportunity, the fact that the opportunity is emergent, and the limited resources controlled by the entrepreneur. And again, the initial way in which the entrepreneur's limited resources are configured can constrain the extent to which they are able to easily adapt as they come to better understand customers and competitors.

It becomes important that intervention efforts focused on fostering entrepreneurship among the poor begin when they are young, initially by fostering alertness and expanding the opportunity horizon. In working with those ready to start something, attention must not just be focused on the business idea, bookkeeping, marketing, obtaining finance or similar business basics. Much more emphasis must be placed on the opportunity recognition stage of the entrepreneurial process. By helping entrepreneurs better understand opportunity, and specifically the underlying causes, nature, size, rate of growth, customer segments, buyer behaviors, and competitive threats that constitute an opportunity, the potential for venture survival and growth will be considerably enhanced.

REFERENCES

Aldrich, H.E. and C. Zimmer (1986), "Entrepreneurship through social networks," in D. Sexton and R. Smilor (eds), *The Art and Science of Entrepreneurship*, New York: Ballinger, pp. 2–23.

Alvarez, S.A. and J.B. Barney (2014), "Entrepreneurial opportunities and poverty alleviation," *Entrepreneurship Theory and Practice*, **38**, 159–84.

Baron, R.A. (2006), "Opportunity recognition as pattern recognition: How entrepreneurs 'connect the dots' to identify new business opportunities," *Academy of Management Perspectives*, **20**(1), 104–19.

Baron, R.A. and M.D. Ensley (2006), "Opportunity recognition as the detection of meaningful patterns: Evidence from comparisons of novice and experienced entrepreneurs," *Management Science*, **52**(9), 1331–44.

Baumol, W.J. (1990), "Entrepreneurship: Productive, unproductive and destructive," *Journal of Political Economy*, **98**(3), 893–921.

Berkman, E. (2015), "It's not a lack of self-control that keeps people poor," *The Conversation*, September 22, accessed June 8, 2018 at https://theconversation.com/its-not-a-lack-of-self-control-that-keeps-people-poor-47734.

Cardon, M.S., J. Wincent, J. Singh and M. Drnovsek (2009), "The nature and experience of entrepreneurial passion," *Academy of Management Review*, **34**(3), 511–32.

Chen, X., X. Yao and S.B. Kotha (2009), "Passion and preparedness in entrepreneurs' business plan presentations: A persuasion analysis of venture capitalists' funding decisions," *Academy of Management Journal*, **52**(1), 199–214.

De Soto, H. (1989), *The Other Path: The Invisible Revolution in the Third World*, New York: Harper & Row.

Eckhardt, J.T. and S.A. Shane (2003), "Opportunities and entrepreneurship," *Journal of Management*, **29**(3), 333–4.

Gaglio, C.M. and J.A. Katz (2001), "The psychological basis of opportunity identification: Entrepreneurial alertness," *Small Business Economics*, **16**(2), 95–111.

Grégoire, D.A., P.S. Barr and D.A. Shepherd (2010), "Cognitive processes of opportunity recognition," *Organization Science*, **21**(2), 413–31.

Grégoire, D.A., D.A. Shepherd and L.S. Lambert (2010), "Measuring opportunity recognition beliefs," *Organizational Research Methods*, **13**(1), 114–45.

Harding, D.J. (2009), "Collateral consequences of violence in disadvantaged neighborhoods," *Social Forces*, **88**(2), 757–84.

Hess, A. (2017), "How WhatsApp founder Jan Koum went from welfare to billionaire," *CNBC*, April 24, accessed June 8, 2018 at https://www.cnbc.com/2017/04/24/how-whatsapp-founder-jan-koum-went-from-welfare-to-billionaire.html.

Kirzner, I. (1979), *Perception, Opportunity, and Profit*, Chicago, IL: University of Chicago Press.

Lee, H., P.M. Herr, F.R. Kardes and C. Kim (1999), "Motivated search: Effects of choice accountability, issue involvement, and prior knowledge on information acquisition and use," *Journal of Business Research*, **45**(1), 75–88.

Minniti, M. (2004), "Entrepreneurial alertness and asymmetric information in a spin-glass model," *Journal of Business Venturing*, **19**(5), 637–58.

Morris, M.H. and J.W. Webb (2015), "Entrepreneurship as emergence," in C.E. Shalley, M.A. Hitt and J. Zhou (eds), *The Oxford Handbook of Creativity, Innovation and Entrepreneurship*, Oxford: Oxford University Press, pp. 457–76.

Morris, M.H., M. Schindehutte and R.W. LaForge (2002), "Entrepreneurial marketing: A construct for integrating emerging entrepreneurship and marketing perspectives," *Journal of Marketing Theory and Practice*, **10**(4), 1–19.

Olson, P. (2014), "Exclusive: The rags-to-riches tale of how Jan Koum built WhatsApp into Facebook's new \$19 billion baby," *Forbes*, February 19, accessed June 8, 2018 at https://www.forbes.com/sites/parmyolson/2014/02/19/exclusive-inside-story-how-jan-koum-built-whatsapp-into-facebooks-new-19-billion-baby/#3dece4f82fa1.

O'Shea, C. (2012), *The Man From Zara: The Story of the Genius Behind the Inditex Group*, London: LID Publishing, Inc.

Pessar, P.R. (1995), "The elusive enclave: Ethnicity, class, and nationality among Latino entrepreneurs in Greater Washington, DC," *Human Organization*, **54**, 383–92.

Raijman, R. (2001), "Mexican immigrants and informal self-employment in Chicago," *Human Organization*, **60**, 47–55.

Ronstadt, R. (1988), "The corridor principal and entrepreneurial time," *Journal of Business Venturing*, **3**(1), 31–40.

Santos, S.C., A. Caetano, R. Baron and L. Curral (2015), "Prototype models of opportunity recognition and the decision to launch a new venture: Identifying the basic dimensions," *International Journal of Entrepreneurial Behavior & Research*, **21**(4), 510–38.

Shane, S. (2003), *A General Theory of Entrepreneurship: The Individual–Opportunity Nexus*, Cheltenham, UK and Northampton, MA, USA: Edward Elgar Publishing.

Sharkey, P. (2013), *Stuck in Place: Urban Neighborhoods and the End of Progress Toward Racial Equality*, Chicago, IL: University of Chicago Press.

Shepherd, D.A. and D.R. DeTienne (2005), "Prior knowledge, potential financial reward, and opportunity identification," *Entrepreneurship Theory and Practice*, **29**(1), 91–112.

Tang, J., K.M. Kacmar and L. Busenitz (2012), "Entrepreneurial alertness in the pursuit of new opportunities," *Journal of Business Venturing*, **27**(1), 77–94.

Webb, J.W., G.D. Bruton, L. Tihanyi and R.D. Ireland (2013), "Research on entrepreneurship in the informal economy: Framing a research agenda," *Journal of Business Venturing*, **28**(5), 598–614.

Webb, J.W., L. Tihanyi, R.D. Ireland and D.G. Sirmon (2009), "You say illegal, I say legitimate: Entrepreneurship in the informal economy," *Academy of Management Review*, **34**(3), 492–510.

Welter, F. (2011), "Contextualizing entrepreneurship – conceptual challenges and ways forward," *Entrepreneurship Theory and Practice*, **35**(1), 165–84.

Yu, T.F.L. (2001), "Entrepreneurial alertness and discovery," *The Review of Austrian Economics*, **14**(1), 47–63.

6.   The challenges of literacy among the poor

> To me, the poor are like Bonsai trees. When you plant the best seed of the tallest tree in a six-inch deep flower pot, you get a perfect replica of the tallest tree, but it is only inches tall. There is nothing wrong with the seed you planted; only the soil-base you provided was inadequate.
>
> (Muhammad Yunus)

INTRODUCTION

Arguably, more important than any other resource when starting a business are the abilities to read and write, use language, numbers, images, and computers, understand and communicate effectively, acquire and assimilate knowledge, and solve mathematical and everyday problems. Being literate in its multiple facets is at the core of the ability to perform entrepreneurial activities, and can be a critical Achilles' heel for the poor who want to start ventures.

As one might expect, literacy levels are lower both in developing and developed countries among ethnic and cultural minorities, women, and the poor – those who are more marginalized in society (Ahmed, 1992). All too often, schools in low-income communities tend to perpetuate the status quo when it comes to illiteracy rather than improve upon it (Neuman, 2006). Evidence suggests that the probability of someone who is a poor reader at the end of Grade 1 remaining a poor reader at the end of Grade 4 is 0.88 (Juel, 1988; Juel, Griffith and Gough, 1986).

Literacy deficits are frequently a generational inheritance. When families suffer long-term unemployment, a child's cognitive development can be negatively affected (Corcoran and Chaudry, 1997). Poor health conditions (hearing problems, ear infections, dental problems, asthma, poor nutrition and housing) also shape the cognitive abilities and achievements of young children and adolescents over time (Duncan and Brooks-Gunn, 1997; Rothstein, 2004). Cognitive development and literacy among the poor are hindered by the family's inability to acquire needed resources to promote a child's development, such as extra lessons, learning materials, resources associated with knowledge acquisition, or extra-curricular activities (Foster, 2002). Researchers have found that while there are more than a dozen books per child in middle-income neighborhoods, in low-income neighborhoods the ratio is closer to one book for every 300 children (Neuman and Celano, 2001). Another key factor involves the emotional resources of the parents, including the impact on children of a parent's depression, physical exhaustion, reduced well-being, lower emotional intelligence or inability to interact in a responsive manner. The negative statistical relationship between having fewer material and emotional resources and cognitive development is well-established (see Jencks and Philips, 1998). It is reflected in large differences in the ability to read, write and general literacy levels of children from low-income compared to middle- and upper-income families.

The impact of reduced literacy and poorer learning habits among children tends to carry through their adult lives (Duncan and Brooks-Gunn, 1997) with a demonstrable effect on job and career advancement opportunities (McIntosh and Vignoles, 2001). Low quantitative literacy skills have been associated with differences in job prospects for young Black Americans when compared to Whites (Rivera-Batiz, 1992).

In this chapter, we explore the nature of literacy and its underlying dimensions. Patterns in literacy levels among the poor are examined. Implications of different aspects of literacy (e.g., reading, communicating) and different types of literacy (e.g., financial, technological) for various aspects of successful venture creation are investigated. Emphasis is placed on the abilities of low-income entrepreneurs to continually learn and adapt as a venture unfolds. Finally, we explore approaches to improving literacy levels among the poor.

WHAT IS LITERACY?

When people think of literacy, they commonly focus on the ability to read and write (Wallendorf, 2001). They may also consider whether they can use what they read and write to function in society, or so-called functional literacy (see Levine, 1982, for a historical note). However, literacy is a complex construct and can have many facets. One of the most integrative definitions originates from UNESCO (2005). It states (p. 21):

> [L]iteracy is the ability to identify, understand, interpret, create, communicate and compute using printed and written materials associated with varying contexts. Literacy involves a continuum of learning in enabling an individual to achieve his or her goals, develop his or her knowledge and potential, and participate fully in community and wider society.

Similarly, the National Assessment of Adult Literacy (NAAL) project in America defines literacy as "using printed and written information to function in society, to achieve one's goals, and to develop one's knowledge and potential" (Kutner et al., 2007, p. 2). Literacy is then a multi-faceted and pluralist construct, as it can be related to technological, health, information, business, finance, media, visual, scientific and other contexts.

There are several aspects of these definitions that warrant elaboration. First, literacy has a social dimension (Ahmed, 2011). That is, there are multiple literacies to be found in a community that emerge outside the formal education system, occurring in the context of home and various social interactions. This social dimension is embedded in the activities and practices of a community (ibid.) where meanings are extracted from printed forms of language and processed by its members (Bernardo, 2000; Scribner and Cole, 1978; Street, 1984). Poor communities typically have their own language. For instance, in the urban ghetto, there are specific language expressions, hidden words and interjections. These can contribute to a group identity. At the same time they create a barrier to outsiders. Further, the use of such expressions, jargon, and vocabulary by someone trying to start a business can work against the individual when dealing with potential suppliers, customers, financiers, mentors, regulators, and other stakeholders.

A second critical aspect of literacy is that it is language based. As such, it is shaped by and affects activities and practices that are dependent on the language. Hence, it is related to critical thinking, oral communication, conversation, interaction, relationships, argumentation, discussion and publicity as each applies to a particular language (UNESCO, 2005). As a case in point, there is a specific literacy related to entrepreneurial activity. Fluency is required in a lexicon that includes such key terms as business models and profitability, cash flow and burn rates,[1] dynamics of market forces, product development and technology commercialization, the articulation of competitive advantage, product positioning, segmentation and differentiation, and mastery of a variety of terms that capture the broader business world. This suggests a need for different literacies depending on the issues and contexts within which the individual is operating.

Third, literacy involves a "continuum of learning," rather than being a binary or static phenomenon (i.e., being literate vs illiterate). It entails a continuous process that requires ongoing learning and application. Improving one's literacy requires effort, commitment, consciousness, and willingness to challenge the status quo in one's life. The challenges here can be illustrated by considering adult literacy programs. To receive funding, heavy pressure can be placed on these programs to accomplish multiple goals, including increasing job skills, moving people from welfare to work, and reducing crime. Showing progress in meeting performance targets can find them ignoring or underserving those with the very lowest skills (Hacker and Yankwitt, 1997). Moreover, attending such programs is difficult without additional support for child care and transportation expenses. Finding time (and energy) when trying to work multiple full- or part-time jobs is also a challenge. However, literacy education moves people out of poverty (Wamba, 2010). When the poor are able to engage in literacy and related education programs, the positive outcomes extend to improved career prospects, better life skills, enhanced critical thinking, more community participation, and a stronger political voice. More entrepreneurial activity is another outcome, and these literate entrepreneurs perform better. A meta-analysis of studies of the impact of education on entrepreneurship performance found that a marginal year of instruction increases enterprise income by 5.5 percent on average (Van der Sluis, Van Praag and Vijverberg, 2005).

TRENDS AND PATTERNS IN LITERACY

The 1992 National Assessment of Adult Literacy from the US Department of Education found that 21 to 23 percent of US adults have only rudimentary reading and writing skills, performing at the lowest level on scales that measure prose, document, and quantitative proficiencies (Level 1 of five levels) (see Kirsch et al., 1993). Some were able to total an entry on a bank deposit slip, locate the time or place of a meeting on a form, and identify a piece of specific information in a brief news article, but others were unable to perform these types of tasks, and some had such limited skills that they were unable to respond to the survey. Another 25 to 28 percent of respondents demonstrated proficiency at Level 2, indicating they are generally able to locate information in a text, make low-level inferences, integrate easily identifiable pieces of information and perform quantitative tasks that involve a single operation. Individuals in literacy Levels 1 and 2 reported working an average 18 to 19 weeks in the year prior to the survey (compared with an average 34 and 44 weeks for those in the three highest levels of literacy), and reported median weekly earnings of about $230 to $245 (compared with earnings between $350 to $680 for those in Levels 3, 4 and 5). In addition, adults in the lowest level on each of the literacy scales were far more likely than those in the two highest levels to report receiving food stamps (17 to 19 percent versus 4 percent). Similarly, only 23 to 27 percent of the respondents who performed in Level 1 said they received interest from a savings or bank account (compared with 70 to 85 percent in Levels 4 or 5). Almost half of all adults in the lowest level on each literacy scale (41 to 44 percent) were living in poverty (compared with 4 to 8 percent of those in the two highest proficiency levels).

In a subsequent study, the 2003 NAAL reported that average quantitative literacy[2] scores of those 16 years and older increased eight points between 1992 and 2003 (from 275 to 283), though average prose[3] and document literacy[4] scores had not meaningfully changed (see Kutner et al., 2007). In 2003, some 30 million American adults had less than basic prose literacy, 27 million had less than basic document literacy, and 46 million had less than basic quantitative literacy. Having below basic literacy indicates that a person ranges from being non-literate in English to being able to (a) locate easily identifiable information in short, commonplace prose texts and simple documents, (b) follow written instructions in rudimentary documents (e.g., charts or forms), and (c) locate numbers and use them to perform simple quantitative operations (primarily addition) when the mathematical information is concrete and familiar. In this national study, almost 27 percent of those who performed at below basic levels lived in households with incomes under $10 000, which is significantly higher than all other income categories (Kutner et al., 2007). A higher percentage of adults with below basic literacy in each of these three areas were unemployed, while those who were employed earned lower salaries on average (less than $300 a week compared to $1950 or more each week).

Literacy is also a problem in other developed economies. The Survey of Adult Skills, conducted by the Organisation for Economic Co-operation and Development (OECD), measures proficiency in literacy, numeracy, and problem solving in technology-rich environments among adults between 16 and 65 years old (see OECD, 2016). Data were collected from 33 countries in 2013 and 2014–15. A considerable proportion of adults (18.5 percent on average) had poor reading skills. While under 5 percent in a number of countries (e.g., Australia, Canada, Germany, England, Japan), the percentage of adults scoring at or below Level 1 (out of 5) in literacy exceeded 20 percent in Chile (53.4 percent), Turkey (45.7 percent), Italy (27.7 percent), Spain (27.5 percent), Israel (27.1 percent), Greece (26.5 percent) and Slovenia (24.9 percent). These are individuals who can only complete reading of relatively short texts to locate a single piece of information that is synonymous with information given in the question, when there is little competing information.

Regarding numeracy skills, 22.7 percent of adults in the OECD countries scored at or below Level 1. In 14 of the countries more than 20 percent of the adults scored only at or below Level 1. These included Chile (61.9 percent), Turkey (50.2 percent), Italy (31.7 percent), Israel (30.9 percent), Spain (30.6 percent), Greece (28.5 percent), France (28 percent), Slovenia (25.8 percent), Ireland (25.2 percent), Northern Ireland (24.4

percent), England (24.1 percent), Canada (22.4 percent), and Poland (23.5 percent). This is a level where individuals at best are only able to carry out basic mathematical processes in common contexts where the content is explicit, and there is little text and marginal distractors. Sample tasks included counting, sorting, performing basic arithmetic operations, or understanding simple percentages.

In this same OECD study, about 10 percent of the participants had no computer experience, and another 10 percent did not feel confident in their ability to use computers. In four countries, more than 30 percent of adults did not have computer experience or did not feel confident in their ability to use computers: Turkey (53.2 percent), Poland (43.3 percent), Italy (39.1 percent) and the Slovak Republic (34.2 percent). Moreover, 42.9 percent of the adults were proficient only at or below Level 1 in problem solving in technology-rich environments. The lowest percentage was in Japan (27.3 percent) and the highest were in Chile (52.4 percent) and Northern Ireland (51 percent). Here, Level 1 indicates individuals who can only use familiar applications to solve problems that involve just a few steps and explicit criteria, such as sorting e-mails into pre-existing folders.

The OECD uses the educational attainment of the respondent's parents as a proxy for socio-economic status. Almost 30 percent of adults with neither parent having accomplished an upper secondary degree scored at or below Level 1 in the literacy assessment (while only 5 percent scored at Level 4 or 5). For adults raised by at least one tertiary-educated parent, 20 percent scored at Level 4 or 5 (while 8 percent scored at or below Level 1). A consistent pattern across countries emerges where adults raised by parents with limited educational backgrounds are themselves likely to be less literate.

On balance, and despite all the advancements in society, literacy remains a serious problem among the poor in developed economies, often resulting in higher unemployment levels, fewer job and advancement prospects, and lower earnings levels. While lack of other opportunities may push them into entrepreneurship, the rigors of successfully launching a business can be overwhelming. This is a topic to which we shall return, but first let us consider the different types of literacies that are especially pertinent in venture creation.

THE FIVE LITERACIES OF ENTREPRENEURSHIP

Literacy contributes to economic development. It raises the productivity of new literates and those with whom they work; enables them to tap more of their creative potential; accelerates the acquisition and transmission of knowledge and useful information; encourages the pursuit of vocational training and technical education; and heightens the impact of performance-based economic incentives (Blaug, 1966). Literacy also contributes to stimulating entrepreneurship. Higher levels of literacy increase the depth and breadth of the individual's opportunity horizon, making it possible to recognize more and better business opportunities. It enables the development of more sophisticated business concepts and models, enhances resource gathering/leveraging and the access to different stakeholders, and opens different possibilities for business growth. In short, literacy is required across all stages of the venture creation process.

Entrepreneurs must compete in environments that are increasingly characterized by dynamic, complex and threatening change. Under such conditions, Roberts (1995, p.413) argues that approaching literacy as a singular, all-encompassing concept is bound to result in failure. He concludes (p. 413) that: "we do better to focus on multiple literacies." Entrepreneurs need the ability to read and write – the so-called functional or general literacy – but are also required to understand, assimilate, solve problems, reason and make decisions on financial and economic aspects, use and develop technology and operate in a digital world. Thus, as illustrated in Figure 6.1, entrepreneurial success is dependent upon at least five literacies: functional, financial, economic, business, and technological.

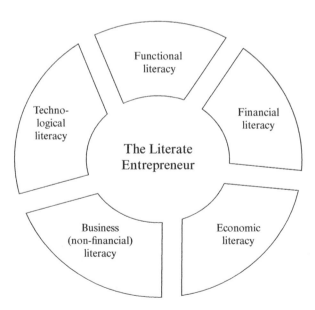

Figure 6.1   The five literacies of entrepreneurship

Functional Literacy

The abilities to read and write, use numbers, interpret images and graphs, understand and communicate effectively, gain and integrate knowledge, and solve mathematical problems come into play in every facet of business operations. Consider basic reading and writing. Without rudimentary skills, how can we expect the low-income entrepreneur to ever do the research and create a business plan? Or, in everyday operations, imagine the entrepreneur who does not understand the terms in a written contract or lease, cannot write a proper business letter to a supplier, misinterprets a written request or complaint from a customer, misreads instructions on installing or operating a piece of equipment, or is unable to study books, manuals and reports on industry trends and company best practices.

Similarly, the implications of one's ability with numbers, which we have noted can be an even greater problem among the poor, are just as significant. Here are just ten of the everyday ways in which numeracy affects entrepreneurial success:

- calculating the size of a market opportunity;
- determining the feasibility of launching the business;
- setting prices in a manner that covers costs and generates an acceptable margin;
- determining shipping volumes, inventory needs and procurement requirements;
- properly preparing an invoice or bid;
- paying employees and suppliers correct amounts;
- recording expenses and revenues and determining if any profit is being made;
- measuring employee performance and operational efficiencies;
- analyzing patterns in customer purchases, business expenditures, customer complaints, or the effectiveness of different promotional approaches;
- paying taxes in correct amounts on dates they are due.

One of the greatest concerns with entrepreneurs having poor numeracy skills is not simply that they make miscalculations, but instead they will entirely avoid key activities that involve numbers. This is an additional reason why it can cost the low-income entrepreneur more than it does others to start and manage a venture.

Poor functional literacy is also manifested in the way the entrepreneur communicates with stakeholders. Lack of understanding of reading, writing and numeracy undermines self-confidence, making the low-income entrepreneur less apt to ask questions or to interact in ways that might expose their perceived shortcomings. For the poor, communication efforts are also hindered by unfamiliarity with both the language of business and of the hidden rules of others who come from middle- or upper-income backgrounds (see Chapter 3).

Financial Literacy

Financial literacy is concerned with the ability to make financially responsible decisions, and requires the learning of a language (e.g., asset versus liability, revenue versus profit, fixed versus variable cost). Weakness here is particularly acute among the poor (Lusardi, 2002; Tang and Lachance, 2012). It begins with fundamentals such as knowing how to save, manage credit and debt obligations, and clearly separate business from personal financial transactions. It helps the entrepreneur determine how much money is needed to start the business and how long it will take to reach breakeven. Two especially critical literacy skills include budgeting and cash flow management. Living week to week on a tight budget is nothing new to a person in poverty, but creating, and then operating in accordance with a budget that accurately anticipates business expenses, tax payments, and receipt of revenues, and allows for unpredictable developments, is a whole new challenge. Good budgeting practices will enable good financial planning. The entrepreneur can better anticipate cash needs in the months to come, or set aside enough money to enable equipment purchases or the hiring of employees.

Cash flow is the difference between how much money comes into the business each day, and how much goes out. The entrepreneur often has to spend money upfront to complete a job for a customer, and only gets paid afterwards. And it may take quite a few jobs before they are actually breaking even. Given small amounts of personal savings and an inability to raise much money (see Chapter 9), the financial strain can be intense, especially in the early days of the venture. Surviving can depend on one's skills in knowing when to pay which bills, how much to pay, and how to stretch payables, together with discipline in making customers remit when payment is due. Poor cash flow management has also destroyed businesses that achieved decent levels of sales, and were growing rapidly, yet had no cash to pay for things. The money was all tied up in the things that make growth possible, such as inventory, expanded capacity, new employees, and additional equipment. A supplier, landlord or banker demands payment, the entrepreneur has no way to pay, and the company gets cut off and perhaps forced into bankruptcy. It is also worth noting that many ventures started by the poor are cash businesses, meaning they do not accept credit cards or other electronic and non-cash forms of payment. This can create more problems in terms of tracking what money comes in, when, and for what purpose, and also creates more opportunities for employee theft.

A cash flow issue that gets some low-income entrepreneurs into trouble involves the payment of various taxes on a monthly, quarterly and/or annual basis. Depending on the country and region or state in which the business is located, different taxes are due. Consider excise, sales or VAT taxes that are collected from customers. There can be a temptation to use this money to cover short-term cash needs. The financially literate entrepreneur will appreciate how dangerous this is, and why these and other taxes (e.g., estimated income taxes, workers compensation and payroll taxes if there are employees) must be paid on a timely basis or the company can be fined large amounts, foreclosed upon, or financially blacklisted.

The poor are also subject to personal financial crises and unpredictable emergencies (e.g., a bill for critical medical services, interruption of food stamp payments, eviction from an apartment or low-income housing project). These kinds of developments have far greater implications for both business and personal cash flows than they would for a middle- or upper-income family. Timing is also a factor, as a reimbursement or payment may be due to a poor person, but will not be available when they actually need the money. As a result, the poor may be less resilient to disruptive financial events. Avoiding the tendency to turn to predatory lenders when these events occur is another benefit of financial literacy (Curley, Ssewamala and Sherraden, 2009).

Last, financial literacy affects the ability of the entrepreneur to read and properly interpret the financial statements of the firm. These statements tell a story from which the entrepreneur can learn and make course corrections. They convey the obligations and value of the firm. They indicate whether money is being made and where, and if bills can be paid. They enable the identification of patterns in terms of sales and key expense categories, payables and receivables, and inventory turnover.

Economic Literacy

Entrepreneurs operate in markets. To function, they must appreciate how markets work and the implications of changes in economic conditions and public policies for business decisions. This is economic literacy, and it includes an ability to identify economic problems, understand economic incentives and disincentives, and weigh the costs and benefits of alternative courses of action (Burkhardt et al., 2003).

Economic literacy begins with an understanding of supply and demand, and how the combination of the two determine the entrepreneur's position in the marketplace. The entrepreneur has to recognize impending changes in supply (competitors and their actions) or demand (customers and their actions) conditions, and what they mean for the prices he or she should be charging, when to invest in equipment, how much to build inventory up or down, and when to expand or reduce staffing (including temporary and part-time staff), among other decisions. The entrepreneur must also incorporate into these decisions the implications of other economic variables, such as changes in interest rates, inflation, unemployment rates, trade barriers and tax policies/incentives.

Another important dimension of economic literacy is cost-benefit analysis. Consider the start-up entrepreneur trying to decide whether to teach themselves to do their own bookkeeping or website maintenance, or if they should outsource these activities to another firm. This is a resource allocation decision. The economically literate entrepreneur is able to systematically evaluate all the costs (e.g., financial, non-financial and opportunity costs) and benefits (e.g., savings, freeing up time, control) in arriving at a decision.

Business (Non-financial) Literacy

Business itself has a language together with a required skill set that encompasses the basics of administration and record-keeping, organizing (e.g., tasks, inventory), selling, hiring, and a wide variety of other tasks. Beyond difficulties in learning these tasks, the low-income entrepreneur who is business illiterate can struggle when interacting with potential stakeholders. Consider some of the terms a supplier, investor or distributor is likely to use in everyday conversation. Examples include: inventory turnover, barriers to entry, differentiation, segmentation and targeting, product positioning, brand equity, customer acquisition cost, broker, early adopter, experience curve, price elasticity, penetration pricing, slotting allowances, exclusive distribution, present value, switching costs and order cycle time. The emergence of the discipline of entrepreneurship has led to the popularizing of a number of additional terms. For instance, terms like business model, angel investor, elevator pitch, cash burn rate, minimum viable product, scalable venture, lean start-up, bootstrapping, buy–sell agreement, and exit strategy are now commonplace. Lack of understanding of such terms can also mean the ideas behind them are not being incorporated into business decisions.

Technological Literacy

Technological literacy includes an awareness and appreciation for the significance of key technologies impacting a business, the ability to use these technologies, and an understanding of the issues raised by their use (Boser, Palmer and Daugherty, 1998). It prepares individuals to interact and function more effectively in what is increasingly a technological world – a world where technology is redefining all aspects of life and virtually everything a business does (Pearson and Young, 2002). More than just information or digital technology, it includes a range of other technological arenas (e.g., nano, energy, chemical, laser, robotic, etc.) that can play a role in the performance of a particular business.

For entrepreneurs, technology literacy is relevant for developing the products or services that they sell, and for enabling many of the operational processes within the business (e.g., production, procurement, logistics, bookkeeping, human resource management, marketing). Of our five literacies, it is arguably the most dynamic – requiring continuous learning to keep abreast of new developments that occur almost daily. As such, it is an area where, even when the low-income entrepreneur develops an adequate level of literacy, they can quickly fall behind. Technology is so central to the start-up of a venture that we explore its role and the implications of technological literacy in more depth in Chapter 7.

LITERACIES, VENTURE CREATION AND THE POOR

Levels of literacy in these five areas vary considerably for people in all income groups. Among the poor, there are many who demonstrate requisite levels of literacy in some if not all of these five areas. As a group, however, those in poverty are disproportionately represented at the lower end of the spectrum for each type of literacy. These low levels can be especially problematic when a poor person attempts to launch a business. Table 6.1 summarizes key obstacles in venture creation as they relate to each of our five literacies.

Importantly, these obstacles significantly impact the low-income entrepreneur at every stage of the entrepreneurial process (see Chapter 2). Let us briefly consider each of these stages:

1. *Opportunity recognition.* Opportunities (unmet needs, gaps in the marketplace) exist in the environments that surround us, but the challenge is to recognize them as they emerge. Of our five literacies, functional and technological literacy play paramount roles in determining the kinds of opportunities recognized by the poor. If one struggles to read, is not adept in use of computers and online search engines, and does not understand the potential applications of a given technology, one's opportunity horizon is severely constrained. Poor and minority

Table 6.1   *Five literacies of entrepreneurship and challenges for the poor*

Type of Literacy	Definition	Sample Challenges for the Low-income Entrepreneur
Functional literacy	Ability to read and write, use numbers, interpret images and graphs, understand and communicate effectively, gain and integrate knowledge, and solve mathematical problems	Struggles in doing research, creating a business plan, calculating the size of market opportunities, determining the feasibility of launching the business; challenges with oral and written communication with stakeholders; difficulty in interpreting a written contract or lease, regulation, set of instructions; reduced ability to set prices in a manner that covers costs and generates an acceptable margin, determine correct shipping volumes, inventory levels and procurement requirements, properly prepare invoices or bids, pay employees and customers correct amounts, record expenses and revenues and determine if profit is being made, measure operational efficiencies, or analyze patterns in data
Financial literacy	Understanding how to interpret financial information, make financially responsible decisions, and manage one's financial obligations and needs on an ongoing basis	Difficulties in knowing how to save, manage credit and debt obligations, and separate business from personal financial transactions; struggling to determine how much money is needed to start the business and how long it will take to reach breakeven; problems in budgeting and cash flow management; difficulties in knowing when to pay which bills, how much to pay, and how to negotiate payment deadlines; lower resilience to disruptive financial events; inability to raise funding
Economic literacy	Understanding of the implications of supply, demand and other market-related variables on business decision-making, and ability to weigh costs and benefits in making resource allocation decisions	Challenges in understanding supply and demand, conditions that affect the entrepreneur's position in the marketplace and the implications for pricing, making investments in the businesses, determining correct inventory and staffing levels; reduced understanding of the implications of changes in interest rates, inflation, unemployment rates, trade barriers and tax policy; less ability to assess costs and benefits surrounding key business decisions

Table 6.1   (continued)

Type of Literacy	Definition	Sample Challenges for the Low-income Entrepreneur
Business (non-financial) literacy	Ability to communicate and interact using the language specific to business operations	Reduced abilities to communicate with key stakeholders and incorporate key business concepts into ongoing decision-making
Techno-logical literacy	Awareness of and ability to use relevant technologies in developing products and managing processes within a venture	Inability to incorporate technology into products and services being developed and sold to customers; inefficiencies in key operational processes within the business; difficulty in keeping pace with the new developments in technology

families are less likely to have access to a computer and the Internet in their homes and less likely to have the necessary skills and knowledge to use these resources (Attewell, 2001; Hesseldahl, 2008). Further, they can struggle to assess the legitimacy of a given information source or the reliability of the information. Not surprisingly then, the poor rely more heavily on information obtained through personal networks compared to other sources (Pigato, 2001). For these reasons, low-income entrepreneurs are more likely to uncover opportunities that are readily observable in their immediate surroundings and less likely to find opportunities involving discovery and creation (see Chapter 5 for more detail on these approaches to uncovering opportunity).

2. *Business concept and business model development.* Literacy is a key contributor to kinds of business ideas conceived, and the nature of the ventures created, by the poor. Especially relevant here are functional, technological and financial literacies and their respective abilities to contribute to innovative business ideas and novel business models. Less functional literacy leads to simpler business ideas, and more informal sector ventures (Servon, 1999). All too often, the ventures of the poor are survival or lifestyle ventures that are effectively selling a "commodity" (e.g., cleaning, transport, hair care) that is not well differentiated, and operate in highly competitive markets. As a result, they find themselves competing on the basis of low price. We discuss this commodity trap in more detail in Chapter 11. Improved financial

literacy would enable the poor to more accurately estimate profit potential and better appreciate the underlying logic of how profits can be made for a given venture concept. It can help estimate the potential of different market segments, and hence where to focus one's limited resources. Improved technological literacy could allow these entrepreneurs to conceptualize ventures with enhanced capabilities and/or the potential to create new sources of value, as well as ventures that reach broader markets and are more scalable. Familiarity with technology can also lead to ventures with lower costs and reduced labor intensity.

3. *Assessing the needed resources.* What are the minimal resources needed to start a venture? While not always the most critical resource, money can be the most problematic for low-income entrepreneurs. They will be unfamiliar with the various sources of money and their requirements based on underdeveloped business literacy. Moreover, the combination of poverty and low financial literacy finds the entrepreneur underestimating how much is needed, and underinvesting in key areas (e.g., basic equipment and facilities). The roles of suppliers, distributors, public authorities, and other stakeholders as resource providers will not be understood based on limited business literacy. Decisions on the trade-offs between working from home and having premises, or between buying a truck and spending more on staff are more difficult based on low economic literacy. Recognition of the importance of intellectual property as a source of advantage and differentiation for the business (and a means to higher margins and more growth) is most affected by technological literacy together with business literacy. As a generalization, the ventures of the poor reflect a greater focus on financial and physical resources and less emphasis on intellectual property.

4. *Acquiring the necessary resources.* When it comes to raising money, as we shall see in Chapter 9, the poor typically do not have access to conventional bank debt or to equity investors at the launch stage. Financial literacy is the key here, particularly in terms of supporting good savings habits, building a good credit rating, establishing some kind of asset base, and finding sources of collateral. Combined with functional literacy, it also affects the ability of the entrepreneur to put together key financial performance data on the proposed venture and communicate this information to bankers or investors (or put together a crowd-funding campaign). The business plan plays a key role here, and its quality is undermined by weak functional, financial and business literacies. As we shall explore in Chapter 10, the poor must rely more heavily on bootstrapping, leveraging, and guerrilla tactics to overcome resource constraints. Even here literacy makes all the difference, especially given the limited social and business networks

of many of those in poverty. Financial literacy can contribute to bootstrapping efforts in such areas as extending payables and shortening receivables. Similarly, the communication and creativity skills involved in leveraging relationships with suppliers to get extended payment terms, getting retailers to hold more of the entrepreneur's inventory, or getting customers to pay in advance of service delivery all require strong functional and business literacy.

5. *Implementation and adaptation.* A successful launch requires knowledge of an increasingly complex regulatory environment. This can include licensing, certification, and inspection requirements, as well as compliance with labor, zoning, taxation and other laws. The entrepreneur is usually executing a number of contracts. Mistakes here are traceable to low functional, business, and economic literacy. Once in business, one must be able to simultaneously produce, sell, buy inventory, maintain facilities, keep records, deal with customer problems, and so forth. Business, financial, and technological literacies become essential. For many poor entrepreneurs, the business is initially launched part-time or in the evenings and weekends, as they continue to work full- and part-time jobs to survive. This can provide them with some initial time to learn (which includes further developing literacies). However, it is the ongoing abilities to learn and adapt that will distinguish the successful venture from the failure, and while facilitated by all the literacies, they both center on functional literacy.

6. *Management and growth.* At this stage, the entrepreneurial skills required to overcome obstacles and get a venture launched must now be supplemented by good management skills. Functional and business literacies can contribute to the entrepreneur's ability to organize, plan, prioritize, and delegate. With low-income entrepreneurs, the kinds of resources on which the initial business is built (i.e., reliance on handcraft or manual labor) can result in a highly labor-intensive operation, which takes time away from planning and organizing. Critical managerial activities do not receive adequate attention. Beyond this, lack of (particularly functional) literacy can undermine the entrepreneur's confidence, making them more cautious towards and fearful of growth and what it could bring in terms of demands and risks. Another key factor in growth is technological literacy, as investment in process and product technologies, together with development of intellectual property, are instrumental in growing or scaling a company. The poor frequently do not have the kind of literacy that enables the understanding, application and use of various technologies and advanced equipment (Servon and Nelson, 2001).

7. *Exit/harvest.* When it comes to exit strategies, the poor most often simply shut the business down and sell off any assets, pass the business to an heir or acquaintance, or arrange for some party to purchase the business. Optimizing the harvest of a venture requires planning, which builds on most of the literacies. The entrepreneur must be prepared in terms of his or her personal financial position, suggesting the importance of financial literacy. Financial, business, and economic literacies are necessary for estimating the value of the business and negotiating terms of a sale or acquisition.

The conclusion from this discussion is that limited functional literacy seriously detracts from every stage in the entrepreneurial process, and the other four literacies play a part that is more or less prominent depending on the stage. Importantly, these literacies are not independent. For instance, functional literacy makes possible the other four. Financial and business literacies can contribute to economic literacy. And technological literacy interacts with business literacy to impact venture development.

IMPROVING LITERACY AMONG THE POOR

Adult literacy, and particularly the functional, financial, and technological areas, has received growing attention in developed economies over the past few decades. Adult literacy programs help individuals get the basic skills they need in reading, writing, doing math, language proficiency, and problem-solving. The available programs tend to be quite diverse, utilizing a variety of pedagogical approaches. These programs also struggle with high drop-out rates (Quigley, 1997; Smith, 1998), while sustainable funding continues to be a major obstacle (Jaffee, 2001).

Low-income adults can encounter distinct difficulties when it comes to learning (Merriam and Caffarella, 1991). Scholarly research with adult literacy and numeracy learners has highlighted how the social, economic, and physical conditions of poverty impact the ability to grasp and retain content and maintain engagement in the learning process (Barton et al., 2007). Engagement and persistence of learners can be positively affected by pedagogical practices that promote social interactions and co-learning practices (e.g., working in pairs or small groups, providing instant feedback, reciprocal teaching and encouraging fluent, oral reading) (ibid.). Where educators and staff help individual learners establish goals, reinforce learner persistence, and focus efforts on development of self-efficacy, there is a positive impact on adult engagement and learning outcomes (Comings, 2009). Effective programs are able to approach literacy in the larger social context of basic learning needs and opportunities, where learning is strengthened and amplified by a network of opportunities for diverse and continuing education, and a network of actors (e.g., lecturers, mentors, coaches, and fellow learners). Balanced emphasis is placed on both the formal and the informal educational settings. Appropriately designed literacy programs can enable vulnerable adults to change their dispositions to learning, achieve personal goals, and transition towards the kinds of futures to which they aspire, including entrepreneurship (Cameron and Cameron, 2006; Crowther, Maclachlan and Tett, 2010).

However, the sad irony is that those who most need access to literacy programs are often the ones most deprived of this access (Ahmed, 1992). Availability of programs varies by locality, online programs require computer and Internet access, scheduling may not be at appropriate or flexible times, and awareness is affected by how heavily programs are promoted through channels reaching the poor. Further, those with the greatest need often require assistance with transportation, paying for educational materials, meals, and daycare for their children. The end result finds that the illiteracy cycle is entangled with the poverty cycle, with illiteracy a common outcome from poverty, and the poverty conditions a barrier to engaging in literacy programs.

Yet, when the poor enroll in literacy programs, the returns are evident: higher individual earnings (Psacharopoulos and Patrinos, 2004), reduced crime (Lochner and Moretti, 2004), improved health of children (Currie and Moretti, 2003), improved civic participation (Dee, 2004), enhanced work possibilities (Moretti, 2004) and higher labor productivity (Coulombe and Tremblay, 2006). Schaffer and Mohs (2016) demonstrate how financial literacy programs aimed at low-income adults can have a positive ripple effect on family financial stability.

A growing volume of adult literacy programs are available in developed countries. Some of them offer additional support to address childcare, transport and other needs beyond the training itself. Table 6A.1 in the appendix at the end of this chapter presents examples in different developed economies of programs targeting functional, financial, digital, technological and economic literacy that are available for low-income entrepreneurs.

THE ONGOING CHALLENGE

Literacy is a cornerstone of development, work, democracy, quality of life, health, technology, science, and importantly, entrepreneurship. Without adequate literacy skills, the individual is essentially excluded from participation in many of the opportunities found in society, and is unable to realize the potential to make a difference through entrepreneurship (Bernardo, 2000). The two great challenges in literacy are, first, to better prepare the poor for the twenty-first century, which means preparing them for the age of entrepreneurship; and second, to reduce the disparities in literacy outcomes between those from disadvantaged and more privileged backgrounds (Murnane, Sawhill and Snow, 2012). With regard to the latter point, if anything, the gaps in our five literacies between the poor and rest of society continue to grow.

As we move forward, increasing the number of poor people in adult literacy programs, and continuing to improve the design and delivery of these programs, are important steps. However, for those in poverty who strive to be entrepreneurs, the need is more complex. Extant literacy programs target the general public, including those in poverty. They emphasize functional literacy. Alternatively, training and development programs for entrepreneurs tend to stress financial and business literacy and sometimes technological literacy, with less emphasis on functional and economic literacy. The ongoing need is for an integrated approach for developing low-income entrepreneurs that reflects the interplay among these literacies, where their interactions are reinforced as the entrepreneurial journey unfolds.

Finally, the multiple literacies of entrepreneurship involve a continuum of learning. The rhythm and intensity of advances in the different literacies of entrepreneurship require that learning be ongoing and immersive. For many of those starting ventures, technology literacy would appear to be the area where they would most quickly fall behind. However, the sheer pace of information provision and new knowledge generation is accelerating, affecting all five literacies. Meanwhile, as this information becomes more complex, the challenges of processing and assimilating it will become even greater. This further reinforces the vital importance of continuing educational opportunities for low-income entrepreneurs.

NOTES

1. The rate at which a new company spends its initial capital.
2. Quantitative literacy – the knowledge and skills required to apply arithmetic operations, either alone or sequentially, using numbers embedded in printed materials; for example, balancing a checkbook, figuring out a tip, completing an order form, or determining the amount of interest from a loan advertisement (Kirsch et al., 1993, p. 3).
3. Prose literacy – the knowledge and skills needed to understand and use information from texts that include editorials, news stories, poems, and fiction; for example, finding a piece of information in a newspaper article, interpreting instructions from a warranty, inferring a theme from a poem, or contrasting views expressed in an editorial (Kirsch et al., 1993, p. 3).

4. Document literacy – the knowledge and skills required to locate and use information contained in materials that include job applications, payroll forms, transportation schedules, maps, tables, and graphs; for example, locating a particular intersection on a street map, using a schedule to choose the appropriate bus, or entering information on an application form (Kirsch et al., 1993, p. 3).

REFERENCES

Ahmed, M. (1992), "Literacy in a larger context," *Annals of the American Academy of Political and Social Science*, **520**, 32–5.

Ahmed, M. (2011), "Defining and measuring literacy: Facing the reality," *International Review of Education*, **57**(1), 179–95.

Attewell, P. (2001), "The first and second digital divides," *Sociology of Education*, **74**, 252–9.

Barton, D., R. Ivanic and Y. Appleby et al. (2007), *Literacy, Lives and Learning*, London: Routledge.

Bernardo, A.B.I. (2000), "On defining and developing literacy across communities," *International Review of Education*, **46**(5), 455–65.

Blaug, M. (1966), "Literacy and economic development," *The School Review*, **74**(4), 393–418.

Boser, R., J. Palmer and M.K. Daugherty (1998), "Students' attitudes toward technology in selected technology education programs," *Journal of Technology Education*, **10**(1), 1–19.

Burkhardt, G., M. Monsour and G. Valdez et al. (2003), *Literacy in the Digital Age*, NCREL and METIRI Group, accessed June 10, 2018 at http://pict.sdsu. edu/engauge21st.pdf.

Cameron, J. and S. Cameron (2006), *The Economic Benefits of Increased Literacy*, 2006 EFA Global Monitoring Report.

Comings, J. (2009), "Student persistence in adult literacy and numeracy programmes," in S. Reder and J. Brynner (eds), *Tracking Adult Literacy and Numeracy Skills: Findings from Longitudinal Research*, New York: Routledge, pp. 160–76.

Corcoran, M.E. and A. Chaudry (1997), "The dynamics of childhood poverty," *Children and Poverty*, **7**(2), 40–54.

Coulombe, S. and J. Tremblay (2006), "Literacy and growth," *Topics in Macroeconomics*, **6**(2), Article 4.

Crowther, J., K. Maclachlan and L. Tet (2010), "Adult literacy, learning identities and pedagogic practice," *International Journal of Lifelong Education*, **29**(6), 651–64.

Curley, J., F. Ssewamala and M. Sherraden (2009), "Institutions and savings in low-income households," *Journal of Sociology and Social Welfare*, **36**(3), 9–32.

Currie, J. and E. Moretti (2003), "Mother's education and the intergenerational transmission of human capital: Evidence from college openings," *Quarterly Journal of Economics*, **118**(4), 1495–532.

Dee, T.S. (2004), "Are there civic returns to education?," *Journal of Public Economics*, **88**(9–10), 1697–720.

Duncan, G. and J. Brooks-Gunn (eds) (1997), *Consequences of Growing Up Poor*, New York: Russell Sage Foundation.

Foster, E.M. (2002), "How economists think about family resources and child development," *Child Development*, **73**(6), 1904–14.

Hacker, E. and I. Yankwitt (1997), "Education, job skills, or workfare: The crisis facing adult literacy education today," *Social Text*, No. 51, 109–17.

Hesseldahl, A. (2008), "Bringing broadband to the urban poor," *Bloomberg Business Week*, December 31, accessed June 10, 2018 at https://www.bloomberg.com/news/articles/2008-12-31/bringing-broadband-to-the-urban-poorbusiness-week-business-news-stock-market-and-financial-advice.

Jaffee, L.L. (2001), "Adult literacy programs and the use of technology," *Adult Basic Education*, **11**(2), 109–24.

Jencks, C. and M. Philips (eds) (1998), *The Black–White Test Score Gap*, Washington, DC: Brookings Institution Press.

Juel, C. (1988), "Learning to read and write: A longitudinal study of 54 children from first through fourth grades," *Journal of Educational Psychology*, **80**(4), 437–47.

Juel, C., P.L. Griffith and P.B. Gough (1986), "Acquisition of literacy: A longitudinal study of children in first and second grade," *Journal of Educational Psychology*, **78**(4), 243–55.

Kirsch, I.S., A. Jungeblut, L. Jenkins and A. Kolstad (1993), *Adult Literacy in America*, Washington, DC: National Center for Education Statistics, US Department of Education, accessed June 9, 2018 at https://nces.ed.gov/pubsearch/pubsinfo.asp?pubid=93275.

Kutner, M., E. Greenberg and Y. Jin et al. (2007), *Literacy in Everyday Life: Results from the 2003 National Assessment of Adult Literacy* (NCES 2007–480), Washington, DC: National Center for Education Statistics, accessed June 9, 2018 at https://nces.ed.gov/pubsearch/pubsinfo.asp?pubid=2007480.

Levine, K. (1982), "Functional literacy: Fond illusions and false economies," *Harvard Educational Review*, **52**(3), 249–66.

Lochner, L. and E. Moretti (2004), "The effect of education on crime: Evidence from prison inmates, arrests, and self-reports," *American Economic Review*, **94**(1), 155–89.

Lusardi, A. (2002), "Increasing saving among the poor: The role of financial literacy," *Poverty Research News*, **6**(1).

McIntosh, S. and A. Vignoles (2001), "Measuring and assessing the impact of basic skills on labour market outcomes," *Oxford Economic Papers*, **3**, 453–81.

Merriam, S. and R. Caffarella (1991), *Learning in Adulthood*, San Francisco, CA: Jossey-Bass.

Moretti, E. (2004), "Workers' education, spillovers, and productivity: Evidence from plant-level production functions," *American Economic Review*, **94**(3), 656–90.

Murnane, R., I. Sawhill and C. Snow (2012), "Literacy challenges for the twenty-first century: Introducing the issue," *Future Child*, **22**(2), 3–15.

Neuman, S.B. (2006), "The knowledge gap: Implications for early education," in D.K. Dickinson and S.B. Neumann (eds), *Handbook for Early Literacy Research, Vol. 2*, London: Guilford.

Neuman, S.B. and D. Celano (2001), "Access to print in low-income and middle-income communities: An ecological study of four neighborhoods," *Reading Research Quarterly*, **36**(1), 8–26.

OECD (2016), *Skills Matter: Further Results from the Survey of Adult Skills*, Paris: OECD Publishing.

Pearson, G. and A. Young (2002), *Technically Speaking: Why All Americans Need to Know More About Technology*, Washington, DC: National Academies Press.

Pigato, M. (2001), "Information and communication technology, poverty, and development in Sub-Saharan Africa and South Asia," *Africa Region Working Paper, Series No. 20.*

Psacharopoulos, G. and H.A. Patrinos (2004), "Returns to investment in education: A further update," *Education Economics*, **12**(2), 111–14.

Quigley, B.A. (1997), *Rethinking Literacy Education*, San Francisco, CA: Jossey-Bass.

Rivera-Batiz, F.L. (1992), "Quantitative literacy and the likelihood of employment among young adults in the United States," *The Journal of Human Resources*, **27**(2), 313–28.

Roberts, P. (1995), "Defining literacy: Paradise, nightmare or red herring," *British Journal of Educational Studies*, **43**(4), 412–32.

Robinson, P. (1998), "Literacy, numeracy and economic performance," *New Political Economy*, **3**(1), 143–9.

Rothstein, R. (2004), *Class and Schools: Using Social, Economic, and Educational Reform to Close the Black–White Achievement Gap*, Washington, DC: Economic Policy Institute.

Schaffer, B.A. and J.N. Mohs (2016), "Exploring the effect of financial literacy programs on low-income adults," *The Journal of Global Business Management*, **12**(2), 61–70.

Scribner, S. and M. Cole (1978), "Literacy without schooling: Testing for intellectual effects," *Harvard Educational Review*, **48**, 448–61.

Servon, L.J. (1999), *Microenterprises and the American Poor*, Washington, DC: The Brookings Institution.

Servon, L.J. and M.K. Nelson (2001), "Community technology centers: Narrowing the digital divide in low-income, urban communities," *Journal of Urban Affairs*, **23**(3–4), 279–90.

Smith, M.C. (1998), *Literacy for the Twenty-First Century*, Westport, CT: Praeger.

Street, B. (1984), *Literacy in Theory and Practice*, Cambridge, UK: Cambridge University Press.

Tang, N. and M.E. Lachance (2012), "Financial advice: What about low-income consumers?," *Journal of Personal Finance*, **11**(2), 121–58.

UNESCO (2005), *Aspects of Literacy Assessment: Topics and Issues from the UNESCO Expert Meeting*, Paris, June 10–12, 2003, Paris: United Nations Educational, Scientific and Cultural Organization.

Van der Sluis, J., M. van Praag and W. Vijverberg (2005), "Entrepreneurship selection and performance: A meta-analysis of the impact of education in developing economies," *World Bank Economic Review*, **19**(2), 225–61.

Wallendorf, M. (2001), "Literally literacy," *Journal of Consumer Behavior*, **27**, 505–11.

Wamba, N.G. (2010), "Poverty and literacy: An introduction," *Reading and Writing Quarterly*, **26**(3), 189–94.

APPENDIX

Table 6A.1   Examples of programs addressing functional, economic, financial, and technology literacy

Name of Program	Services	Location	Type of Literacy	Website
MoneyMinded	MoneyMinded is an adult financial education program developed by ANZ (Australia and New Zealand Group) in 2002 in consultation with community and government stakeholders and education experts	Australia	Financial	http://www.moneyminded.com.au/
Saver Plus	Saver Plus is a matched savings and financial education program, offered locally by community organizations in every state and territory	Australia	Financial	http://www.bsl.org.au/services/money-matters/saver-plus/
You're the Boss	The Salvation Army has developed an app as part of the You're the Boss program. The app is free and provides financial tips, information and other resources to help you stay on top of your money	Australia	Financial	http://salvos.org.au/need-help/financial-assistance/financial-literacy/
The Smith Family	Participating families receive eight hours of skills training with an accredited trainer and 12 months of free Internet access and technical support to ensure they can get the most out of using the equipment	Australia	Digital	https://www.thesmithfamily.com.au/programs/technology/tech-packs

Table 6A.1 (continued)

Name of Program	Services	Location	Type of Literacy	Website
Cira	Provides orientation, training, and support in the use of computers and mobile technology to adults who are looking to build their digital literacy skills	Canada	Digital	https://cira.ca/build-better-internet/community-investment-program/find-project/adult-digital-literacy-bridging-gaps
Media Awareness Network	Media Awareness Network (MNet) is a Canadian not-for-profit center for media and digital literacy. Its vision is to ensure children and youth possess the necessary critical thinking skills and tools to understand and actively engage with media	Canada	Digital	https://mediasmarts.ca/sites/mediasmarts/files/pdfs/publication-report/full/digitalliteracypaper.pdf
ABC Life Literacy Canada	ABC Life Literacy Canada is a non-profit organization that inspires Canadians to increase their literacy skills	Canada	Family/financial/workplace/health/civic/digital	https://abclifeliteracy.ca/
Prosper Canada	Prosper Canada works with business, government, and non-profit partners to increase access to high-quality, unbiased, and free financial information, education and counselling for Canadians living on low incomes	Canada	Financial	http://prospercanada.org/Our-Work/Centre-for-Financial-Literacy.aspx
Your Financial Toolkit	A comprehensive learning program that provides basic information and tools to help adults manage their personal finances and	Canada	Financial	https://www.canada.ca/en/financial-consumer-agency/services/financial-toolkit.html

	gain the confidence they need to make better financial decisions			
Toronto Public Library	The Adult Literacy Program offers free, one-on-one tutoring in basic reading, writing and math for English-speaking adults 16 years or older	Canada	Functional	https://www.torontopubliclibrary.ca/adult-literacy/
Project Adult Literacy Society	To create a community in which all adults are functionally literate so that they can meet their full potential	Canada	Functional/technological	https://palsedmonton.ca/
Digital Literacy Training for Adults	Guidelines concerning adult literacy teaching strategies for people aged over 55	Europe	Digital	http://www.geengee.eu/geengee/geengee-docs/contenuti/comune/G&G%20Research%20Report.pdf
Telecentre Europe	Supports Europeans who have an insufficient level of digital skills	Europe	Digital	http://www.telecentre-europe.org/
European Charter for Media Literacy	Supports the establishment of media literacy across Europe	Europe	Digital/technological	http://www.euromedialiteracy.eu/
EMEDUS	Several large-scale studies have been carried out in recent years into the topic of media and film literacy in Europe. This webinar highlights a number, pointing to their main findings, conclusions and recommendations	Europe	Digital/technological	https://www.media-and-learning.eu/category/resource-uncategorised/emedus
Financial Literacy Programme	These teams work together to advance knowledge on what works in financial literacy based on different countries'	Europe	Financial	https://www.globalfinancialliteracyproject.org/

Table 6A.1 (continued)

Name of Program	Services	Location	Type of Literacy	Website
	experiences. This international collaboration is designed to generate creative, multidisciplinary approaches to improving financial literacy and financial education programs			
EURead	EURead is a consortium of European reading promotion organizations who believe that reading is a prerequisite for full participation in today's media-led and culturally diverse society	Europe	Functional	https://www.euread.com/about-us/
European Basic Skills Network (ESBN)	An association of policy-level stakeholders engaged in basic skills training for adults	Europe	Functional	http://www.basicskills.eu/
EveryoneOn	A national non-profit organization whose work focuses on increasing access to free and low-cost Internet service and free digital literacy courses	US	Digital	http://everyoneon.org/adulted
Digital Promise	Works to improve digital learning opportunities for low-skilled, underserved adults in the United States	US	Digital	http://digitalpromise.org/
LiteracyLink	Provides an integrated instructional system of video and online computer technology	US	Digital	http://www.pbs.org/learn/literacy

	to help adult students advance their general educational development (GED) and workplace skills. Also provides professional development resources and training to literacy educators			
American Institute of CPAs	Helps people understand their personal finances through every stage of life	US	Financial	http://www.360financialliteracy.org/
Choose to Save	Encourages savings through all stages of life	US	Financial	http://www.choosetosave.org/
The Financial Education Evaluation Toolkit	An online resource that shows how to apply evaluation techniques to programs to document learner impact	US	Financial	https://toolkit.nefe.org/
Money Smart	A financial education curriculum designed to help individuals outside the financial mainstream enhance their financial skills and create positive banking relationships	US	Economic/financial	http://www.fdic.gov/consumers/consumer/moneysmart/index.html
Native Financial Education Coalition (NFEC)	A group of local, regional, and national organizations and government agencies that have joined together to promote financial education in native communities	US	Financial	http://www.ncai.org/initiatives/nativefinancial-ed/nfec
The NeighborWorks Financial Capability Program	Helps individuals and families develop sound personal financial management skills	US	Financial	http://www.neighborworks.org/Homes-Finances/Financial-Security

Table 6A.1 (continued)

Name of Program	Services	Location	Type of Literacy	Website
Operation Hope – Banking on Our Future	A private non-profit financial empowerment organization, offers a national financial literacy education program for elementary, middle and high school students, and adults	US	Financial	https://www.operationhope.org/banking-on-our-future
Financial Football	An NFL-themed educational video game, uses the NFL's structure and rules to teach money skills and to improve financial literacy	US	Financial	http://www.practicalmoneyskills.com/games/trainingcamp/ff/
Adult Reading Program	Self-taught learning program	US	Functional	http://www.practicalmoneyskills.com/games/trainingcamp/ff//
Literacy Information and Communication System (LINCS)	LINCS is a national dissemination, resource gathering, and professional development system providing information on a wide variety of literacy relevant topics, issues, and resources for educators of adult learners	US	Functional	http://lincs.ed.gov/

Barton Reading and Spelling System	The Barton System is an Orton-Gillingham-based program designed for volunteer tutors in adult literacy programs. Training is provided on videotape with fully scripted lesson plans	US	Functional	http://www.bartonreading.com/
Project Read	Project Read is a method of teaching that is systematic, multi-sensory, concrete and involves direct instruction. It is a language arts program based on the theories of Samuel Orton	US	Functional	http://www.projectread.com/
GCFLearnFree.org	Online educational website focusing on technology, job training, reading, and math skills. The site is a program of Goodwill Industries of Eastern NC Inc. and the Goodwill Community Foundation Inc.	US	Functional	http://www.gcflearnfree.org/

Note: All websites accessed June 10, 2018.

113

7. Technology and the poor

> Human beings are extremely creative and resilient, especially when they are
> operating within an institutional framework that encourages and supports
> their actions.
> (Muhammad Yunus)

TECHNOLOGY AS OPPORTUNITY AND CHALLENGE

Technology seeps through every segment of society, equipping organizations with new tools to increase their productivity and innovativeness, and providing individuals with new options for their personal and professional development. It is usually associated with the development and use of tools and machinery such as hammerstones in the Stone Age, the steam engine during the Industrial Revolution, or the smartphone in the contemporary digital age. More formally, it has been defined as the collection of techniques, skills, methods, and processes used in the production of goods or services or in the accomplishment of objectives, such as scientific inquiry (Hughes, 2004).

Technological change never stops – it is evolutionary (and sometimes revolutionary) in nature. Recent decades have witnessed dramatic advances in technology, and the pace of these developments appears to be accelerating. Examples include the transition from 78 rpm records to cassette tapes to downloadable music or the movement from room-sized computers to hard-drive actuators that can fit in someone's pocket. Entrepreneurs are at the forefront of technological change as they either bring new technologies to market or monetize them through their ventures. Further, their ventures are transformed as they incorporate the latest technologies into operations.

The often uncompromising nature of technological change is both a threat and an opportunity. On the one hand, new technologies frequently lead to a disruption in ways of doing things, replacing low-skill jobs with automation technology and changing the ways other jobs and tasks are performed. On the other hand, technological advances make new products and services possible, and result in the emergence of new career and entrepreneurial opportunities. Moreover, modern technologies make it easier than ever to start and grow a venture, accomplish more with less in terms of assets, and reach markets and customers virtually anywhere.

For the poor, technology offers similar promise, but brings with it unique difficulties. First, they often lack the necessary technology skills. Although the poor are frequent users of smartphones and other technological devices, they often lack the knowledge and experience regarding how to leverage an array of technologies for their ventures. Second, using new technology in one's business can be expensive, which given the financial constraints of the poor reduces the likelihood of technology adoption.

In this chapter, we explore how those in poverty can integrate technology into their ventures. Attention is devoted to understanding technology as a product versus a process and what this distinction means for poverty entrepreneurs. The many aspects of a venture that are affected by technology are examined. The concepts of technological literacy and the digital divide, and how both apply to low-income entrepreneurs, are examined. We take a closer look at how technology affects the low-income entrepreneur's opportunity horizons and decision-making processes. Finally, we outline available tools and options the poor have to leverage technology in their ventures.

NEW TECHNOLOGY: PRODUCTS VERSUS PROCESSES

At its simplest level, technology is a means of translating inputs into outputs. If one needs to translate an idea into a written statement, an earlier approach involved a quill and inkwell, while a ballpoint pen was a subsequent technology, and today voice recognition software allows a person to speak into a device and then converts the oral input into printed words. Each of these represents a different technology.

From an entrepreneurial perspective, we can distinguish product and process technologies. Entrepreneurs use technology to develop innovative new products or improve existing products (adding new features or capabilities) to sell in the marketplace. This is product technology. The focus is on advancing technology and incorporating it into the entrepreneur's product offering. The use of laser technology to design a new surgical tool for sale to hospitals, or development of an app that reminds people when to take medicines would be examples.

However, entrepreneurs also incorporate technologies into the ways in which they operate their businesses, and this is process technology. So, when the entrepreneur buys a software package to enhance bookkeeping processes in their construction business, installs a new point-of-sale system in their retail store, or uses a new environmentally safe cleaning product to sterilize their gym equipment, they are using technology to lower costs or improve process performance within their ventures. This distinction suggests that all firms are involved with technology, not just high-tech firms.

Table 7.1 provides examples of areas within a business that are affected by product and process technologies. Here, we have broken out areas of the business, sample products or services, and some of the key benefits deriving from use of the technology. Literally any activity within a firm can be improved or enhanced by incorporating such technologies, with new innovations continually becoming available. The latter point suggests that technology is a moving target that entrepreneurs may struggle to stay on top of.

USE OF TECHNOLOGY BY ENTREPRENEURS AND THE COSTS OF AVOIDANCE

Entrepreneurs are embedded in technology environments – whether it is innovating themselves or applying the innovations of others to build and grow their businesses. Let's consider the case of someone who attempts to build a successful restaurant. Although not a business typically thought of as technology-centric, in fact technology is potentially everywhere in this business. Meal preparation takes raw ingredients and converts them into finished, custom-made products. Novel cooking technologies can enhance what the chef creates, such as molecular gastronomy or different forms of sous vide (cooking in a plastic pouch and placing in a steamer). Kitchen operations utilize innovative (e.g., smart, energy efficient, or having other unique features and capabilities) types of industrial-grade ranges, ovens, fryers, broilers, specialty burners, microwaves, steamers, freezers and refrigerators. Bots may be used to make pancakes while beverage dispensers might be automated. Computerized approaches to portion control and inventory management can ensure consistency and help contain food expenses. Beyond food preparation, technology is embedded in kitchen display systems and order prioritization software, self-order kiosks, touchscreen terminals as part of integrated point-of-sale systems, receipt printers, server tablets to take orders, and the communication system at a drive-up window. It is incorporated into the employee payroll system, the bookkeeping process and generation of financial statements, and the chemicals used in cleaning floors, counters and kitchen equipment. Restaurant marketing efforts include new forms of (and tools for managing) social media and email automation, online coupon platforms, and approaches to co-marketing. The inside and outside signage of the

Table 7.1   Examples and benefits of product and process technologies for
entrepreneurs

		Function	Examples	Benefits/Outcomes
Technology	Operating Processes	Customer relationship management	Salesforce.com; SAP; Oraclem; HubSpot	Sales leads; more systematic and effective coordination of customer information; deeper and longer-term relationships
		Marketing	Facebook; Hootsuite; MailChimp, Fiverr; WebiMax	Better message content; greater reach; more closed sales
		Administration, billing	Appointments-Plus, Bill4Time, Zoho	Improved scheduling, more accurate billing, better communications
		Bookkeeping and financial planning	QuickBooks; Excel; XERO	More accurate picture of expenses, margins, cash flow needs, management of growth
		Human resource management	Cezanne; Namely; Zenefits, Sage Payroll	Model employee retention
		Logistics and fulfillment	Amazon Marketplace; Alibaba; ShippingEasy	Time and cost savings, third-party liability, improved product shipping
	Product creation	Concept testing	Concept Pulse, Socratic Technologies	Better identify and evaluate new product concepts and customer reaction
		Prototyping and product testing	Origami, Rapid Prototyping Services; fab labs with 3D printers	Cost savings, access to skills and expertise in developing products
		Manufacturing and inventory management	Alibaba, Fishbowl	Cost savings, support for scaling production

business as well as the camera-based security system can also reflect the latest technologies.

Now consider the low-income entrepreneur attempting to launch a restaurant. Having invested any money he or she has, run up credit card debt, and mustered what might be available from friends and family, he or she opens at a location that is likely more affordable than desirable. Leaning heavily on family members to staff operations, the entrepreneur may know more about preparing food than procurement, inventory, marketing, bookkeeping, managing cash, and other facets of running a successful venture. By necessity, much is typically learned about all of these areas of the business as things unfold. However, the performance of the restaurant, and the owner's ability to learn, are significantly impacted by the technologies that are adopted. The extent to which they are integrated into operations or avoided will depend upon the entrepreneur's awareness of, understanding of, sense of the perceived importance of, willingness to adopt, and ability to employ different technological solutions. As things unfold, these decisions can be further constrained by the technological approach currently in place.

Yet, technological avoidance can be quite costly. Box 7.1 highlights some of the key costs. Absence of technology generally means most of the activities of running a business become more labor intensive, which can slow things down while also increasing the chance for human error and inconsistency. This labor intensity means less time is available for underdeveloped areas of the business, such as selling and record-keeping. Using our restaurant example, a lack of money finds the business dependent upon (used) cooking and baking equipment that cannot produce large volumes, and may limit menu options, extend customer waiting times, drive up unit costs, and limit room for experimentation. The entire scope of operations is constrained. Beyond this, the ability to accurately keep track of business expenses and revenues, prepare invoices, and pay bills and taxes on a timely basis could be compromised without basic accounting software such as QuickBooks or Wave Accounting (which is free). Record-keeping and inventory tracking are also more challenging when the business is not employing integrated point-of-sale hardware and software. Poor inventory management can lead to higher procurement costs and unavailability of items on the menu. Errors and gaps in data and financial records can result in incorrect projections, errant conclusions, and bad decisions. They can impact whether the business has adequate cash to meet financial obligations. Further, lack of technology undermines the ability to track performance in a variety of business areas. All of this can compromise the entrepreneur's grasp on the business and where it is going – he or she remains preoccupied

BOX 7.1   THE COSTS OF TECHNOLOGY AVOIDANCE

The failure to incorporate key technological advances into the business results in real costs to the entrepreneur. Below are ten examples of how a business is adversely affected by either lack of knowledge regarding technology or the unwillingness or inability to incorporate technology into the venture:

1. Reduced capabilities in terms of value that can be created for customers.
2. Higher costs in production or service delivery, payroll, key administrative tasks and other areas because of labor-intensive practices and reduced capabilities.
3. Slowness in completing operational tasks (e.g., order fulfillment, client checkout, billing, responding to client inquiries, etc.) resulting in lower volumes, higher costs, and less satisfied customers.
4. Lack of sufficient time for addressing key business needs (e.g., record-keeping, selling, hiring, quality control) because of labor-intensive practices.
5. Errors and gaps (e.g., in data, invoices, financial records) due to lack of automation and reliance on manual and paper-based administrative systems that can lead to wrong projections, inappropriate conclusions, and mis-statements to customers, suppliers and others.
6. Reduced marketplace reach and customer follow-up intensity by failing to adequately take advantage of social media, automated email and other digital technologies in marketing efforts.
7. Less effective inventory management, excess supply of certain items and shortages of others when customers want them.
8. Weaker ability to track employee, product, and marketing performance and other efficiencies in the business.
9. Less ability to anticipate cash flow needs and meet financial obligations on a timely basis.
10. Poorer image among customers and other stakeholders because of perception that business is not up-to-date and is less efficient.

with operational matters and cannot transition to a more strategic perspective. Marketing efforts may also suffer when not adequately employing social media platforms such as Facebook or Instagram and customer relationship management software such as Salesforce. This can be costly in terms of market reach, the identification of new prospects, timely follow-up communications, and the development of longer-term customer loyalty. Even the inability to install a proper security system can drive up insurance costs and result in more loss due to theft. While these are but a few examples, the bottom line is that the absence of technologies can mean it costs the entrepreneur more to a run a business that is able to deliver less value to customers.

Technology has also enhanced the potential for outsourcing – frequently to companies remotely located and with whom the entrepreneur has little in-person interaction. Outsourcing of key business functions is much more prevalent today than has historically been the case (Jiang and Qureshi, 2006). Although it allows entrepreneurs to do much more with less, outsourcing tends to be underutilized by low-income entrepreneurs. Yet it can offer cost savings and lower the entrepreneur's capital requirements, as they do not have to pay for key facilities and equipment, while also reducing the costs of wages, training, and benefits. It can enable access to advanced skills that he or she does not possess. For instance, consider an entrepreneur running a clothing business that either resells or produces new clothing. Technology can provide access to low-cost manufacturers and designers in various parts of the world, such as China, Malaysia, Mexico, or Vietnam. Various technology platforms such as Amazon Marketplace and Alibaba (see Table 7.2) offer a full range of manufacturing, logistics, inventory management and fulfillment services. Beyond this, firms can outsource the management of digital marketing campaigns, their salesforce requirements, bookkeeping, employee hiring, training and payroll, and virtually any other business activity. All this gives entrepreneurs operational relief and the opportunity to focus more on other core aspects of their venture.

VENTURE TYPES AND TECHNOLOGY

The adoption of technology tends to be tied to the type of venture being created. In Chapter 4, we explored the distinctions between survival, lifestyle, managed growth and aggressive growth ventures. Technology is a significant factor enabling firms to transition from one type to the next. Table 7.2 illustrates how, as we move across the four types, different technological tools are used to increase automation, reduce manual labor, and enhance capabilities. Stated differently, these tools or innovations are what make the scaling of the venture possible.

In essence, new technologies are largely absent from the survival venture, while the aggressive growth venture is defined by technologies both in terms of what they sell and how they operate. In between these two end-points, the lifestyle business adopts relatively basic, off-the-shelf technological solutions for select problems or needs, such as bookkeeping, local marketing, and the handling of point-of-sale transactions. With the managed growth firm, we see a more comprehensive integration of off-the-shelf technological solutions throughout the firm (e.g., accounting, finance, payroll, operations, logistics, human resource management, marketing), and some development of proprietary technology both for

Table 7.2 Technology usage in select areas across different venture types

	Survival	Lifestyle	Managed Growth	Aggressive Growth
Operations	Mostly manual labor with little to no equipment	Manual labor with use of basic commercial equipment	Shrinking manual labor, growing reliance on technology, more standardized outputs	Highly labor efficient, extensive automation, leading-edge equipment
Financial transactions	Cash	Cash and electronic	Cash and electronic	Largely electronic
Financial management	Mostly paper based	Some paper, but largely electronic	Electronic	Electronic
Customer communications	Personal	Personal and online (e.g., social media and website)	Increased use of customer relationship management (CRM) systems	Online through CRM systems, interactive video communications
Market feedback	Little to no technology involvement	Personal, paper based, use of social media and online surveys	Use of social media, electronic employee and online feedback	Use of social media, electronic employee, and online feedback
Employee management	One-on-one (if any employees)	One-on-one	Some integration of electronic human resource management (HRM) systems	Predominant use of electronic HRM systems
Employee recruiting	Personal networks	Personal networks as well as online and print media employment ads	Online and print media as well as online and offline employment portals	Online and print media as well as online and offline employment portals

Table 7.2   (continued)

	Survival	Lifestyle	Managed Growth	Aggressive Growth
New product/ service development	Little to no innovation	New products/ services sourced from others	Limited development of own proprietary systems and products	Intense focus on advancing proprietary new products and process technologies
Technology usage	LOW	LOW TO MEDIUM		HIGH

operations and in the product or service they are selling. Employees tend to be a source of physical labor in the survival and lifestyle ventures, while they become more a source of intellectual capital in the managed and aggressive growth ventures. As we progress across these four types, the viability and associated benefits from outsourcing various functions are also going up. Meanwhile, the adaptability and speed of the organization are being enhanced. Ultimately, as its importance increases across these four types, technology is opening up new possibilities in terms of what can be done, how it is done and for whom.

As we have seen, low income entrepreneurs disproportionately create survival and lifestyle ventures and their ventures rarely make the transition to managed or aggressive growth. Technology is a key factor behind these tendencies. Part of the problem is the cost of adopting various technologies, but a bigger obstacle tends to be technology literacy.

THE CONCEPT OF TECHNOLOGY LITERACY

For low-income entrepreneurs, the first priority must be to enhance their technology literacy. This type of literacy, introduced in Chapter 6, has different conceptualizations. For some, technology literacy is associated with computer literacy, or that knowledge and ability a person has to use computers, or to use computer programs and other applications associated with computers (e.g., McMillan, 1996). Others prioritize information and communication technology (ICT) literacy, or the person's ability to gather, organize, analyze, and report information using technology (Leu and Kinzer, 2000). Hansen (2003, p. 117) takes a more comprehensive view, defining technology literacy as "an individual's abilities to adopt, adapt, invent, and evaluate technology to positively affect his or her life, community, and environment." Eisenberg and Johnson (2002, p. 1) suggest that a technologically literate person can "use technology as a tool for organization, communication, research, and problem solving." Therefore, technology-literate people know what the technology is capable of, they are able to use the technology proficiently, they make intelligent decisions about which technology to use and when to use it, and they can leverage technology in the creation of new entrepreneurial ventures.

Acquiring technological literacy tends to be a function of socio-economic status, with low-income neighborhoods often trailing in the development of the necessary knowledge and skills. The so-called "digital divide" has led various government and non-government organizations to develop and implement educational initiatives to enhance technology-related knowledge and skills among the poor. The European Union, in particular, has embraced the notion of technology as a vehicle for social inclusion (see European Commission, 2010). Similarly, the government of Brazil has launched a national digital inclusion project (see Governo do Brasil, 2017). In the United States, the federal government's National Telecommunications and Information Administration (NTIA, 2000), which first popularized the notion of a digital divide, has also shifted to the terminology of digital inclusion.

The digital divide refers to social and economic inequality when it comes to access, the use of, and the impact of technologies on individuals, households, neighborhoods and communities (NTIA, 2000). As economies are more driven by e-commerce and the widespread use of an array of technological devices with each passing year, the digital disadvantage of the poor is especially worrisome (Molla and Licker, 2005). It persists despite the fact that costs of technology have come down and continue to decline. As demonstrated in Figure 7.1, even with relatively basic technologies such as smartphones and desktop or laptop computers, there is a significant gap in usage by those with low incomes. Close to half of African American and Hispanic households in the US do not have broadband access, while more than half of educators in low-income schools struggle to incorporate technology into their teaching because of student lack of access (Soltan, 2016). In an OECD study involving 40 countries, 30 of which have developed economies, the evidence suggests that the poor in these countries had more Internet access compared to the US (Hutt, 2016).

Much attention is devoted to expanding affordable (or free) Internet access in low-income neighborhoods. The dissemination of smartphones has somewhat helped in this regard – and for some it is their only avenue to the Internet (Falaki et al., 2010; Smith, 2015). However, the problem is more complex. For instance, McCloud et al. (2016) report evidence that individuals from a low socioeconomic position (SEP) use the Internet

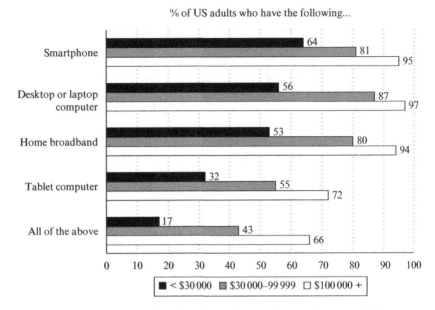

Source: Based on survey conducted by the Pew Research Center, September 29–November 6, 2016.

Figure 7.1   Technology adoption and low-income Americans

less for beneficial capital-enhancing activities such as helping with career advancement or utilizing financial services than high SEP individuals. Similarly, Hutt (2016) reports evidence from the OECD that the poor in developed economies use the Internet in different ways. Specifically, low-income teenagers are more likely to use the Internet to chat or play games and less likely to search for practical information or read news, when compared to their high-income counterparts. The author notes that these usage patterns also correlate with academic performance. Appreciating the potential of the Internet is also affected by teacher preparation. Herold (2017) cites evidence that teachers in high-poverty schools are less likely than those in wealthier schools to have received training in how to integrate technology into their classroom instruction.

Beyond use of the Internet, social media, and downloadable apps, potential entrepreneurs need exposure to innovative approaches for facilitating transactions electronically, building and mining databases, and using software to accomplish basic business activities such as keeping records and accounts and managing payroll. Further, while most discussions of technology and the poor primarily stress information, communication and digital-related technologies, these tend to be especially critical for managing *processes* within start-up ventures. However, if we consider many of the highest potential *products and services* being developed by entrepreneurs today, they often incorporate nano, energy, bio-related, chemical, polymer, medical, laser, sonar, robotic, advanced manufacturing and other technologies. The implication is that more effort must be devoted to science and mathematics in primary and second schools attended by the poor, and to getting more of those from poverty backgrounds into science and engineering fields in colleges. While so-called STEAM (science, technology, engineering, the arts and math) learning is getting more attention in low-income schools, it is not enough. Herold (2017, p. 7), in comparing the use of technology in a poorer school district with one that is economically better off, concludes that other problems tend to take precedence in the poor district, while the transformative potential of newer models of hands-on, technology-infused, project-based learning is less appreciated.

The learning challenge is to help low-income entrepreneurs advance through at least three, and in some cases four, levels of technology literacy:

1. The first of these levels involves developing a solid understanding of how to perform basic tasks like writing, communicating, searching for information using contemporary technology devices such as desktop and laptop computers, smartphones, tablets or similar electronic or technical equipment.
2. The second level concerns the mastery of more complex tasks such as completing economic transactions (e.g., buying and selling goods), use of web applications and basic financial management and planning software.
3. Level 3 entails developing the ability to collect and process data, and/ or use complex equipment such as medical devices, machining tools and 3D printers.
4. The final level addresses the ability to (a) use coding language to develop new software that gets computers and products to do things, and/or (b) build complex physical prototypes for new innovation.

With respect to the poor in developed economies, technology literacy is frequently limited to levels 1 or 2. This helps explain the very low proportion of technology ventures that are created in economically disadvantaged neighborhoods (Tang and Koveos, 2004). However, many of the product and process technologies used in start-up ventures are increasingly accessible with a level 1 or 2 mastery of technology. The first level represents the upper limit on what is accomplished in many low-income schools. The second level includes the use of software for managing a range of business activities of a venture, from accounting to customer relationship management (CRM). There are some natural barriers for low-income entrepreneurs at this level of technology engagement, starting with the cost of software licensing and affordable training. E-commerce platforms such as Amazon, eBay, Shopify, Magento, Squarespace, and Symphony Commerce offer low-income entrepreneurs the opportunity to access a wider target audience for their products and/or services. Community programs such as the Watts Entrepreneur Business Accelerator (WEBA) in Los Angeles can also make a difference. The WEBA program provides technical assistance and access to capital for residents of the high-crime Watts neighborhood in South Los Angeles. The emphasis is to introduce local entrepreneurs to social media platforms as well as online technical assistance tools to help them grow their businesses online.

The highest levels of literacy find the entrepreneur using and/or actually developing new technologically intensive products and services. The creation of application software has been the focus of many high-growth technology ventures, often operating from technology incubators/accelerators in specific geographic regions such as the Silicon Valley or the Research Triangle. With respect to low-income entrepreneurs, this can be most challenging, as it can require a combination of seed funding, mentoring, technology literacy and skills, and access to incubator and accelerator space. Research has shown that entrepreneurial ecosystems are not very permeable to entrepreneurs from poverty-stricken areas (Light and Dana, 2013; Neumeyer, He and Santos, 2017). Yet, computer coding is increasingly accessible. An interesting example can be found with the efforts of the Raspberry Pi Foundation in the United Kingdom. Working with educational partners, they attempt to bring very low-cost computing, basic mastery of coding, and digital-maker projects to those who might otherwise be excluded, including the poor.

TECHNOLOGY ILLITERACY, OPPORTUNITY RECOGNITION, AND VENTURE TYPES

As we saw in Chapter 4, opportunity recognition is a key competency of entrepreneurs. Entrepreneurs scan their environments, recognize patterns that others often miss, and subsequently pursue these opportunities. They use a variety of tools such as direct observation, information exchange through formal and informal networks, public sources, personal and professional experience, and participation in training and education programs to expand their opportunity horizons and exploit these patterns. Technology literacy enables the entrepreneur to explore the digital dimension of all these tools, saving time and accessing a wider and deeper array of information. This is particularly important for entrepreneurs in low-income areas that often operate in a constrained economic environment and disproportionately rely on the access to virtual resources such as the World Wide Web to explore new trends and uncover opportunities (Schön, Sanyal and Mitchell, 1999). Unfortunately, as Hutt (2016, p. 3) concludes, even when they have access, the poor "may not have the knowledge or skills required to turn online opportunities into real opportunities."

Opportunity horizons can be extended through creative use of search engines (e.g., Google, Bing, Yahoo!) and social media. The latter can enable insights on and interactive relationships with prospective consumers, investors, and other stakeholders to better understand the gaps in the market (Fischer and Reuber, 2011; Piller, Vossen and Ihl, 2011). For example, a systematic analysis of product reviews on ecommerce platforms (e.g., Amazon, Magento, Vokart) can help poverty entrepreneurs assess current deficits or unmet needs in the market. Beyond this, e-commerce platforms create opportunities for poverty entrepreneurs to engage in various forms of arbitrage, avoiding the costly investment in a physical location and decoupling themselves from the limitations of their local economy.

Related to the limits it can place on opportunity horizons is the effect technology illiteracy can have on the kinds of ventures launched by low-income entrepreneurs. As we saw earlier in this chapter, the role of technology changes rather significantly as we move from survival, lifestyle, managed growth and then aggressive growth ventures. Consider the person who starts a cleaning venture – again a very basic kind of activity that is not generally considered to be high tech. Figure 7.2 envisions cleaning businesses that reflect our four different venture types. In fact, the amount and sophistication of technology increases markedly in moving from Clara's Cleaning, a home-based survival venture, to Merry Maids, an international franchise chain with an aggressive growth model – and the demands on the entrepreneur in terms of technology literacy are correspondingly increasing. Low-income entrepreneurs who lack either the awareness and understanding of, interest in, or ability to spend money on technology can find themselves pushed into a survival or, at best, lifestyle venture. Such ventures usually only require level 1 or level 2 technology literacy. Size and scale are virtually impossible without technology. Again, this is at least part of the reason why, when compared to entrepreneurs in higher-income categories, poor entrepreneurs tend to disproportionately create survival and lifestyle businesses.

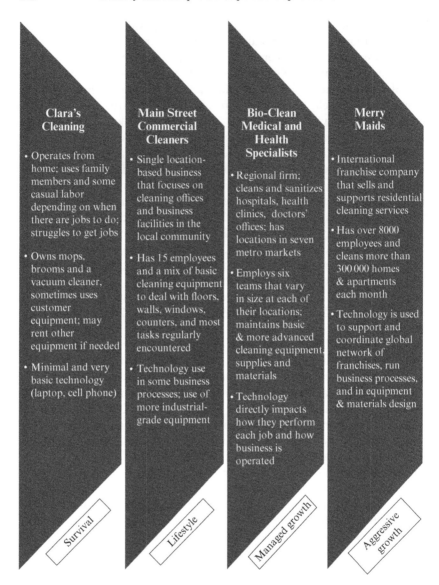

Clara's Cleaning

- Operates from home; uses family members and some casual labor depending on when there are jobs to do; struggles to get jobs

- Owns mops, brooms and a vacuum cleaner, sometimes uses customer equipment; may rent other equipment if needed

- Minimal and very basic technology (laptop, cell phone)

Survival

Main Street Commercial Cleaners

- Single location-based business that focuses on cleaning offices and business facilities in the local community

- Has 15 employees and a mix of basic cleaning equipment to deal with floors, walls, windows, counters, and most tasks regularly encountered

- Technology use in some business processes; use of more industrial-grade equipment

Lifestyle

Bio-Clean Medical and Health Specialists

- Regional firm; cleans and sanitizes hospitals, health clinics, doctors' offices; has locations in seven metro markets

- Employs six teams that vary in size at each of their locations; maintains basic & more advanced cleaning equipment, supplies and materials

- Technology directly impacts how they perform each job and how business is operated

Managed growth

Merry Maids

- International franchise company that sells and supports residential cleaning services

- Has over 8000 employees and cleans more than 300,000 homes & apartments each month

- Technology is used to support and coordinate global network of franchises, run business processes, and in equipment & materials design

Aggressive growth

Figure 7.2   Four types of cleaning ventures and technologies they employ

MOVING FORWARD

The many struggles that must be overcome by low-income entrepreneurs are magnified when technology cannot be leveraged in their businesses. The solution begins with more and much better education on types and uses of technology in the middle and high schools attended by the poor, and with better access to technology in disadvantaged neighborhoods and communities. But for the entrepreneur in the middle of trying to start something, these systemic solutions will only come to fruition in the coming decades. In the meantime, these entrepreneurs have some options at their disposal. Costs are coming down on many technology solutions for small businesses, and products are becoming more user friendly. At the same time, various technology tools such as open source software for word processing, spreadsheets and financial planning are available. For instance, companies such as Wave Accounting offer free accounting software that can help the entrepreneur better understand their business and move from a preoccupation with operational matters to a more strategic perspective that includes financial and business modeling. Free software is available online to do everything from finding a company name and generating invoices to correcting grammar, sending emails, creating logos and getting the public to vote on things (e.g., how much they like a product name, logo, or business idea).[1] Furthermore, a variety of (inexpensive or free) online platforms such as Coursera, the Khan Academy, and YouTube can provide poverty entrepreneurs with the necessary background knowledge on how to use and implement many technologies in their businesses. In the US, the Small Business Administration has teamed with Microsoft and other tech companies to create Business Technology Simplified, a set of online modules and downloadable resources to help small business owners navigate technology in their ventures.[2]

Further, while there is much more to be done, low-income entrepreneurs can increasingly find education, training, incubation and mentoring opportunities offered by various organizations and institutions in their local regions. The Deep Dive Coding Bootcamps in New Mexico represent a case in point. The program combines basic training in several coding languages, physical prototyping, and entrepreneurship skills to help develop technology entrepreneurs in the Albuquerque area. Residents receive financial assistance if their total household income is 200 percent of federal poverty guidelines or less. Other programs target the youth, hoping to train technology entrepreneurs from low-income neighborhoods during their formative years. For example, Tech Square Labs, a Georgia-based initiative offers a coding program targeting young low-income adults from underserved communities and school districts, helping them to access software-oriented high-demand job markets as well as technology entrepreneurship opportunities. The program goes beyond tactical skills and teaches students how to think like a software engineer and innovator, where students also receive training in the areas of ideation, design thinking, business model generation, financial responsibility, diversity, inclusion, and career readiness.

Finally, in urban areas within developed economies across the globe, more emphasis is being placed on the development of entrepreneurial ecosystems (see Chapter 8). While these ecosystems tend to exclude or ignore the poor, this is slowly changing. For the low-income entrepreneur, being tenacious in trying to connect to this ecosystem can open doors in terms of gaining access to (observing, sharing, borrowing, receiving for free) the technologies and knowledge of existing small businesses, emerging technology firms, non-profits working in the economic development and entrepreneurship spaces, and local universities.

NOTES

1. See Mese, A. (2015), "300 awesome free things: A massive list of free resources you should know," TNW, February 18, accessed June 11, 2018 at https://thenextweb.com/dd/2015/02/18/300-awesome-free-things-massive-list-free-resources-know/.
2. See US Small Business Administration (n.d.), "Learning Center," accessed June 11, 2018 at https://www.sba.gov/tools/sba-learningcenter/search/training.

REFERENCES

Eisenberg, M.B. and D. Johnson (2002), *Learning and Teaching Information Technology*, Syracuse, NY: ERIC Clearinghouse on Information and Technology.
European Commission (2010), *Joint Report on Social Protection and Social Inclusion 2010*, accessed June 14, 2018 at ec.europa.eu/social/BlobServlet?docId=5503&langId=en.
Falaki, H., R. Mahajan and S. Kandula et al. (2010), "Diversity in smartphone usage," in *Proceedings of the 8th International Conference on Mobile Systems, Applications, and Services*, Association for Computing Machinery, pp. 179–94.
Fischer, E. and A.R. Reuber (2011), "Social interaction via new social media: (How) can interactions on Twitter affect effectual thinking and behavior?," *Journal of Business Venturing*, 26(1), 1–18.
Governo do Brasil (2017), *Programa de Inclusão Social e Digital* [Social and Digital Inclusion Program], accessed June 14, 2018 at https://www.governodigital.gov.br/cidadania/inclusao-digital/programa-de-inclusao-social-e-digital.
Hansen, J.W. (2003), "To change perceptions of technology programs," *Journal of Technology Studies*, 29(2), 116–19.
Herold, B. (2017), "Poor students face digital divide in how teachers learn to use

technology," *Education Week*, June 12, accessed June 11, 2018 at https://www. edweek.org/ew/articles/2017/06/14/poor-students-face-digital-divide-in-teacher-technology-training.html.

Hughes, T.P. (2004), *Human-Built World: How to Think About Technology and Culture*, Chicago, IL: University of Chicago Press.

Hutt, R. (2016), "Rich and poor teenagers use the web differently – here's what this is doing to inequality," *World Economic Forum*, July 27, accessed June 11, 2018 at https://www.weforum.org/agenda/2016/07/rich-and-poor-teenagers-spend-a-similar-amount-of-time-online-so-why-aren-t-we-closing-the-digital-divide/.

Jiang, B. and A. Qureshi (2006), "Research on outsourcing results: Current literature and future opportunities," *Management Decision*, **44**(1), 44–55.

Leu, D.J. and C.K. Kinzer (2000), "The convergence of literacy instruction with networked technologies for information and communication," *Reading Research Quarterly*, **35**(1), 108–27.

Light, I. and L.-P. Dana (2013), "Boundaries of social capital in entrepreneurship," *Entrepreneurship Theory and Practice*, **37**(3), 603–24.

McCloud, R.F., C.A. Okechukwu, G. Sorensen and K. Viswanath (2016), "Entertainment or health? Exploring the Internet usage patterns of the urban poor: A secondary analysis of a randomized controlled trial," *Journal of Medical Internet Research*, **18**(3).

McMillan, S. (1996), "Literacy and computer literacy: Definitions and comparisons," *Computers & Education*, **27**(3–4), 161–70.

Molla, A. and P. Licker (2005), "eCommerce adoption in developing countries: A model and instrument," *Information & Management*, **42**(6), 877–99.

National Telecommunications and Information Administration (NTIA) (2000), *Falling Through the Net II: Toward Digital Inclusion*, accessed September 29, 2004 at http://www.ntia.doc.gov/ntiahome/fttn00/contents00.html.

Neumeyer, X., S. He and S.C. Santos (2017), *The Social Organization of Entrepreneurial Ecosystems*," in *Proceedings of the Technology & Engineering Management Conference (TEMSCON), 2017 IEEE*.

Piller, F., A. Vossen and C. Ihl (2011), "From social media to social product development: The impact of social media on co-creation of innovation," *Die Unternehmung*, **66**(1), 7–25.

Schön, D.A., B. Sanyal and W.J. Mitchell (eds) (1999), *High Technology and Low-Income Communities: Prospects for the Positive Use of Advanced Information Technology*, Cambridge, MA: MIT Press.

Smith, A. (2015), "US smartphone use in 2015," *Pew Research Center*, April 1, accessed June 2018 at http://www.pewinternet.org/2015/04/01/us-smartphone-use-in-2015/.

Soltan, L. (2016), "Digital divide: The technology gap between rich and poor," *Digital Responsibility*, accessed June 11, 2018 at http://www.digitalresponsibility. org/digital-divide-the-technology-gap-between-rich-and-poor/.

Tang, L. and P.E. Koveos (2004), "Venture entrepreneurship, innovation entrepreneurship, and economic growth," *Journal of Developmental Entrepreneurship*, **9**(2), 161–71.

8. Building supportive infrastructure for low-income entrepreneurs

> One cannot but wonder how an environment can make people despair and sit
> idle and then, by changing the conditions, one can transform the same people
> into matchless performers.
> (Muhammad Yunus)

INFRASTRUCTURE AND THE ENTREPRENEUR

Entrepreneurship is about individual action, adaptation, perseverance, and resilience. The sustained efforts of the entrepreneur are essential for venture success. At the same time, supportive infrastructure also plays an important role. Infrastructure refers to the physical and organizational structures, systems, and facilities that enable the effective operation of a society, community, or, in this case, a business enterprise. It includes things like schools, law enforcement, financial structures, and transportation systems, among many other components. For an entrepreneur, it can facilitate the development and refinement of new business ideas, acquisition of resources, launch of the business, production and distribution of products and services, targeting of customers, and ongoing growth of the business over time.

Infrastructure is not static or fixed. It is continually developing and changing, and can rapidly decline or decay. New elements are being added and others become obsolete. Components are adapted as the characteristics and needs of the community change, and ongoing efforts are made to enhance compatibility among different parts of the infrastructure. It is costly to build, and requires ongoing investment to operate and maintain. Investments come from public, non-profit and private sources, and can be mutually reinforcing. Interdependency among parts of the infrastructure can mean that a decline in any one element (e.g., schools, public transit) undermines the ability of other elements (e.g., banks, health care institutions) to serve their purpose.

For their part, the poor are typically surrounded by weak, underdeveloped, and decaying infrastructure (e.g., underperforming schools, substandard housing, unsafe neighborhoods, lack of nearby, affordable medical care). Where quality infrastructure does exist, the poor may not have the same kind of access that those in higher income brackets will generally have. And when it comes to the specific kinds of infrastructure elements that can help people start and grow entrepreneurial ventures, the problem is worse.

In this chapter, we explore how general and entrepreneurship-specific infrastructure components affect the poor and their ventures. The challenges of the poor in accessing the elements of an entrepreneurial ecosystem are examined. We assess the role of infrastructure components across the stages of venture development, and then draw implications for those in poverty when attempting to start and grow ventures.

COMPONENTS OF INFRASTRUCTURE RELEVANT FOR ENTREPRENEURSHIP

In entrepreneurship, supportive infrastructure refers to the complete range of community-based resources needed to sustain a venture from launch to exit. We will divide these into general or basic and entrepreneurship-specific elements. General infrastructure includes facilities and buildings where businesses can operate, including factories, retail locations, warehouses, and office space. These facilities need power and energy, water and security systems every day, and police and fire services in case of emergency. Infrastructure also includes roads, bridges, viaducts, parking spots and public transportation services that allow for distribution, moving products from point A to B and to get customers to the business. Creating and managing a business daily further requires broadband access, as well as information and communication technologies such as Internet, phone and fax. Additional elements of a supportive infrastructure include access to quality educational and training institutions, which are critical for the five literacies of entrepreneurship (see Chapter 6), and to financial institutions, such as banks and credit institutions, where the entrepreneur can manage the daily financial operations of the business and have access to capital. A legal system and courts ensure contracts are enforceable, property rights can be protected, and other legal safeguards are provided. These general elements are vitally important for the daily operations of a venture, but they are not enough.

Entrepreneurial ventures also benefit from a more specialized infrastructure that has come to be called an "entrepreneurial ecosystem." It is defined as the agglomeration of interrelated individuals, institutions, organizations, and regulatory entities in a particular geographic area that act upon and promote entrepreneurial initiatives and actions (Isenberg, 2010; Malecki, 2011). Like a biological ecosystem, an entrepreneurial ecosystem includes highly interdependent components that interact with the larger environment to enable ventures to start, grow and exit (see Isenberg, 2010 and Neck et al., 2004 for examples). We typically consider entrepreneurial ecosystems at a community level, although the concept is also relevant at regional and national levels, and there are interdependencies among elements at these different levels.

Focusing on the local community, a number of institutional structures play a role in fostering entrepreneurial activity, including chambers of commerce, local economic development agencies, small business development centers, and non-profits involved in various entrepreneurial support activities. The availability of incubators and accelerators, as well as access to facilities such as fablabs, makerspaces or other facilities where prototypes and products can be developed, is important. Entrepreneurs also need elements that help them build social capital such as venture pitch and business plan competitions, mentoring and apprenticeship programs and social forums dedicated to the entrepreneurial community (Neumeyer et al., 2018). Here, entrepreneurs can develop their business ideas and plans, get feedback and counseling from experts, access resources, and establish partnerships. When it comes to money to support the venture, infrastructure components include microcredit programs, grants, venture capital and angel investors (see Chapter 9). Universities and colleges contribute to the ecosystem through research, inventions, and trained student talent, as well as academic entrepreneurship programs. Another key element is the local small business community, which provides networking and mentoring opportunities, as well as the potential for collaboration with new start-ups. Finally, the broad scope of professional service providers in such areas as legal, accounting, marketing, design and branding help entrepreneurs navigate the entrepreneurial journey. Figure 8.1 presents an overview of the general as well as the entrepreneurship-specific components of an effective infrastructure.

Low-income neighborhoods generally have underdeveloped infrastructures (both general and entrepreneurship specific) and often lack fundamental infrastructure components. A major force shaping many low-income neighborhoods has been the transformation of the urban economy. For the past 50 years and especially in the past two decades, urban economies have become more decentralized, global, and heavily reliant on finance, services, and technology rather than on the once larger and more powerful manufacturing base (Abramson, Tobin and VanderGoot, 1995; Massey and Eggers, 1993). This has affected basic infrastructure investments in low-income neighborhoods, where the poor have to deal with deficient roads and parking facilities, insufficient public transportation options, frequent power outages, deficits in sewers and drains, reduced access to Internet or the phone, lack of security and police surveillance.

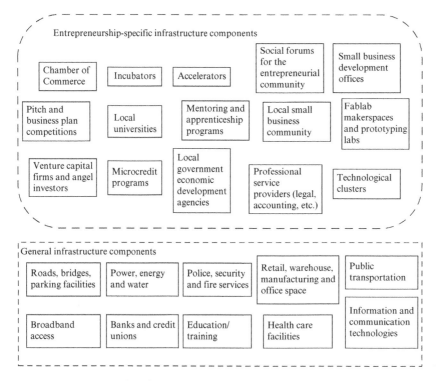

Figure 8.1   General and entrepreneurship-specific infrastructure components

The poor can encounter other differences in the available infrastructure, such as when payday loan issuers replace banks; dollar stores replace grocery and office supply stores; and government-assistance programs replace private sector investment. Further, neighborhood effects, or the coupling of neighborhood socioeconomic disadvantage with other social problems – such as high rates of unemployment, crime, or adolescent delinquency – play an important (often-detrimental) role in ongoing infrastructure development. Major financial institutions avoid opening branches in poor neighborhoods, as they fear robberies or vandalism, as well as low deposits or levels of capital to work with. And other entrepreneurship-specific infrastructure elements, such as incubators and accelerators are missing entirely, preferring to locate in areas with easy transportation access, good parking, locations close to conference centers and universities, and proximity to the creative community.

GENERAL INFRASTRUCTURE: CHALLENGES FOR THE POOR ENTREPRENEUR

While most of the general or basic infrastructure components are taken for granted by those who live in middle- or higher-income neighborhoods, the poor struggle to deal with infrastructure deficits on a daily basis. These deficits have significant implications for the ability of low-income entrepreneurs to create and grow ventures (see Figure 8.2). Let us examine six prominent areas of difficulty:

Transportation

One such struggle involves securing reliable and affordable transportation. In a large and ongoing study of upward mobility, it was demonstrated that commuting time is the single most important factor in the odds of escaping poverty. Specifically, the longer the average commute time in a given county, the lower are the chances of a low-income family moving upwards on the economic ladder (Chetty and Hendren, 2015). Transportation impacts employment, social mobility, security, the ability to address family needs, and pursuit of opportunities in general. For entrepreneurs, it affects their ability to do research, connect with potential resource providers and other stakeholders, obtain supplies, and serve customers, among many other critical activities.

Many of the poor rely on public transportation or friends and family to get to work, commute, and manage their everyday lives, thereby limiting their overall mobility as well as creating uncertainty and disruption. And when residing outside dense urban areas, housing, employment, and other opportunities are more dispersed and harder to access. According to the National Household Travel Survey (2009), individuals in poverty take about three times as many transit trips as those in the higher-income groups, have the greatest rate of bicycle trips, and walk to destinations about 50 percent more than their higher-income counterparts. While these results are for the US, similar patterns exist in other developed economies (e.g., Australian Bureau of Statistics, 2008). Unfortunately, public transit can be unreliable and infrequent, which poses a significant problem for low-income residents who have multiple jobs and/or work overnight shifts. For women in poverty, transportation issues complicate the ability to balance work, childcare, and elder care (Casper, McLanahan and Garfinkel, 1994; Pendall, Blumenberg and Dawkins, 2016). For their part, transit agencies increasingly prioritize investments and service improvements that target riders who might otherwise drive, paying for these upgrades by sacrificing routes serving low-income neighborhoods. At the same time, residents of these neighborhoods have less political and financial power when attempting to muster opposition to these changes, and may just abandon public transit (Taylor and Morris, 2015).

Cars would offer an alternative solution, and evidence shows that car access improves employment prospects (Baum, 2009; Ong, 2002), wages and earnings (Gurley and Bruce, 2005; Raphael and Rice, 2002), and access to safe neighborhoods with good schools and environmental quality (Dawkins, Jeon and Pendall, 2015). Affordable and reliable car access is therefore a pervasive issue for low-income households in the United States. Families above the federal poverty level, on average, have one car per adult in the household; those below poverty, by contrast, have only 0.52 cars per adult (Klein and Smart, 2017). According to the National Household Travel Survey (2009), about 24 percent of households in poverty do not own a vehicle. Comparatively, 98 percent of the $100000+ households own at least one vehicle. Moreover, when using personal vehicles, individuals in poverty are twice as likely to travel in a multi-occupant versus a single occupant vehicle. The average vehicle occupancy for those at or below the poverty level is 2.37 persons per vehicle mile versus 2.07 for those with incomes above $100000. In Europe, the pattern is similar. Countries with the least equitable car availability, also have the least equitable income distribution (Portugal, Greece and the UK), while those with more equitable car availability also have a more equitable income distribution (Italy, Germany, France and Luxembourg) (Dargay, Hivert and Legros, 2008).

To address the deficit in car ownership many low-income households turn to predatory lenders for loans to purchase vehicles or take out risky title loans to provide a ready source of cash, increasing their financial vulnerability. For families living in low-income neighborhoods, the costs of driving are further increased because of discriminatory practices or "redlining" in the setting of automobile insurance premiums (Ong and Stoll, 2007). In addition, owning a car means adding expenses to the household budget, crowding out the ability to address other needs.

Car sharing offers some potential, and these programs have grown significantly in metropolitan areas in the last ten years (Shaheen and Cohen, 2013). With very few exceptions, car-sharing services are still an anomaly in low-income neighborhoods. Several reasons exist, including the need for a smartphone and credit card, requirements on where the car is accessed and returned, sufficient user density to make them financially feasible, and high crime and hence higher insurance rates in low-income neighborhoods. Notable exceptions exist, including the Los Angeles' EV Car Sharing Pilot for Disadvantaged Communities and Chicago's Shared Use Mobility Center. Kim (2015) concludes that car sharing can make a difference in low-income neighborhoods if rental prices can be kept low or subsidized.

Affordable Energy

Research suggests that the overwhelming majority of low-income households and households of color experience higher-than-average energy burdens. The percentage of household income that low-income households in the US pay on their home energy bills is more than three times what their higher-income counterparts pay (Drehobl and Ross, 2016). For low-income households, this average burden can be as high as 30 percent, according to a survey conducted by the Center of Neighborhood Technology (CNT) of 28 metropolitan areas (Drehobl and Ross, 2016). What has been termed "energy poverty" is also a significant issue in Europe (Bouzarovski, 2013). There, the share of household budgets spent on domestic energy services has been growing disproportionately among the lowest-income quintile of the population, from 6 percent in 2000 to 9 percent in 2014, compared to an average increase from 5 percent to 6 percent for the entire population (European Commission, 2015). The results from the EU Survey on Income and Living Conditions (EU-SILC) indicate that 9.4 percent of the EU population were unable to keep their home adequately heated in 2015, 9.1 percent accumulated debts on their utility bills and 15.2 percent lived in homes with a leaking roof, damp walls, and porous window frames or floors.

These conditions have detrimental effects on physical and mental health, capacity to find or maintain a job, and on creating social connections (Dhéret and Giuli, 2017). They also affect new businesses started by the poor. Inefficient and poorly maintained heating, ventilation and air-conditioning (HVAC) systems, poor insulation, inefficient large-scale appliances, utility rate design practices (e.g., high customer fixed charges), lack of awareness of bill assistance or energy efficiency programs, as well as a lack of knowledge about energy conservation measures, and an inability to incorporate new technologies (see Chapter 7) contribute to the challenge.

Education

Education and training are at the forefront of most government and institutional initiatives focused on poverty alleviation. The need to address functional literacy as well as the other four literacies crucial for entrepreneurship (see Chapter 6) is paramount. As discussed in Chapters 1 and 3, inadequate schools and high dropout rates significantly hinder the poor throughout their lifetime. Many of those living in low-income neighborhoods lack comprehensive access to education, experience underfunded and lower-quality educational institutions, and their ability to learn is hindered by socioeconomic factors such as housing, nutrition, employment, health care, and heightened exposure to environmental stress (e.g., crime, domestic violence, a missing parent) (Duncan and Magnuson, 2005; Hoff, 2003). The educational infrastructure often fails to adapt to distinct learning needs and styles, and reflect diverse professional paths, when it comes to the poor. It fails to offer the kinds of learning spaces (physical and virtual), core content, and experiential opportunities that can bridge the learning gap and compensate for the learning complexities imposed by poverty conditions.

Educational and training deficits among the poor are particularly important for entrepreneurship, as they have a direct effect on functional, financial, business, economic, and technological literacies that dramatically impact every stage of the entrepreneurial process, from opportunity recognition to implementation and harvesting (see Chapters 2 and 6). At a more basic level, without sufficient literacy it is difficult to write a business plan, get access to incubators and accelerators, participate in a pitch competition, attend a workshop provided by a local small business development agency, or bid on a government contract. Moreover, deficits in other general infrastructure components (i.e., public transportation, energy, broadband access, safety and security), can compromise both access to education and the ability to learn.

Housing

Access to decent and affordable housing is another important component of a supportive infrastructure. The evidence suggests that increasing access to affordable housing is the most cost-effective strategy for reducing childhood poverty in the US (Yentel, 2016). Benefits of a stable, affordable home include better health and educational outcomes, greater access to economic opportunities, better mental and physical well-being, and stronger communities. And yet, in spite of considerable government investment in housing projects, rent subsidies, vouchers, tax credits, and other support, a majority of the poor do not get the housing assistance they need. Further, Crump (2002) argues that the geographic concentration of low-income, minority residents in public housing projects within the inner city constitutes a fundamental dilemma facing US cities, serving as a major contributor to the economic and social pathologies observed in urban poverty (Wacquant, 1997).

Solving housing deficits among the poor is a vexing policy goal. Developed economies around the world have found that government housing policies in the form of rent subsidies and state support for moderate-income housing construction have contributed to alleviating the inequalities of class. One approach has involved demolishing substandard inner city housing projects and relocating residents to areas with better infrastructure conditions, thereby diluting the concertation of poverty. A residential mobility project in Yonkers, New York randomly assigned low-income minority families residing in public and private housing in high-poverty neighborhoods to publicly funded attached row houses in seven middle-class neighborhoods (Fauth, Leventhal and Brooks-Gunn, 2004). Results controlling for individual- and family-level background character-istics indicated that families relocated to low-poverty neighborhoods were less likely to be exposed to violence and disorder, have health problems, consume alcohol abusively, receive cash assistance, and were also more likely to show satisfaction with neighborhood resources, perceive higher housing quality, and be employed, when compared to a comparison group who remained in high-poverty neighborhoods. Yet, this policy is not without critics. Crump (2002) raises concerns about an inadequate under-standing of the role of space and of spatial influences on poverty and on the behavior of poor people, suggesting that simplistic spatial solutions and geographic rearrangements are not enough, by themselves, to solve complex social, economic, and political problems.

The effects of poor housing are also prominent in other developed countries. Stephens and Van Steen (2011) found that quality housing exerts a greater poverty-reducing impact compared to disposable income by itself in England and the Netherlands, where government involvement in housing has been substantial over the years. Government housing poli-cies in the form of rent subsidies and state support for moderate-income housing construction have contributed to alleviating the inequalities of class. A particular successful case was in Oeiras, a municipal county in the suburbs of Lisbon, Portugal, where more than 5000 families lived in slums and were subsequently relocated between 1986 and 2003. This was the first municipality in Portugal to successfully eradicate the slums following the Shelter Eradication Program (Programa de Erradicação de Barracas) (Câmara Municipal de Oeiras, 2010), and became a case study for developed nations.

Access to Basic Technology

Poverty entrepreneurs also lack sufficient access to broadband and associ-ated information and communication technology (ICT). Weak infrastruc-ture is arguably the main barrier causing low broadband penetration, and the major reason for broadband exclusion (Kyriakidou, Michalakelis and Sphicopoulos, 2011). Broadband access is related to location, and in general people in low-income neighborhoods and rural areas are least well served (Kenny, 2002; Townsend et al., 2013). Moreover, the availability of hardware such as computers, laptops, smartphones or tablets in poor neighborhoods is limited, while poor functional and technological literacy undermines the ability to use the technology (see Chapter 6). This deficit in infrastructure is a leading cause of the digital divide between low-income and other neighborhoods (see Chapter 7). As a solution to the reduced access to broadband in poor neighborhoods, public libraries are often the ICT hubs in these communities (Becker et al., 2010). Yet, demand exceeds supply in most instances, which can mean long waiting times. While basic access may be available through libraries and community agencies, the poor are often unable to take advantage of online resources to support their entrepreneurial pursuits, such as key online databases, free or low-cost software (e.g., for accounting, scheduling, design of marketing materials) that can be downloaded, and free or low-cost online service providers (e.g., for logos, legal assistance, assistance with the use of social media).

Banks and Financial Institutions

Basic banking services are another shortcoming in low-income communities (NPR, 2013; Schwartz, 2011). Caskey (1994) found that bank branches are significantly underrepresented in low-income and minority urban communities in the United States and the problem is worsening. The same has been found in Europe. An analysis by Reuters shows that Britain's largest banks are disproportionately closing branches in the lowest-income areas (90 percent of the closures) while expanding in richer ones, taking bricks-and-mortar services away from communities where they are arguably most needed (MacAskill and White, 2016). Separately, Ergungor (2010) found that the favorable effects of a bank branch presence get stronger as the branch becomes more connected to the neighborhood. These findings support previous evidence indicating that in the small business lending market, relationships are associated with greater availability of credit (Petersen and Rajan, 2002). Yet, the opposite is more often the case, producing significant implications. The lack of financial infrastructure undermines the early establishment of bank accounts, development of good savings and credit habits, and the building of good credit scores. It reflects insufficient investment by banks in the financial literacy of the poor. For the low-income person starting a venture, beyond the issues of savings and establishing a good credit history, the lack of financial infrastructure negatively affects the availability of bank debt, lines of credit, and company credit cards, as well as the potential to develop a relationship with a banker that can yield benefits over time (see Chapter 9 for a discussion on access to banking among the poor). Instead, poverty entrepreneurs have to rely on their limited savings, personal credit cards, family and friends, sparse microloan programs or take out expensive payday loans that significantly limit the financial viability of their venture (Bruton, Ketchen and Ireland, 2013; Lawrence and Elliehausen, 2008).

In order to counter some of the challenges the poor face with respect to basic infrastructure, there are communities that have undertaken innovative programs within the different infrastructure categories. Table 8.1 presents an overview of some of the programs available for the poor in various developed economies.

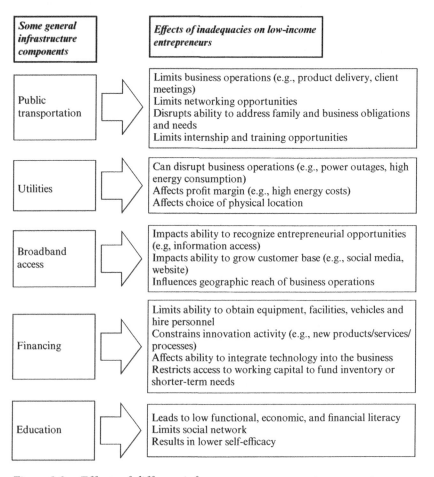

Some general infrastructure components	Effects of inadequacies on low-income entrepreneurs
Public transportation	Limits business operations (e.g., product delivery, client meetings) Limits networking opportunities Disrupts ability to address family and business obligations and needs Limits internship and training opportunities
Utilities	Can disrupt business operations (e.g., power outages, high energy consumption) Affects profit margin (e.g., high energy costs) Affects choice of physical location
Broadband access	Impacts ability to recognize entrepreneurial opportunities (e.g, information access) Impacts ability to grow customer base (e.g., social media, website) Influences geographic reach of business operations
Financing	Limits ability to obtain equipment, facilities, vehicles and hire personnel Constrains innovation activity (e.g., new products/services/processes) Affects ability to integrate technology into the business Restricts access to working capital to fund inventory or shorter-term needs
Education	Leads to low functional, economic, and financial literacy Limits social network Results in lower self-efficacy

Figure 8.2   Effects of different infrastructure components on poverty entrepreneurs

Table 8.1   Examples of general infrastructure support programs for the poor

Infrastructure Components	Programs	Target Outcomes
Transportation	EV Car Sharing Pilot for Disadvantaged Communities, Los Angeles, CA Shared Use Mobility Center, Chicago, IL Vehicles for Change, US, national More Than Wheels, Boston, MA Transit Low-Income Fare Programs for Public Transportation, US ORCA LIFT, Seattle Calgary's Low-Income Monthly Transit Pass, Canada Hamilton's Affordable Transit Pass Program, Canada Social+ Carris, special fares in public transportation in Lisbon, Portugal	Increase the use of car sharing Collect and redistribute donated cars Use public transportation at a reduced fare for low-income individuals
Energy	Low Income Home Energy Assistance Program (LIHEAP), US Modified rate design, rate discounts or waivers, and modified billing methods for the low-income population Weatherization Assistance Programs (WAP), US Low-income energy efficiency programs, US Low Income Energy Efficiency Program, Australia Low Income Household Rebate, Australia Green Communities, Canada Ontario Electricity Support Program (OESP), Canada Caritas-Stromspar-Check program, Germany Fonds de solidarité logement (FSL – Solidarity Funds for Housing), France Household energy bill subsidy to pay fuel heating bills, Hungary Fuel Allowance for an extra subsidy during winter months, Ireland Household Benefits Package, Ireland, a free basic supply of energy annually Warm Up New Zealand program focused on improving insulation in homes; low-income households offered grants for insulation	Reduce energy costs Increase energy efficiency Design and delivery of low-income energy efficiency programs, including social housing, owner-occupied and private rental housing Low-income consumers with a monthly on-bill credit to reduce their electricity bill Offer advice to low-income households, and provide simple energy-saving appliances including installation at no cost

Table 8.1   (continued)

Infrastructure Components	Programs	Target Outcomes
Broadband access, information and communication technology	Connect to Compete initiative: EveryoneOn, US Connect Home, US Google Fiber – broadband service option to low-income neighborhood residents in Kansas City Life-Changing Connections – Start Broadband, Australia InfoxChange: Technology for Social Justice, Australia Telstra: Access for Everyone, Australia Low-income broadband program, Canada Telus Corp., Alberta, Canada Better Broadband Subsidy Scheme, UK Un computer in famiglia, Italy L'Internet accompagné (Internet Accompanied), France E-oportunidades program, Portugal UK Online Centres Network EURO 200 program, Romania	Free high-speed broadband for low-income families Designed to assist people on a low income or facing financial hardship maintain tele-communications access Increase broadband access through subsidies Promote access to Internet and technologies in disadvantaged areas
Housing	Wells Fargo Housing Foundation, US US Department of Housing and Urban Development (HUD) Vienna's Unique Social Housing Program, Austria Social housing programs such as the Programa de Erradicação de Barracas – New Urban Renting Regime and Rehousing Programme, Portugal Housing Finance and Development Centre of Finland Housing First model in Finland Habitation à loyer modéré (rent-controlled housing), France, Switzerland and Quebec Vivienda de Protección Pública (publicly protected housing), Spain	Create affordable and sustainable housing initiatives serving low- and moderate-income households

Note: For education and training programs, see Appendix Table 6A.1 in Chapter 6.

Finally, in examining these basic infrastructure components, the independencies among them become all the more apparent. A disruption or deficit in one of these components has implications for the others – suggesting a kind of domino effect. Further, for the low-income entrepreneur, inadequacies in the basic infrastructure can seriously impact the relevance and value of the entrepreneurship-specific infrastructure, a subject to which we now turn.

ENTREPRENEURSHIP-SPECIFIC INFRASTRUCTURE: DO ECOSYSTEMS SERVE THE POOR?

If we consider the components of entrepreneurial ecosystems, cities and regions across the globe are witnessing increases in both the number and quality of these components, as well as in the interconnectedness among them. Incubators and accelerators are appearing that specialize in everything from biotech start-ups to food and restaurant concepts. New forms of angel networks and microcredit schemes are being developed. Service providers (e.g., law firms, consultants, web and app development companies) are focusing on the unique needs of different kinds of start-ups and early-stage firms. Universities are getting engaged with local ecosystems in a variety of ways. And, while components of these ecosystems often operate as silos, with relatively weak coordination among the components representing the biggest shortcoming in most ecosystems, we are seeing progress here as well. The different players are learning how to better communicate, collaborate, eliminate duplication of effort, reinforce one another, and collectively contribute to the fostering of ventures at different stages in the start-up and development process.

Components of these ecosystems can enable the entrepreneur at every stage of the venture development process (Figure 8.3). In the ideation stage, participating in local pitch competitions, experimenting in a fablab, talking with a mentor from the small business community, or participating in a training program sponsored by a small business development center can help identify flaws and ways to adapt the business idea. When in the pre-start-up stage, business plan competitions, incubators, microcredit programs, fablabs, universities, mentors and professional service providers can help with plans, prototypes, seed funding, business registration, and other preparatory activities for a launch. During the start-up phase, the entrepreneur can benefit from community social forums, microcredit programs, small business development centers, local small businesses, and municipal government for everything from shared facilities and

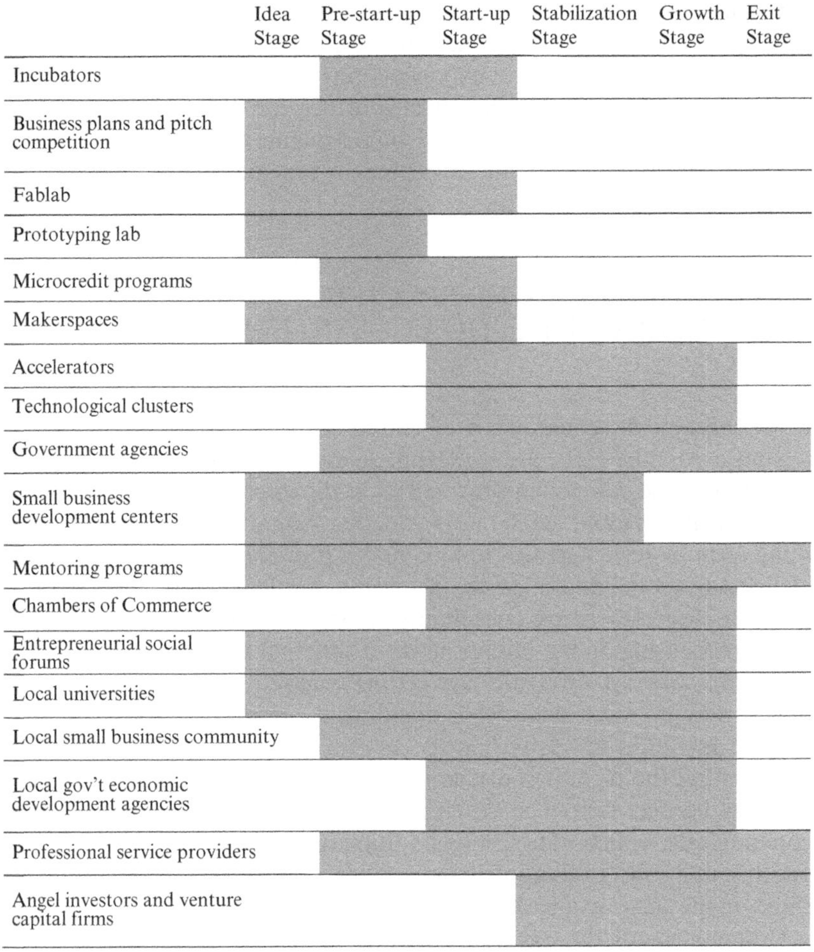

	Idea Stage	Pre-start-up Stage	Start-up Stage	Stabilization Stage	Growth Stage	Exit Stage
Incubators		▓	▓			
Business plans and pitch competition	▓	▓	▓			
Fablab	▓	▓	▓			
Prototyping lab	▓	▓	▓			
Microcredit programs		▓	▓			
Makerspaces	▓	▓	▓			
Accelerators			▓	▓	▓	
Technological clusters			▓	▓	▓	
Government agencies		▓	▓	▓	▓	
Small business development centers	▓	▓	▓	▓	▓	
Mentoring programs		▓	▓	▓	▓	▓
Chambers of Commerce		▓	▓	▓	▓	▓
Entrepreneurial social forums		▓	▓	▓	▓	▓
Local universities	▓	▓	▓	▓	▓	▓
Local small business community		▓	▓	▓	▓	▓
Local gov't economic development agencies		▓	▓	▓	▓	▓
Professional service providers		▓	▓	▓	▓	▓
Angel investors and venture capital firms				▓	▓	▓

Note: Gray shading represents high relevance in that stage of the venture development.

Figure 8.3 Relevance of entrepreneurial ecosystem components across venture stages

equipment, to help with marketing and sales, to assistance with getting government contracts and regulatory compliance. As the entrepreneur makes adjustments and the business stabilizes, he or she leans on professional service providers (legal, accounting services), mentors (advice), local government (contracts, tax abatements), chambers of commerce (contacts), other small businesses (shared resources, contacts) and banks (loans). If real growth happens, universities provide employees, angels and other equity investors provide capital, and government bodies provide economic incentives. Even in the exit stage, professional service providers, government agencies, and locally based potential acquirers can facilitate the harvest of the business.

For the most part, the poor have been left out of entrepreneurial ecosystems. There are a number of possible reasons for this exclusion. The biggest factor is the kinds of businesses they want to pursue (survival and lifestyle ventures, which again tend to be ignored by ecosystems). Beyond this, the limitations of their social networks are such that the poor are often not connected directly or even indirectly to key individuals within the ecosystem. They often work one or more jobs during hours that components of the ecosystem are accessible, while also being reliant on public transit. Literacy shortcomings affect interactions with members of the ecosystem. Problems here include not understanding the nature of one's needs for a venture, who to communicate with for a particular need, what to ask for, and how to request and obtain resources (including information) that could address these needs.

However, the problem is often more fundamental. Elements of the entrepreneurial ecosystem are simply not set up to serve the poor, and they make little effort to reach out to those in poverty. The knowledge and experiences of the people within the ecosystem, the nature of the services and assistance they offer, and even more basic things like the kinds of speakers they feature at forums, do not reflect an appreciation for the poverty condition and its implications for entrepreneurial action. This reality is not necessarily intentional or reflective of a lack of concern for the poor. It is more often due to the objectives, sources of funding, time horizons, and backgrounds of the people running the organizations that constitute the ecosystem. They are set up to support high-growth ventures that commercialize new technology, will create lots of jobs, bring visibility to a community, and attract creative people and other companies to the region. Ironically, these kinds of ventures represent a very small percentage of start-ups. The ventures of the poor do not qualify for most incubators or accelerators, are uninteresting to angel networks, have little chance of winning business plan or pitch competitions, and do not require the services of specialized law firms or tax consultants.

However, there are a growing number of exceptions to this overall pattern. Let us consider just a few of these. Within the US, the South Side Innovation Center in Syracuse, New York is a university-supported facility serving low-income start-ups in a distressed part of the city with space, training, microcredit and product testing capabilities. A non-profit food incubator in California called La Cocina houses up to 12 businesses per year that are owned by low-income and immigrant women. La Cocina cultivates low-income food entrepreneurs as they formalize and grow their businesses by providing affordable commercial kitchen space, industry-specific technical assistance and access to market opportunities. Another example is Hot Bread Kitchen in East Harlem, New York that requires membership to include 30 percent low-income entrepreneurs and will subsidize their use of the incubator's resources. It offers the usual kitchen space and storage but also hosts monthly workshops and one-on-one business advice. Many examples exist in other developed economies as well. For instance, in Portugal, Amadora Empreende is a municipal incubation program that serves beneficiaries of social support and those residing in degraded or resettled neighborhoods, while FabLab Lisboa refurbished an abandoned slaughterhouse in a decaying inner-city neighborhood to create a facility that enables low-income entrepreneurs to work on prototypes. Malaga, Spain has created Promálaga Urban Incubators, which is designed to foster retail ventures in newly created neighborhoods, where the social and economic fabric does not yet exist.

Other initiatives offer training, mentoring, development and connections. The CHARO Community Development Corp. provides career and business assistance to help generate economic development in low-income neighborhoods in Los Angeles County; and the Bronx Business Bridge is part of New York City Economic Development Corporation's Low Income Fast Track Entrepreneurship Program (LIFT), designed to connect New Yorkers from low-income neighborhoods with opportunities to grow their businesses. Some chambers of commerce have adjusted their target demographic, with chambers in a number of cities now focusing efforts on supporting entrepreneurship among underserved population groups. The Service Corps of Retired Executives (SCORE), supported by the US Small Business Administration, is a large network of business experts that provide free business mentoring through over 300 chapters across the country. Small Business Development Centers are also located in communities throughout the US and offer no-cost counseling for existing small business owners, including the poor.

There are also positive signs with regard to university engagement with low-income entrepreneurs. Rutgers University has launched the Center for Urban Entrepreneurship & Economic Development, a multifaceted initiative that includes technology training, incubation, assistance in pursuing government and private funding, and other resources to the economically and socially disadvantaged in Newark, New Jersey. The University of Florida coordinates the Gainesville Entrepreneurship and Adversity Program (GEAP), an integrated six-part program involving faculty, graduate students, and community partners with a goal of empowering those living in adverse circumstances to create and grow their own businesses. Princeton University is pursuing a similar program in Trenton, New Jersey.

In the financing arena, local governments, non-profit organizations and community banks are creating novel types of microcredit programs to provide low-interest loans and grants to poor entrepreneurs. Developments here are explored in Chapter 9. In addition, local governments, universities and larger private companies are supporting the ventures of minorities, women and the disabled with efforts to award contracts for a wide range of products and services. Some of the more proactive efforts give training and assistance to low-income entrepreneurs on how to win contracts, and include them in mentor–protégé programs where they work with companies that have won contracts in the past.

While promising, these examples tend to be isolated programs. They are not always well embedded into low-income neighborhoods, reflecting unique historical, cultural, political and demographic characteristics and associated needs of particular poor communities. Just as critically, they are rarely well integrated into the larger entrepreneurial ecosystem of the city or region. Doing so would find many players in the ecosystem identifying ways their services might be adapted to reflect unique needs of the poor. It would also find connections among elements of the ecosystem that could help the low-income entrepreneur through different stages and problems in the entrepreneurial process. Finally, it would extend the ecosystem to include new components, such as programs that address the five literacies discussed in Chapter 6, or ones that can help with the transport and daycare needs of the person in poverty. The alternative would be to develop dedicated entrepreneurial ecosystems just with the low-income community, which could be prohibitively expensive.

OVERCOMING THE INFRASTRUCTURE DIVIDE

Infrastructure must be the beginning point in any effort to make entrepreneurship a viable pathway out of poverty. The basic infrastructure provides a foundation for building a company, while the entrepreneurial ecosystem specifically facilitates the venture creation process. The foundation enables literacy, efficient transportation, space to conduct operations and an ability to conduct them in relative safety, financial transactions, utilities to fuel operations, and access to the world through broadband and information and communication technologies. And, as we have seen, the entrepreneurial ecosystem can help address a wide range of issues encountered throughout the entrepreneurial journey.

Low-income neighborhoods have inadequate infrastructures, while those in poverty rarely benefit from whatever entrepreneurial ecosystem exists within the larger community or region. These shortcomings help explain why the poor disproportionately create survival ventures and marginal lifestyle ventures (see Chapter 4) that fall into the commodity trap (see Chapter 11), with unsustainable profit models (see Chapter 12). To change this state of affairs a more holistic approach is needed for fostering entrepreneurship among the poor.

As we shall examine in more depth in Chapter 13, holism implies approaches that are both comprehensive in the needs they consider and integrative in reflecting the ways needs affect and are affected by one another. It means solutions that simultaneously consider foundational and venture development needs. It can be problematic for people to grasp key business concepts in a start-up training program if attendees have fundamental literacy problems. Affordable space is less valuable if utilities are undependable or too costly, or one is not also addressing issues of broadband access and proximity to customers. Offering mentors or access to incubators may be unwise if one does not also take into account the need for transportation, daycare and access at times when the low income entrepreneur is not at work. Microcredit and other forms of financial assistance must be tied to developing financial and business literacies. And all these efforts must be designed in ways that reflect the unique context and experiences of those in poverty. Alternatively, much can be invested with little result in terms of sustainable enterprises.

REFERENCES

Abramson, A.J., M.S. Tobin and M.R. VanderGoot (1995), "The changing geography of metropolitan opportunity: The segregation of the poor in the US metropolitan areas, 1970 to 1990," *Housing Policy Debate*, **6**(1), 45–72.

Australian Bureau of Statistics (2008), "Public transport use for work and study," *Australian Social Trends 2008*, Canberra: Australian Bureau of Statistics, accessed June 11, 2018 at www.abs.gov.au/AUSSTATS/abs@.nsf/Lookup/4102.0Chapter10102008.

Baum, C.L. (2009), "The effects of vehicle ownership on employment," *Journal of Urban Economics*, **66**(3), 151–63.

Becker, S., M.D. Crandall and K.E. Fisher et al. (2010), *Opportunity for All: How the American Public Benefits from Internet Access at US Libraries*, Washington, DC: Institute for Museum and Library Services.

Bouzarovski, S. (2013), "Energy poverty in European Union: Landscapes of vulnerability," *Wiley Interdisciplinary Reviews: Energy and Environment*, **3**(3), 276–89.

Bruton, G.D., D.J. Ketchen Jr. and R.D. Ireland (2013), "Entrepreneurship as solution to poverty," *Journal of Business Venturing*, **28**(6), 683–9.

Câmara Municipal de Oeiras (2010), *Habitação em Oeiras – 25 Anos* [Housing in Oerias – 25 Years], Lisbon, Portugal.
Caskey, J.P. (1994), "Bank representation in low-income and minority urban communities," *Urban Affairs Review*, **29**(4), 617–38.
Casper, L.M., S.S. McLanahan and I. Garfinkel (1994), "The gender–poverty gap: What we can learn from other countries," *American Sociological Review*, **59**(4), 594–605.
Chetty, R. and N. Hendren (2015), "The impacts of neighborhoods on intergenerational mobility: Childhood exposure effects and county-level estimates," accessed June 11, 2018 at http://www.equality-of-opportunity.org/images/nbhds_exec_summary.pdf.
Cohen, B. (2006), "Sustainable valley entrepreneurial ecosystems," *Business Strategy and the Environment*, **15**(1), 1–14.
Crump, J. (2002), "Deconcentration by demolition: Public housing, poverty, and urban policy," *Environment and Planning D: Society and Space*, **20**, 581–96.
Dargay, J., L. Hivert and D. Legros (2008), "The dynamics of car availability in EU countries: A comparison based on the European Household Panel Survey," *IATSS Research*, **32**(2), 44–55.
Dawkins, C., J.S. Jeon and R. Pendall (2015), "Transportation access, rental vouchers, and neighborhood satisfaction: Evidence from the Moving to Opportunity experiment," *Housing Policy Debate*, **25**(3), 497–530.
Dhéret, C. and M. Giuli (2017), "The long journey to end energy poverty in Europe," *EPC Policy Brief*, 16 June, accessed June 12, 2018 at http://aei.pitt.edu/87904/1/pub_7789_energypovertyineurope.pdf.
Drehobl, A. and L. Ross (2016), *Lifting the High Energy Burden in America's Largest Cities: How Energy Efficiency Can Improve Low-Income and Underserved Communities*, Washington, DC: American Council for an Energy-Efficient Economy.
Duncan, G.J. and K.A. Magnuson (2005), "Can family socioeconomic resources account for racial and ethnic test score gaps?," *Future Child*, **15**(1), 35–54.
Ergungor, O.E. (2010), "Bank branch presence and access to credit in low- to moderate-income neighborhoods," *Journal of Money, Credit and Banking*, **42**(7), 1321–49.
European Commission (2015), "Working paper on energy poverty – Vulnerable Consumers Working Group," accessed June 11, 2018 at https://ec.europa.eu/energy/sites/ener/files/documents/Working%20Paper%20on%20Energy%20Poverty.pdf.
Fauth, R.C., T. Leventhal and J. Brooks-Gunn (2004), "Short-effects of moving from public housing in poor to middle-class neighborhoods on low-income, minority adults' outcomes," *Social Science and Medicine*, **59**(11), 2271–84.
Gurley, T. and D. Bruce (2005), "The effects of car access on employment outcomes for welfare recipients," *Journal of Urban Economics*, **58**(2), 250–72.
Hoff, E. (2003), "The specificity of environmental influence: Socioeconomic status affects early vocabulary development via maternal speech," *Child Development*, **74**, 1368–78.
Isenberg, D.J. (2010), "How to start an entrepreneurial revolution," *Harvard Business Review*, **88**(6), 40–50.
Kenny, C. (2002), "Information and communication technologies for direct poverty alleviation: Costs and benefits," *Development Policy Review*, **20**(2), 141–57.
Kim, K. (2015), "Can carsharing meet the mobility needs for the low-income

neighborhoods? Lessons from carsharing usage patterns in New York City," *Transportation Research Part A: Policy and Practice*, **77**, 249–60.

Klein, N.J. and M.J. Smart (2017), "Car today, gone tomorrow: The ephemeral car in low-income, immigrant and minority families," *Transportation*, **44**(3), 495–510.

Kyriakidou, V., C. Michalakelis and T. Sphicopoulos (2011), "Digital divide gap convergence in Europe," *Technology in Society*, **33**, 265–70.

Lawrence, E.C. and G. Elliehausen (2008), "A comparative analysis of payday loan customers," *Contemporary Economic Policy*, **26**, 299–316.

MacAskill, A. and L. White (2016), "Britain's poorer communities, hit hardest by closures, may face shutout," *Reuters UK*, June 20, accessed June 12, 2018 at https://uk.reuters.com/article/uk-britain-banks-branches/britains-poorer-communities-hit-hardest-by-bank-closures-may-face-shutout-idUKKCN0Z60BP.

Malecki, E.J. (2011), "Connecting local entrepreneurial ecosystems to global innovation networks: Open innovation, double networks and knowledge integration," *International Journal of Entrepreneurship and Innovation Management*, **14**(1), 36–59.

Massey, D.S. and M.L. Eggers (1993), "The special concentration of affluence and poverty during the 1970s," *Urban Affairs Review*, **29**(2), 299–315.

National Household Travel Survey (2009), *Mobility Challenges for Households in Poverty*, accessed June 12, 2018 at http://nhts.ornl.gov/briefs/PovertyBrief.pdf.

National Public Radio, Inc. (NPR) (2013), "'Banking deserts' spread across low-income neighborhoods," *NPR*, November 13, accessed June 12, 2018 at https://www.npr.org/2013/11/13/244947836/dayton-ohio-is-latest-area-suffering-from-banking-desert.

Neck, H.M., G.D. Meyer, B. Cohen and A.C. Corbett (2004), "An entrepreneurial system view of new venture creation," *Journal of Small Business Management*, **42**(2), 190–208.

Neumeyer, X., S.C. Santos, A. Caetano and P. Kalbfleisch (2018), "Entrepreneurship ecosystems and women entrepreneurs: A social capital and network approach," *Small Business Economics*, at https://doi.org/10.1007/s11187-018-9996-5.

Ong, P.M. (2002), "Car ownership and welfare-to-work," *Journal of Policy Analysis and Management*, **21**(2), 239–52.

Ong, P.M. and M.A. Stoll (2007), "Redlining or risk? A spatial analysis of auto insurance rates in Los Angeles," *Journal of Policy Analysis and Management*, **26**(4), 811–30.

Pendall, R., E. Blumenberg and C. Dawkins (2016), "What if cities combined car-based solutions with transit to improve access to opportunity?," *The Urban Institute*, June 22, Metropolitan Housing and Communities Policy Center.

Petersen, M.A. and R.G. Rajan (2002), "Does distance still matter? The information revolution in small business lending," *Journal of Finance*, **57**, 2533–70.

Raphael, S. and L. Rice (2002), "Car ownership, employment, and earnings," *Journal of Urban Economics*, **52**(1), 109–30.

Schwartz, N.D. (2011), "Bank closings tilt toward poor areas," *New York Times*, February 22, accessed June 12, 2018 at http://www.nytimes.com/2011/02/23/business/23banks.html.

Shaheen, S.A. and A.P. Cohen (2013), "Carsharing and personal vehicle services: Worldwide market developments and emerging trends," *International Journal of Sustainable Transportation*, **7**(1), 5–34.

Stephens, M. and G. van Steen (2011), "'Housing poverty' and income poverty in England and the Netherlands," *Housing Studies*, **26**(7–8), 1035–57.

Taylor, B.D. and E.A. Morris (2015), "Public transportation objectives and rider demographics: Are transit's priorities poor public policy?," *Transportation*, **42**(2), 347–67.

Townsend, L., A. Sathiaseelan, G. Fairhurst and C. Wallace (2013), "Enhanced broadband access as a solution to the social and economic problems of the rural digital divide," *Local Economy*, **28**(6), 580–95.

Wacquant, L.J.D. (1997), "Three pernicious premises in the study of the American ghetto," *International Journal of Urban and Regional Research*, **21**, 341–53.

Yentel, D. (2016), *Opportunities to End Homelessness and Housing Poverty in a Trump Administration*, Washington, DC: National Low Income Housing Coalition.

9. Financing the ventures of the poor

> People . . . were poor not because they were stupid or lazy. They worked all
> day long, doing complex physical tasks. They were poor because the financial
> institution in the country did not help them widen their economic base.
> (Muhammad Yunus)

INTRODUCTION

Finding the necessary financial resources is typically emphasized as the single biggest obstacle to starting a business. This need not be the case, as we shall discuss in Chapter 10, as there are many available approaches to leveraging resources, and non-financial factors also derail the launch of new ventures. Further, the National Federation of Independent Business (NFIB) estimates that more than 25 percent of new ventures start with $500 or less. However, money certainly matters. The vast majority of start-ups struggle to get the needed financing, but financing is even more challenging for those in poverty. Given the daily struggle to address basic needs, allocating money to a venture is especially difficult.

Financing comes into play in three fundamental ways. It impacts whether or not a venture is started, the type of venture that gets launched (see Chapter 4), and the amount and pace of growth the venture achieves. For the poor, lack of access to money adversely affects all three, leading to lower start-up rates, and many more survival-type ventures that only grow nominally, if at all. They often lack collateral, suffer from low credit scores, have limited income streams, have no established relationships with lending institutions (or loan histories), and have underdeveloped financial management skills (Fafchamps, 2013). Correspondingly, traditional sources of financing do not cater to the needs of the poor, and in some cases they actually discriminate against or create barriers for low-income individuals trying to start ventures (Bates and Robb, 2013; Servon, 2006, 2013).

In this chapter, we examine the financing needs of low-income entrepreneurs together with the possible sources of money. Attention is devoted to new emerging sources, including microcredit schemes and crowdsourcing. A staged model is introduced to distinguish financing needs at different points in the evolution of a venture. Issues and approaches to becoming "bankable" are examined. Ongoing gaps in funding are identified.

FINANCIAL NEEDS AND STAGES OF VENTURE DEVELOPMENT

Determining how much money one needs to start a business is a universal problem for entrepreneurs. While having both too little or too much can be problematic, the more common problem is having too little. Things almost always cost more than anticipated, and there are expenses that come up for which the entrepreneur did not plan. Especially with low-income entrepreneurs, it is crucial to distinguish expenses that are critical and absolutely must be spent, and those that are supplementary and can be deferred to later in the journey. For instance, with many start-ups, it is possible to initially run the business from home or in someone else's facility rather than pay rent.

The financial needs of these entrepreneurs change with the evolution of the venture. In Table 9.1, we have specified five key stages in the venture creation process: developing the idea, pre-start-up, start-up, stabilization, and growth. Each stage represents a different set of demands, problems and requirements – suggesting that the amount of money required and the priorities in terms of how it is spent vary depending upon the stage.

At the idea and pre-start-up stages, the entrepreneur is trying to assess different business ideas and lay the foundation for what the business might look like (determine the products/services to be sold, target markets, price points, operational requirements, etc.). Resources are needed to refine and validate the core business concept, interact with potential customers, attend conferences and trade shows, research the competition, identify any licensing and regulatory requirements, prepare a business plan, develop product prototypes or samples (or design the service delivery process if a service business), and perhaps attend basic entrepreneurship training courses or seminars. For low-income entrepreneurs, most of this is accomplished with very little spending, although lack of money and business expertise at this stage often results in them taking shortcuts that end up constraining the venture or costing a lot more money down the road.

As the entrepreneur actually launches the venture, the key financial priorities include one-time start-up costs and then ongoing operating costs. Included here are the costs of licenses and business registration, rent, equipment, vehicles, wages, inventory, utilities, the grand opening, advertising and marketing materials, copyrights and trademarks, creation of a website, prepaid expenses (e.g., insurance, taxes) and professional fees

Table 9.1   Stages of development and financing needs and sources

Stage of Development	Sample Financial Needs	Key Financing Sources
Idea stage	Research and planning expenses (e.g., travel, surveys), meetings, trade show attendance, prototype development, expenses for short courses or training	Self
Pre-start-up stage	As above	Self, family/friends, microcredit, crowdfunding, local saving schemes
Start-up stage	Location, equipment, vehicles, grand opening, professional fees, licensing and registration, inventory, advertising, website, prepaid expenses (e.g., insurance), wages	Self, family/friends, crowdfunding, microcredit, local saving schemes, grants
Stabilization stage	Rent, advertising, selling, wages and salaries, additional inventory, seasonal cash needs, prepaid expenses, bookkeeping, taxes	Self, family/friends, local saving schemes, microcredit, commercial bank, reinvestment into the business, grants
Growth stage	Facility expansion, larger inventories and new warehousing, additional marketing, introduction of new systems and technologies, new products and services, management and staff expansion, extended distribution, additional locations	Self, reinvestment into the business, microcredit, grants, commercial bank, angels

(e.g., lawyers, accountants). Unfortunately, many of these costs are higher for low-income entrepreneurs, as they must often buy from suppliers in very small quantities, struggle to qualify for credit terms, have little collateral, and operate businesses in high crime areas. It becomes important to minimize these cash needs, finding ways to do more with less, reuse and repurpose resources, and use the resources of others (see Chapter 10). Examples include using a kitchen table as a desk, leasing or renting equipment, relying on computers at the public library, partnering with a high school teacher to have students design a logo, adapting free templates downloaded from the Internet (e.g., for invoices, fliers, or simple business agreements), sharing office space, using students as consultants or interns, selling on consignment,[1] and figuring out how to build one's own website or do one's own bookkeeping. At the same time, the entrepreneur must be willing to spend money on those things that are most central to ensuring value is being delivered to customers, quality levels are acceptable and consistent, and laws/regulations are complied with. This generally leads to vexing decisions regarding what one can do without and what is absolutely necessary (is it more important to have a vehicle or rent office space, spend money on marketing or buy a piece of equipment, hire an employee or pay for insurance?).

Once the business is up and running, it takes time to get things right (see Chapter 2). The entrepreneur is having to adapt the business model as he or she interacts with customers and competitors and learns what works and does not. Unexpected developments are also affecting the business and forcing adjustment. During this stabilization stage, in addition to many of the operating expenses from the launch stage, the business may be hiring staff, doing more (trying different approaches) with advertising, adding additional inventory, and addressing seasonal cash needs. More resources are devoted to collecting and remitting sales, franchise and employee-related taxes, and money may be spent to ensure proper bookkeeping and financial reporting. For some, the decision is made at this point to move from a home-based business to a formal office or other business location.

Growth poses its own distinct financial demands. The business is spending money on developing and introducing new products and services, facility expansion, new warehousing, additional marketing, introduction of new systems and technologies, larger inventories, management and staff expansion, extended distribution, and additional locations, among other expenses. Skills in cash flow management become especially critical at this stage, as we shall discuss later in this chapter. Growth is associated with significant cash needs, as money must be spent ahead of the realization of revenues. A 50 percent increase in revenues requires an even bigger increase in the amount of cash needed to fuel the revenue growth.

TRADITIONAL SOURCES OF ENTREPRENEURIAL FINANCE

Four traditional sources of money are relied upon when starting a new business: (1) personal savings; (2) bootstrapping from friends and family (informal capital); (3) formal debt, where money is borrowed via bank loans, bank overdrafts, leasing[2] and invoice discounting[3] (formal capital);

and (4) equity, where investment is raised either by taking on a partner who has money, or selling shares in the business to private investors (sometimes called angels) who will make a return through dividends and future sale of their shares at an increased valuation. For the poor, as we shall see, there are serious issues surrounding each of these sources, which explains why they put less money into the venture at start-up, which limits their abilities to grow and succeed (Barr and Blank, 2009; Robb and Fairlie, 2007).

Personal Savings and Personal Credit Cards

Personal savings is typically the first and far away most prominent source of new venture finance. It can include the regular savings that one has accumulated by setting money aside, funds from an inheritance or sale of some asset (e.g., a home or vehicle), as well as money generated by cashing in retirement accounts (e.g., an IRA or 401(k) in the United States) or insurance policies. For founders, using their own savings is a means of maintaining control over the venture and avoiding the burden of debt repayment. Alternatively, it demonstrates to lenders and investors their commitment to the venture (that they have so-called "skin in the game"). For the poor, relying on personal savings may be their only option.

Savings habits vary across developed countries (Trading Economics, 2017). In countries such as Germany, France, Austria, Belgium and Sweden, household saving rates (as a percentage of income) average between 10 and 13 percent. In Japan the rate is just under 12 percent. Britain's longer-term average is about 9 percent but this has fallen significantly to under 5 percent in the past few years. By contrast, saving rates in the United States have historically been about 8 percent, but recent years have seen an average closer to 3 percent. If we consider the poor, the picture is bleaker. Just under three-fourths (73 percent) of the lowest-income adults in the US (those with $24999 or less earnings per year) have less than $1000 in savings (Huddleston, 2016).

Founders also use personal credit cards as a source of funding, and over the past two decades low-income families have been issued a greater volume of cards as more credit was extended to riskier customers. Yet, this is an expensive option, as credit card interest is high, and can be even higher on the cards held by the poor. Further, they can spend disproportionately more over time because of a tendency to pay only the minimum required amount each month. Not surprisingly, they are among the most profitable customers for the credit card industry (Mann, 2006). Low-income families are aware of the risks in assuming too many credit products (inability to pay, harm to their credit rating) but they often do so (Littwin, 2007). They can also demonstrate a cognitive bias (of which they are aware) where a stronger weight is given to payoffs closer to the present moment compared to a bigger required expenditure at some future time (O'Donoghue and Rabin, 1999). As a result, the poor frequently enroll in different credit programs – sometimes using a high-interest credit card to pay previous debts, or paying the required monthly amount on one credit card using another credit card, generating a vicious cycle of increasing debt. When such behavior is relied upon to pay the expenses of running a business, especially on an ongoing basis, the seeds are sown for business failure. In addition, many low-income entrepreneurs fail to completely separate their personal from their business finances, especially in the early days of the venture. Ultimately, then, unwise use of a credit card in either the personal or business domains will likely have an adverse effect on the business.

Family and Friends

Having exhausted individual savings as a source of funding, entrepreneurs are forced to turn to their extended family and personal friends. This is a type of bootstrapping strategy – a method for meeting the needed financial resources without depending on external finance from bank debt or sharing ownership with equity investors, neither of which may be available to the poor (Ebben and Johnson, 2006). We will further explore bootstrapping in Chapter 10. Money from family and friends is most typically structured as debt, often with an open-ended repayment date. These individuals normally settle for lower returns than formal investors, and sometimes no returns, as they are motivated by the personal relationship with the entrepreneur and a desire to see him or her succeed. They generally have little understanding of business. The risks to the entrepreneur of this kind of funding are also lower, although the failure to repay this money can damage family relationships and end friendships (Winborg, 2009). For the poor entrepreneur, family and friends are an important yet very limited source of money. Karlan, Ratan and Zinman (2014) highlight how social ties and norms among the poor can promote bargaining and sharing within and across households, especially given their lack of access and distrust of financial institutions. The bigger challenge for the poor is that their family and friends may not have money to give, as they are typically also in a low-income condition and struggle with the same economic realities: limited cash flow for daily expenses and reduced or no savings. Further, awareness that the entrepreneur is poor coupled with the perception that business failure rates are high can result in a feeling that the chances are low that the family member or friend will get their money back.

Debt Financing from Banks

Bank loans are a vital source of financing for small businesses. The bank does not take an ownership interest in the business, but requires the amount of the loan to be repaid over a defined time period and charges interest at a variable or fixed rate. Unlike private investors, however, banks are not in the business of taking risks or making big returns. Their key concern is getting the money back and earning an amount of interest that reflects the cost of money in real terms. As a result, they require collateral in the form of the entrepreneur's business and personal assets, an established credit history and high credit score, clear evidence that the business will continue to perform well enough to repay the loan, personal guarantees from everyone with an ownership stake, and sometimes a co-signer to guarantee the loan. All this means that it is harder to get bank loans for any start-up, and easier once the business is up and running and has a proven cash flow. It is especially hard for the poor.

Banks offer a variety of products to entrepreneurs, but the three most common are conventional small business loans, lines of credit, and business credit cards. With small business loans, the term of the loan will vary from three to seven years, the amount of the loan can range from $15 000 to over $1 million (but are typically over $100 000), and the interest rate will chiefly depend on the loan size (higher for smaller loans), loan term (higher for shorter terms), type of business, nature of any collateral, and the entrepreneur's credit score/history. A line of credit is a type of short-term financing that gives the business owner access to a pre-approved amount of money that they can use as they need it. Interest is paid only on the amount used and more can be borrowed as the principal is paid down. It is helpful for businesses that have cash needs that are seasonal or cyclical (e.g., a toy manufacturer may see a lot more money coming in around Christmas, while it is spending a lot more on production and inventory in earlier months), or to cover short-term expenses such as meeting payroll. In effect it helps to even out cash flow over the months of the year. A business credit card is a form of unsecured borrowing provided by banks. Shane (2008) reports that small businesses have up to $35 000 in balances on company credit cards, while Scott (2009) indicates that nearly 60 percent of new businesses use them to fund up to a third of their debt in the first year. They are relative easy to obtain, but more expensive than loans or lines of credit.

Governments also work with financial institutions in providing guarantees for small business loans. This enables a bank to make loans to someone who would otherwise not qualify, and offer a competitive interest rate. In Europe, where is it estimated that between 400 000 and 700 000 small and medium-sized enterprises (SMEs) cannot obtain a loan from the formal financial system, the European Commission supports loan guarantees through the Competitiveness of Enterprises and Small and Medium-sized Enterprises (COSME) program, and provides a number of other financial support programs for start-up and early-stage firms (European Commission, 2017). Similarly, in the US, the Small Business Administration (SBA), which is part of the US Department of Commerce, offers a number of loan guarantee programs to support new and emerging start-ups. For instance, the 7(a) program supports loans up to $5 million through banks and credit unions, while the Microloan Program supports amounts up to $50 000 through approved non-profit lenders who also provide business training. The latter is focused on women, low-income, veteran, and minority entrepreneurs. Craig, Jackson and Thomson (2007) provide empirical evidence of a positive impact of the 7(a) program on economic performance in low-income markets. Further, the SBA's 8A program helps socially and economically disadvantaged entrepreneurs get government contracts, financial assistance, mentoring and other forms of support. Many individual states and cities in the US also manage their own small business loan funds, although they vary in the extent to which someone in poverty would qualify.

Despite the growth in these government-sponsored programs, it can still be quite difficult for a person in poverty to qualify for financial assistance. Baradaran (2013, p. 483) argues that the United States has two banking systems – one for the haves and one for the have nots. Bankers do not generally develop innovative products that reflect the unique needs and ability to pay of the poor. All too often, they court low-income customers with products that have high fees, even where lower-cost solutions are available from other providers (Silver-Greenberg and Protess, 2012). Bhatt, Painter and Tang (1999) provide evidence of considerable loan bias (a disproportionately low percentage of the total amount of loans) in low-income communities. Servon (2013) concludes that those with low-income are, for the most part, financially excluded. In 2015, 7 percent (approximately 9.0 million) of US households were unbanked, meaning no one in the household had a checking or savings account, and an additional 19.9 percent (24.5 million) were underbanked, where in spite of having a checking or savings account they were forced to obtain financial products outside the banking system (Burhouse et al., 2016). In low-income areas, such as South Bronx, more than half the residents have no bank account, as banks are often more expensive than check cashers or other services (Servon, 2013). Some of this has contributed to the emergence of payday lenders, check-cashing services, and other fringe credit players who provide financial services to the poor at exorbitant costs.

At least five major barriers keep the poor from fully accessing mainstream banking services (Anderloni and Carluccio, 2006; Baradaran, 2013). These include the following:

- *Profitability.* Mainstream banks are profit oriented, but they earn much lower returns from the smaller loans needed by the poor.
- *Discrimination and redlining.* In some instances, banks have denied loans to creditworthy individuals due to their race and offered less attractive products to minorities. Redlining refers to the practice of rejecting services or raising prices to residents of certain neighborhoods characterized by poverty or race.
- *Formality and paperwork.* Banks require extensive documentation to open an account or provide particular products, and poor people and minorities may have trouble with compliance based on educational and literacy shortcomings.
- *Democratization of credit.* Availability of new forms of credit, and particularly the payday lending industry, can worsen the debt position of the poor. These services are marketed aggressively and the providers can be easier to work with in terms of paperwork and documentation, making their very high-cost products appealing to those with limited options.
- *Financial knowledge.* Limited knowledge of and experience with the banking system on the part of the poor leaves them more suspicious and less trusting of financial institutions, while also limiting their awareness of options and understanding of the nature and implications of different financial products.

A growing body of research supports the significance of these barriers. Bates and Robb (2013) find that business owners from minority neighborhoods experience higher costs when they borrow, receive smaller loans, and have their loan applications rejected more often. Blanchflower, Levine and Zimmerman (2003) demonstrate that Black-owned small businesses were twice as likely to be denied credit even after controlling for differences in creditworthiness and other factors. Blanchard, Zhao and Yinger (2008) also provide evidence of discrimination in loan approvals and suggest that some of this might be traceable to lender stereotypes regarding the ability of businesses owned by the poor to succeed.

Equity Investors

When establishing a new business, the sale of equity (shares) to external investors is a typical source of funding. The investors can be individuals or companies, and they are taking a stake in the new venture. Unlike a loan, the investment is not a liability and does not need to be paid back. This means the investor is taking much more of a risk than would a bank or lender. Leading sources of equity investment include private individuals, private equity companies, other companies, and venture capital firms.

The equity investor gets a return either from dividend payments from the venture, which are typically unlikely because all profits (if there are any) are being reinvested in the business, or from appreciation in the value of the shares they own in the venture. So, the returns to investors are dependent on the profitability and growth rate of the venture. For the share value to increase enough to offset the significant risk being taken by the investor, the venture must be growing at a very high rate. It typically must be a scalable venture. As we saw in Chapter 4, low-income entrepreneurs generally start ventures that do not have the kind of growth potential required by equity investors. Again, there are numerous exceptions, but if the entrepreneur is starting a survival or lifestyle business, the likelihood of attracting equity funding is almost zero. Even managed growth ventures struggle to get equity investors.

For low-income entrepreneurs that have unique venture concepts and high-growth aspirations, the most likely source of equity investment is likely to come from angel investors. Business angels are wealthy individuals who want to invest their own money in high-growth businesses. They bring money, expertise, skills, and contacts to the business. Finding a right business angel is key, as it is just as much about the relationship between the angel and the entrepreneur, as it is about the venture itself. While difficult to find in low-income neighborhoods, the larger urban region is likely to have many angels, and today most have angel networks (groups of angels that collaborate in reviewing and investing in start-ups). This is another example of how the low-income entrepreneur's social network and opportunity horizon limit the venture possibilities unless they are expanded. Yet, with tenacity these angels can be reached.

A different equity-based approach is to involve a partner in the business who has money. Usually someone from the local community, this happens with low-income entrepreneurs more often than one might expect. The entrepreneur finds a person with both business experience and money who believes enough in him or her and the business concept that they will partner with the entrepreneur, putting money into the venture and taking a share of the ownership. Such partners are generally active in running the business (although they need not be, serving instead as behind-the-scenes advisors), and so it is important to find people who complement the skills of, and have consistent goals and values with, the entrepreneur.

Much more problematic are venture capital firms and private equity companies as sources of money for the poor (Ratcliffe, 2007). Venture capitalists (VCs) manage large funds (often over $100 million) where the minimum investment in a venture is $1 to $3 million, usually in businesses that have already achieved significant revenues. They demand a large proportion of the entrepreneur's equity, and want to see rates of return on their investment of 40 percent or higher. Not surprisingly, low-income communities normally do not have access to venture capital (Rao, 2016), and the VC investment model does not fit the needs of the low-income entrepreneur. Yet, there are exceptions. For instance, the New Markets Venture Capital program (NMVC), administrated by the US Small Business Administration, was created to encourage venture capital investment in low-income urban and rural communities in order to create jobs and entrepreneurial capacity in places where traditional venture capital funds typically do not invest. In 2006, the NMVC funds invested more than $48 million in 75 companies in poor areas of the US, and were able to leverage $136 million in investments from other sources (CDVCA, 2006). This suggests that equity investments in low-income, underinvested settings are viable, and that a contagious effect can result once the investments begin.

EMERGING SOURCES OF FINANCE FOR LOW-INCOME ENTREPRENEURS

The explosive interest in entrepreneurship around the world has also produced a growing focus on alternative ways to fund start-up activity, with a number of developments that directly affect the poor. Four important sources of money have emerged: microcredit, crowdsourcing, small business grants, and customer funding. Let us consider each in turn.

The Microcredit Revolution

Another form of debt financing is called microcredit or microfinance. Microcredit is the provision of relatively small loans to impoverished borrowers who do not meet conventional bank requirements in terms of collateral, income, and credit history (Brown, 2010). It came to prominence based on the highly successful work of Nobel Prize winner Muhammad Yunus and the Grameen Bank in Bangladesh. The Grameen Bank self-supports a diverse mix of poor people by means of very small loans on easy, extended terms without requiring collateral. Their work is based on the assumption that the poor can manage their own finances and develop their own futures through sustainable ventures. Their trademark methodology of group lending (a small number of individuals who want to start businesses constitute a group, receive training together, and each receives a loan from Grameen Bank) allows the poor to start a business without having to engage in expensive moneylender programs. Group lending uses the trust of fellow members as collateral, and the members receive loans as long as all members continue current payments. In reflecting on the success of microcredit, Yunus posits that "there are roughly 160 million people all over the world in microcredit, mostly women. And they have proven one very important thing: that we are all entrepreneurs" (Cosic, 2017).

The impressive results of these programs caught the attention of policymakers and a variety of organizations across the globe (Bhatt et al., 1999). Subsequently, microenterprise development organizations have emerged not only throughout the developing world, but also in developed economies such as the United States, Canada, the European Union, South Korea, Japan and Australia. In these developed countries, the past 30 years have witnessed dramatic increases in the number of microcredit programs, the amount of funding available, and the volume of entrepreneurs who have been assisted (Edgcomb, 2002; Frisch and Servon, 2006). These include the poor, women, minorities, the disabled, victims of disasters, displaced workers, public assistance recipients, immigrants, farm workers, and others. Search portals have also appeared that enable people to locate microcredit providers, including the Microfinance Gateway,[4] which covers all regions of the world, and the Association for Enterprise Opportunity[5] in the US.

Microcredit programs can offer a range of services, including savings accounts, insurance, credit and loans, money transfers, financial advice, mentoring, procurement assistance (i.e., for government and corporate contracts), business incubators, and personal financial management training. The latter is an especially critical reason for the success of these programs, as giving people money when they do not have the appropriate skills and knowledge can be counterproductive. Through such training the poor learn to save, manage money, understand cash flow, separate personal from business finances, interpret simple financial statements, keep proper records, and master the basic terms (language) related to finance and accounting.

A large number of international organizations are involved in microfinance. For example, the Grameen Bank now has operations in multiple countries, including some developed economies such as the US and Japan. ACCION helps launch and makes investments in microfinance institutions around the world, helping them achieve scale and sustainability, and to broaden the range of financial products and services they offer to their clients. The CrediAmigo microfinance program offered by Brazil's Banco do Nordeste, with support from the World Bank, has become the largest provider of microfinance in South America.

In the United States, there are over 600 microcredit programs today, with significant data to support their effectiveness (Aspen Institute, 2017). Their typical loans range from $1000 to $50 000 (the average is just over $7000 with an average interest rate of 8 percent), and they are most typically run by non-profit organizations with funding coming from government agencies, foundations, businesses, and private citizens. Microcredit initiatives also exist at the national, regional, and local levels. For instance, Self-Help, which is a community development financial institution (CDFI) operating in four different states, has a model where they act as a credit union and non-profit loan fund, and provide support both for mortgages and business (including non-profit ventures) ownership. An example at a local level is The Loan Fund in the city of Albuquerque, New Mexico, which makes loans of $5000 to $100 000 to low-income people, women, and minorities who may not qualify for conventional financing.

A variety of different models exist for microfinance lending, and new and hybrid approaches continue to appear. Box 9.1 summarizes these different models.

At the same time, challenges exist with microcredit in developed countries (Servon, 2006). Six problem areas include: fragmentation (i.e., too many small programs that have insufficient capacity to properly serve their purposes); insufficient data (lack of valid, comprehensive and representative data on the outcomes, relative success and best practices of microcredit programs); lack of accreditation (the microenterprise development field lacks accreditation and enforcement of consistent standards and practices, which affects raising money for these funds); narrow product lines (the offerings of many of the funds are limited in terms of addressing the full range of funding, training and development needs of entrepreneurs); inconsistent or unreliable funding streams (most of the programs are dependent on government and philanthropic subsidies that are one-time, shorter-term, or non-renewable allocations, or their renewability is uncertain); and transition to mainstream credit (entrepreneurs receiving microcredit are not prepared to transition to commercial banks or more conventional sources of finance beyond the initial microcredit loan). Regulation of microcredit also differs significantly from country to country, sometimes with specific rules for microcredit schemes, and other times based on the same rules applied to banks.

The growth and sophistication of microcredit as a form of finance is likely to further accelerate in the coming years. Despite the fact that the organizations making these loans are not self-sufficient, they are producing noteworthy results. Data from the Field Program of the Aspen

BOX 9.1   MICROFINANCE LENDING MODELS

Model 1: Associations
An association is formed by the poor in the target community to offer microfinance services (microsavings, microcredit, microinsurance, etc.) to themselves. The association, which can be formed on the basis of gender, religion, or political and cultural orientation of its members, then gathers capital and intermediates between banks, microfinance institutions (MFIs) and its members.

Model 2: Bank guarantees
A donor or government agency guarantees microloans made by microfinance institutions/commercial banks to individual or groups of borrowers. Compulsory deposits by borrowers in such banks are included in this model.

Model 3: Community banking
Community banks/village banks are formal versions of "associations" created by members of a target community who wish to improve living standards and generate employment. By offering microfinance services, these banks seek to develop their communities. Guarantees are provided by social collateral (peer pressure) as services are distributed through five-member groups (i.e., Grameen) where each member's eligibilities for loans is based on his or her peers' performance.

Model 4: Online community platforms
Borrowers are screened and then the loan is crowdfunded with small contributions from a large audience. An example is Kiva microfinance.

Model 5: Cooperatives
Similar to associations and community banks except ownership structure does not include the poor. A group of middle- and/or upper-class individuals form a co-op to offer microfinance services to the poor.

Model 6: Credit unions
Members of a target community gather their money and make loans to one another at low interest rates. Compared to community banks, credit unions are smaller and non-profit oriented, charging interest rates that allow sustainability of the lending enterprise.

Model 7: Non-governmental organizations (NGOs)
Unlike community-based models, NGOs are external organizations that offer microfinance services (loans, insurance, savings, etc.) to improve credit ratings of the poor, training, education and research. NGOs may also act as intermediaries between the poor and donor agencies (e.g., UN, World Bank) and operate locally and globally (through physical or online presence).

Model 8: For-profit banks
Commercial banks, as well as specialized microfinance banks, offer various financial services to the poor but the main purpose may be to generate a return on investment. Unlike other models, the aim is social development as well as financial gains beyond what is necessary for institutional sustainability.

Model 9: Rotating savings and credit associations (ROSCAs)
ROSCAs are small groups where each member makes regular monthly (or weekly, quarterly or annually) contributions into a common fund, which is given entirely to one member at the start of each cycle (e.g., weekly, monthly, quarterly). A benefit is the matching of a client's cash flow with the loan, the ability to structure the deal without interest rates, and the absence of overhead costs.

Source: Adapted from Srinivas (2015).

Institute indicate that microloans yield significant increases in income and job creation for start-up ventures, while improving credit scores for the entrepreneurs (Aspen Institute, 2017). A sizeable percentage (as much as 60 percent) of poor entrepreneurs receiving these loans move out of poverty, with dramatic decreases in reliance on public assistance or welfare.

When done properly, microcredit also influences the development of other policies and programs to alleviate poverty in impoverished neighborhoods, and can serve as a core element of an integrative strategy to build social and financial capital in these problematic communities (Servon, 1999). Relationships within programs are formed among and between borrowers, program staff, and a larger support network. These relationships can contribute to self-efficacy among the poor, provide vicarious learning and role models, and enable partnerships and the leveraging of other community resources by entrepreneurs. They represent an important opportunity for the poor to enlarge their opportunity horizon (see Chapter 5) as they are exposed to different realities, stories, information, and knowledge. In general, microfinance programs have helped large numbers of people escape poverty through self-employment, and contributed in important ways to the economic development of distressed regions (Servon and Doshna, 2000).

Crowdfunding

Another important non-traditional source of financing that is rapidly growing is crowdfunding. It represents an "an open call, mostly through dedicated platforms on the Internet, for the provision of financial resources, either in the form of donations or in exchange for the future product or some form of reward" (Belleflamme, Lambert and Schwienbacher, 2014, p. 588). The basic idea is to raise small amounts of money (as low as $1) from large numbers (potentially millions) of people. From a business perspective, crowdfunding is beneficial because it gives access to financial resources, and it also provides a good opportunity for comments and suggestions from the public to fine-tune projects, services or products, serving as a community-building activity.

Today there are over 1000 of these platforms. These include equity-based crowdfunding platforms (i.e., underwriting by the crowd of the risk capital issued by a company); lending-based crowdfunding platforms (i.e., underwriting of debt contracts between two parties, as the lender and the borrower); reward-based crowdfunding platforms (i.e., financing is provided in the expectation of some kind of reward or prize to the individual funder); and donation-based crowdfunding platforms (i.e., project funding motivated by philanthropy or sponsorship, without any other remuneration for the crowdfunders) (e.g., Belleflamme, Lambert and Schwienbacher, 2014). The donation-based crowdfunding platforms are the most common when it comes to ventures created by those in poverty. Funds are raised for start-up activities, to support growth, and to assist ventures that are in trouble. Yet, the availability of crowd-based funds for the poor is much less prominent than the use of these platforms to support other types of ventures and activities.

Crowdfunding can support the poor in different ways. Benevolent is a platform that helps low-income individuals overcome economic hurdles, such as helping them buy a car or acquire a computer. The Wishbone platform provides funding to help poor high school students attend special university programs (Thorpe, 2013). GoFundMe promotes itself as the world's largest social fundraising platforms, and raises money for everything from a medical emergency or funeral to schooling and community events. They include categories for entrepreneurial start-ups and existing small businesses, and many of these are not high-tech and/or higher-growth types of ventures that are typically funded through such popular platforms as Kickstarter, RocketHub, AngelList and MicroVentures. IndieGoGo also funds an eclectic mix of projects, including local businesses. The platform that most caters to the ventures of the poor is arguably Kiva, which combines microlending with crowdfunding. Loans are crowdfunded in amounts of $25 or more, and when borrowers repay, the money can be used for new loans, as donations, or withdrawn by the lender.

The use of the crowdfunding model as a vehicle to support the poor is producing promising results, clearly indicating that there is a willingness and ability to gather a high number of people donating a small amount of money to support entrepreneurship under adverse conditions (Attuel-Mendès, 2014). Yet, their potential is significantly unrealized when it comes to adapting these platforms to reflect the distinct needs of the poor at a local level.

Grants for Small Businesses

Low-income entrepreneurs are often surprised to find there is a relative dearth of grant programs to support entrepreneurs, and particularly low-income entrepreneurs who are not working on advancing a technology or developing a leading edge innovation. Someone starting a non-profit is more likely to find grant money than a person launching a for-profit venture. Grants are attractive because they do not involve debt or equity. They generally have few strings, in that they do not need to be paid back, while other restrictions, if any, tend to be limited to specifying what the money can be spent on. They are highly competitive, usually with a set of criteria the applying entrepreneur must meet to be eligible, and most often requiring a written business plan and a follow-up report on outcomes once the money is spent.

In the United States, hundreds of grant programs for entrepreneurs exist, but when spread across the entire country or whole states, it is enough to support only a very small percentage of start-ups. Moreover, the majority of these programs are not focused on the poor. The Small Business Administration has small business grants for innovation and technology transfer projects for entrepreneurs already in business. However, they also administer the PRIME Program, which provides grants to state and local organizations to support programs that benefit entrepreneurs from disadvantaged backgrounds. The Minority Business Development Agency (also part of the US Department of Commerce) has regular grant competitions for minority business owners and attempts to connect minority entrepreneurs to other funding sources. Also at a federal level, the National Science Foundation, NASA, the National Institutes of Health, the Department of Defense, Homeland Security, and other federal government departments have competitive grant programs for businesses that address particular problems or needs that each agency has prioritized – and most of these focus on technology and innovation (e.g., green technologies for the Environmental Protection Agency, cyber security for the Department of Homeland Security). Programs also exist to support particular venture categories, such as farmers and ventures that provide services to at-risk children. Most individual states run grant programs. A few have a broad mandate that includes minorities and the poor, such as the Maryland Economic Development Assistance Fund. Most encourage ventures with a specific focus, such as those involved in export activity, community infrastructure needs, tourism-related activities, recycling, transportation, child care, technology development, and agriculture, among other specific areas of emphasis. Some also emphasize particular groups, such as veterans or women. At a community level, many cities, local economic development offices, minority assistance agencies, and some chambers of commerce provide grants to small businesses that create jobs, improve their facilities, or locate in particular areas – most often businesses that are already operating, but also start-ups.

Private companies have also introduced grant programs, and these are highly selective and small in number. For example, each year Fedex offers grants of up to $25000 to ten small businesses, while Chase Bank provides $3 million to 20 main street businesses having a community impact, Kimberly-Clark offers 12 grants of $15000 to mothers attempting to start businesses, and Eileen Fisher has $100000 for ten women-owned ventures. Some companies, such as Anheuser-Busch with its Miller Lite Tap the Future Competition, award money to winning entrepreneurs for their ventures. A large number of local business plan or pitch competitions with cash prizes can be found in many cities. Again, the ventures of the poor struggle to be competitive in such competitions. Finally, a few foundations have grant programs for defined groups, such as the Open Meadows Foundation (for women) and StreetShares Foundation (veterans).

The picture in Europe is somewhat similar to that of the United States. Grants for poor entrepreneurs are relatively scarce and highly competitive. The European Union offers a range of grants to small businesses pursuing activities that align with EU priorities, such as the EXCITE initiative for young entrepreneurs or the Erasmus for Young Entrepreneurs Exchange Program. In terms of the poor, however, the tendency is more to provide financial support to local organizations offering entrepreneurship initiatives that may or may not reach low-income entrepreneurs. Particular countries also have specialized grant opportunities, some more extensive than the US. The United Kingdom represents a good case in point. At a national level, the priority is on grants that support entrepreneurs working with technology-based innovation, which often does not include the poor. Examples include Innovation Vouchers that help entrepreneurs get advice from an expert or consultant, Smart Grants for major innovations, and Catalyst Grants in particular technical fields. Industry-specific programs exist (e.g., forestry, energy, tourism, arts/fashion/design) as well as grants for ventures attempting to export, those serving the aged, and entrepreneurs who work and live in the British countryside, among others. Social entrepreneurs also see considerable support. When it comes to the disadvantaged or low-income individuals, the Prince's Trust offers loans and grants to those between the ages of 18 and 30 (and over 50) who want to start a venture, with special attention given to the disadvantaged. There are also grants for affordable broadband Internet access and for community-based businesses. A greater abundance of programs can be found in particular regions and municipalities, including small awards for start-ups by unemployed, disabled, minority, and low-income individuals residing in these areas.

While not an actual grant, another noteworthy set of initiatives attempts to award government contracts or tenders to economically disadvantaged entrepreneurs. For instance, the US government offers the 8(a) Business Development Program that provides a range of assistance to disadvantaged entrepreneurs. Included here are access to sole-source (non-competitive) and competitive contracts to provide products or services to government agencies. Many local governments, universities, and private corporations also have special set-aside programs to award contracts to minority and disadvantaged business owners, some of which also include mentor–protégé programs where potential entrepreneurs get mentored by successful entrepreneurs and other experts.

Customer Funding

While often overlooked, another vehicle for financing a venture is through customer funding. Some highly successful ventures have relied on this approach, including Airbnb, Dell Computers, and the Banana Republic. Mullins (2014) has identified some general approaches to customer funding. For the poor, the most relevant is probably the pay-in-advance model, where customers pay for a product or service and then the entrepreneur produces or acquires it. This approach is sometimes used with crowdfunding campaigns where people are incentivized to contribute funds with the offer of a product once the fundraising is successfully completed. A variation of having customers pay in advance is requiring customers to put a deposit down prior to receiving a product or service. Also relevant is the subscription model, where the customer agrees to buy the product or service over an extended period of time, paying a monthly, quarterly or annual subscription fee ahead of actually receiving all of the goods or services. So-called matchmaker models find the entrepreneur serving as a type of intermediary, earning money from buyers and sellers for bringing them together (such as with Airbnb), while not actually owning what is being sold. Playing a go-between role is not uncommon among people in poverty (Chau, Goto and Kanbur, 2016), but here the focus is generating cash flow from the activity. The deliver-and-resell model involves winning a contract to create something for one customer and then reselling a variant of that product to a broader market.

Local Community Savings Schemes

Last, different versions of rotating savings and credit associations (ROSCAs) can be a means for low-income entrepreneurs to raise money for a venture. Let's say eight individuals are each trying to acquire an asset of some kind (e.g., a vehicle, computer, power-washing system, or sewing machine). Here, the group of individuals decides to partner for a defined period of time. Each pays an equal amount of money into a common fund on a weekly, monthly or otherwise regular basis. Once the fund has accumulated enough money, one of the entrepreneurs is able to use the money to make a purchase, while all of them continue to make their regular payments into the fund. It then rotates to the next person, and then the next, until all have been able to buy the asset. ROSCAs are a form of peer-to-peer lending where many variations are possible depending on the capabilities and needs of the individuals involved. For instance, the group might simply pay into a fund without anyone taking money out until someone needs funds for a particular purpose. Alternatively, the group might each pay in monthly, with one person taking this month's total to use in their venture and the next person taking next month's total.

FUNDING THE VENTURES OF THE POOR IN STAGES

These various sources of money become relevant depending on the stages of development of the low-income entrepreneur's venture. That is, as the entrepreneur makes more progress, certain types of financing can become available. Table 9.1, presented earlier in our discussion of funding needs, illustrates this concept.

When in the idea stage, the entrepreneur is principally dependent on personal savings. He or she may qualify for assistance from government and non-profit organizations for small business-related training courses. The pre-start-up planning stage is also heavily dependent on money from personal savings, but now friends and family become a more likely source. As the entrepreneur successfully refines a business concept, completes market research, writes a business plan, develops samples or prototypes, and engages in other activities that help translate an idea into a possible company, additional money sources become viable. Beyond the entrepreneur's own money, these include friends and family as a primary source, but can also include microcredit, crowdfunding, and local savings schemes (i.e., ROSCAs). When launching the venture, the same set of sources remain relevant, with a greater chance of getting microcredit, crowdfunding and grants at this stage. If eligible for government-guaranteed loans, such as those offered by the Small Business Administration in the US, a loan may be possible from a participating bank. With the stabilization stage, a key is that any profits be reinvested in the venture. The money sources from preceding stages remain relevant, but this is the first stage where conventional loans from commercial banks might become relevant. The question then becomes the extent to which the entrepreneur seeks and is ready to accomplish growth. Again, most start-up ventures fail to achieve meaningful growth, and this is even more the case for impoverished entrepreneurs. But with both the desire for growth and a venture that has growth prospects, the entrepreneur is in a stronger position at this stage to attract both bank financing and perhaps angel investors.

Entrepreneurs can waste considerable time and effort when they fail to appreciate the perspective of the financier. As a case in point, low-income entrepreneurs often feel frustrated with, and develop cynicism towards, bankers, believing they do not care about the ventures of the poor (and perhaps discriminate against them). Awareness of when in the entrepreneurial process a source is most likely to consider providing money, and what exactly they are looking for at that stage, can produce much more investment in low-income start-ups.

THE ONGOING GAP IN FUNDING

Funding a business is a big challenge for anyone, but for those in poverty the task can be overwhelming. As we have seen in this chapter, a variety of financing sources are available to low-income entrepreneurs, depending on how far along they are in the process. As a generalization, the earlier the entrepreneur is, the less money is available. The person in poverty typically has little personal savings and few assets (including intellectual property) to invest in a business, and the same is generally true for their friends and families. They have a more difficult time qualifying for credit-based financing, and characteristics of their ventures (and their limited social networks) make obtaining equity finance much more unlikely. The bias in traditional venture funding is towards established ventures that have significant growth prospects. It is also towards technology-based businesses with exciting new innovations. Some of the newer or emerging sources of money, such as microcredit, grants and crowdfunding, while promising, are able to fund only a very small number of low-income start-ups each year.

A large gap continues to plague people in poverty who want to start something. Some of this is due to shortcomings in their backgrounds and experience. Financial literacy is paramount in this regard, and is examined in more depth in Chapter 6. Another contributor is the types of ventures started by the poor, especially when they operate in highly competitive and relative mature markets, are labor intensive, lack differentiation, attempt to compete on price, and are able to spend little on technology (as we shall address in Chapter 11).

There is a critical need not just for more investment in the start-up concepts of the poor, but funding that reflects the needs of these entrepreneurs as they progress through their entrepreneurial journey. Simply distinguishing those in the pre-venture stage from those already in business is insufficient. An integrated approach, particularly at the local level, should include a combined mix of microcredit, grants, and crowdfunding opportunities. Both funding and the connected training, mentoring, apprenticeship, and contracting set-aside initiatives should then be specifically tailored to the ideation, pre-start-up, start-up, stabilization, and growth stages of the venture. Amounts of funding should be directly tied to goals and deliverables produced by the entrepreneur at each stage. The community of low-income entrepreneurs, once successful, could play an instrumental role in helping to guide these programs.

NOTES

1. When one sells on consignment, one provides one's product to a distributor or retailer, who in turn makes it available to customers, but one only gets paid when the product is actually sold.
2. Like leasing a car instead of buying it, the business is signing a lease to obtain an asset (e.g., a truck, a piece of equipment) and makes monthly payments on the lease. When the lease expires, they must return the asset (the truck or piece of equipment) to the owner.
3. Invoice discounting involves the company using its accounts receivable (money owed to it by customers) as collateral with a bank in order to get a loan, so the bank has a claim on those receivables.
4. See their website at http://www.microfinancegateway.org/; accessed June 13, 2018.
5. See their website at https://aeoworks.org/; accessed June 13, 2018.

REFERENCES

Anderloni, L. and E. Carluccio (2006), "Access to bank accounts and payment services," in L. Anderloni, E. Carluccio and M. Braga (eds), *New Frontiers in Banking Services: Emerging Needs and Tailored Products for Untapped Markets*, Berlin: Springer Verlag, pp. 5–105.

Aspen Institute (2017), "Microloan Underwriting," Washington, DC: Field at the Aspen Institute, September 21, 2017, accessed October 8, 2018 at https://assets. aspeninstitute.org/content/uploads/2017/09/FIELD-Microloan-Underwriting-Webinar-2017-2.pdf.

Attuel-Mendès, L. (2014), "Crowdfunding platforms for microfinance: A new way to eradicate poverty through the creation of a global hub?," *Cost Management*, **28**, 38–47.

Baradaran, M. (2013), "How the poor got cut out of banking," *UGA Legal Studies Research Paper No. 2013-12*.

Barr, M. and R. Blank (eds) (2009), "Savings, assets, credit, and banking among low-income households: Introduction and overview," in R. Bland and M. Barr (eds), *Insufficient Funds: Savings, Assets, Credit, and Banking Among Low-Income Households*, New York: Russell Sage Foundation, pp. 1–22.

Bates, T. and A. Robb (2013), "Greater access to capital is needed to unleash the local economic development potential of minority-owned businesses," *Economic Development Quarterly*, **27**(3), 250–59.

Belleflamme, P., T. Lambert and A. Schwienbacher (2014), "Crowdfunding: Tapping the right crowd," *Journal of Business Venturing*, **29**(5), 585–609.

Bhatt, N., G. Painter and S.Y. Tang (1999), "Can microcredit work in the United States?," *Harvard Business Review*, **77**, 26–7.

Blanchard, L., B. Zhao and J. Yinger (2008), "Do lenders discriminate against minority and woman entrepreneurs?," *Journal of Urban Economics*, **63**(2), 467–97.

Blanchflower, D.G., P.B. Levine and D.J. Zimmerman (2003), "Discrimination in the small-business credit market," *The Review of Economics and Statistics*, **85**(4), 930–43.

Brown, G. (2010), "When small is big: Microcredit and economic development," *Technology Innovation Management Review*, November 2010, accessed June 13, 2018 at http://timreview.ca/article/392.

Burhouse, S., K. Chu and K. Ernst et al. (2016), *FDIC National Survey of Unbanked and Underbanked Households 2015*, Federal Deposit Insurance Corporation, Division of Depositor and Consumer Protection.

Chau, N.H., H. Goto and R. Kanbur (2016), "Middlemen, fair traders, and poverty," *The Journal of Economic Inequality*, **14**(1), 81–108.

Community Development Venture Capital Alliance (CDVCA) (2006), "The New Markets Venture Capital Program: Providing equity capital and expertise to entrepreneurs in low-income urban and rural communities," *CDVCA*, July, accessed June 13, 2018 at https://community-wealth.org/sites/clone.community-wealth.org/files/downloads/paper-cdvca.pdf.

Cosic, M. (2017), "We are all entrepreneurs: Muhammad Yunus on changing the world one microloan at a time," in *Sydney Peace Foundation*, 28 March, accessed June 13, 2018 at http://sydneypeacefoundation.org.au/we-are-all-entrepreneurs-muhammad-yunus-on-changing-the-world-one-microloan-at-a-time/.

Craig, B.R., W.E. Jackson and J.B. Thomson (2007), "On government intervention in the small-firm credit market and its effect on economic performance," *Federal Reserve Bank of Cleveland Working Paper No. 07-02*.

Ebben, J. and A. Johnson (2006), "Bootstrapping in small firms: An empirical analysis of change over time," *Journal of Business Venturing*, **21**(6), 851–65.

Edgcomb, E.L. (2002), *Scaling up Microenterprise Services*, Washington, DC: Aspen Institute.

European Commission (2017), "COSME financial instruments," accessed June 13, 2018 at https://ec.europa.eu/growth/access-to-finance/cosme-financial-instruments_en.

Fafchamps, M. (2013), "Credit constraints, collateral, and lending to the poor," *Revue d'Economie du Developpement*, **21**(2), 79–100.

Frisch, M. and L. Servon (2006), "CDCs and the changing context for urban community development: A review of the field and the environment," *Community Development*, **37**(4): 88–108.

Huddleston, C. (2016), "69% of Americans have less than $1,000 in savings,"

GoBankingRates, September 19, accessed June 16, 2018 at https://www.gobank ingrates.com/saving-money/savings-advice/data-americans-savings/.

Karlan, D., A.L. Ratan and J. Zinman (2014), "Savings by and for the poor: A research view and agenda," *The Review of Income and Wealth*, **60**(1), 36–78.

Littwin, A. (2007), "Beyond usury: A study of credit-card use and preference among low-income consumers," *Texas Law Review*, **86**, 453–505.

Mann, R.J. (2006), *Charging Ahead: The Growth and Regulation of Payment Card Markets*, New York: Cambridge University Press.

Mullins, J. (2014), *The Customer-Funded Business*, Hoboken, NJ: John Wiley and Sons.

O'Donoghue, T. and M. Rabin (1999), "Doing it now or later," *American Economic Review*, **89**(1), 103–24.

Rao, D. (2016), "Growing high-potential businesses in low-capital communities: A strategy for social entrepreneurship," *Forbes*, June 14.

Ratcliffe, J. (2007), "Who's counting? Measuring social outcomes from targeted private equity," *Community Development Investment Review*, **1**, 23–37.

Robb, A.M. and R.W. Fairlie (2007), "Access to financial capital among US businesses: The case of African American firms," *The Annals of the American Academy of Political and Social Science*, **613**(1), 47–72.

Scott III, R.H. (2009), *The Use of Credit Card Debt By New Firms*, Kansas City: Ewing Marion Kauffman Foundation.

Servon, L. (1999), *Microenterprises and the American Poor*, Washington, DC: The Brookings Institution.

Servon, L. (2006), "Microenterprise development in the United States: Current challenges and new directions," *Economic Development Quarterly*, **20**(4), 351–67.

Servon, L. (2013), "The high cost, for the poor, of using a bank," *The New Yorker*, October 9, accessed June 13, 2018 at https://www.newyorker.com/business/currency/the-high-cost-for-the-poor-of-using-a-bank.

Servon, L. and J.P. Doshna (2000), "Microenterprise and the economic development toolkit: A small part of the big picture," *Journal of Developmental Entrepreneurship*, **5**(3), 183–208.

Shane, S. (2008), *The Illusions of Entrepreneurship. The Costly Myths That Entrepreneurs, Investors, and Policy Makers Live By*, New Haven, CT: Yale University Press.

Silver-Greenberg, J. and B. Protess (2012), "Chasing fees, banks court low-income customers," *The New York Times*, April 25, accessed June 13, 2018 at http://www.nytimes.com/2012/04/26/business/chasing-fees-banks-court-low-income-custom ers.html?_r=1andhp.

Srinivas, H. (2015), "Microfinance – credit lending models," *GDRC Continuing Research Series E0059*.

Thorpe, D. (2013), "Three young entrepreneurs fighting poverty have big impact," *Forbes*, November 23, accessed June 13, 2018 at https://www.forbes.com/si tes/devinthorpe/2013/11/23/three-young-entrepreneurs-fighting-poverty-have-big-impact/#72c43cd7746f.

Trading Economics (2017), "Personal savings by country," accessed June 13, 2018 at https://tradingeconomics.com/european-union/personal-savings.

Winborg, J. (2009), "Use of financial bootstrapping in new businesses: A question of last resort?," *Venture Capital*, **11**(1), 71–83.

10. Overcoming resource constraints

> If we want to help poor people out, one way to do that is to help them explore and use their own capability. [A] human being is full of capacity, full of capability (and) is a wonderful creation . . . But many people never get a chance to explore that.
> (Muhammad Yunus)

SEEING RESOURCES DIFFERENTLY

Based on the discussion in the preceding chapter, those in poverty frequently have very limited access to formal or informal sources of investment. Given this reality, is it realistic to expect someone who has little to nothing in terms of financial resources to start and grow a business? If a person cannot afford the utility bill and is unsure about his or her ability to feed the family this week, how can he or she be expected to start a venture? The obvious answer is, as we saw in Chapter 3, that many people from poverty have found a way to do so.

Yet, starting a business can be intimidating, with things almost always costing more than the entrepreneur anticipates, and where a wide range of obstacles are encountered that have to be overcome no matter whether one has resources or does not. In addition, new ventures are plagued by what are termed the liabilities of newness and smallness, both of which reflect severe resource constraints in start-up ventures. The liability of newness concerns the vulnerabilities of the business based on its lack of market identity, reputation, legitimacy, established routines, and an accumulated body of relevant tacit knowledge (Freeman, Carroll and Hannan, 1983). Liability of smallness refers to disadvantages the firm experiences in achieving visibility given its size, its relatively weak position in bargaining with suppliers, distributors and customers, and the lack of scale economies in production and distribution (Rauch, Unger and Rosenbusch, 2007).

Overcoming these resource constraints brings us back to the entrepreneurial mindset, introduced in Chapter 2. In discussing the essence of entrepreneurship, Stevenson and Gumpert (1985) draw a distinction between those who tend to be more "resource driven" compared to those who are more "opportunity driven." The resource-driven person allows a lack of resources to severely constrain the actions they are willing to pursue. Resources currently owned or controlled become the filter for evaluating any new possibility, such as starting a venture. If what is needed does not fit what one currently has, the venture idea is rejected. The opportunity-driven person sees a possibility in which they believe, and will do whatever is necessary to find or martial the resources necessary to pursue it.

The entrepreneur must be opportunity driven – willing to pursue opportunity regardless of resources controlled. Doing so requires the entrepreneur to focus on developing skills in three key areas:

- the ability to see things as resources where others do not see them as such;
- the ability to stretch resources and apply them in new and different ways;
- the ability to utilize the resources of others without paying for them, or paying much less than they are worth.

In this chapter, we explore the resource shortcomings of those in poverty when it comes to starting a business. The range of resources needed by the entrepreneur are considered, both financial and non-financial. While in Chapter 9 we discussed ways to obtain financial resources, here we are especially concerned with acquiring resources when the entrepreneur has no money. A variety of approaches for acquiring or gaining access to critical resources are examined.

RESOURCES NEEDED TO START A VENTURE

A venture can be considered a bundle of resources. The particular resources an entrepreneur is able to acquire, and how these resources are combined and deployed, determines the viability and competitive advantage of the venture being created (Sirmon, Hitt and Ireland, 2007). While it is normal to assume that a discussion of resources is all about money, it is often the case that financial resources are not the most critical ones in explaining an entrepreneur's success. Many relatively wealthy or well-resourced individuals fail at entrepreneurship in spite of the amount of money they are willing to spend on the venture. Consider the entrepreneur who invents a better toy or game. He or she may find that success requires the ability to get into stores such as Toys"R"Us or Walmart. The entrepreneur is unable to buy their way into the retail channel, but instead must have the right product and be able to develop a relationship with the retailers.

The many potential resources required to launch a business can be grouped into six basic categories:

- *Physical resources.* Includes land, buildings, office space, trucks, point of sale systems, tools, equipment, computers, and a valuable location, among others. While they can usually be acquired for money, there are often other ways to gain access to them.
- *Relational resources.* The entrepreneur's network, including relationships with suppliers, key customers, distributors, financiers, opinion leaders, and gatekeepers (people who control access to other people), is arguably his or her most important resource. For instance, a relationship with a supplier might lead to special terms where the entrepreneur does not have to pay for materials or inventory purchased for up to four weeks.
- *Organizational resources.* Entrepreneurs are sometimes able to develop new processes, methods, and technologies for use in making a product, providing a service, or accomplishing a task that save time, reduce costs, or enhance the value a customer receives.
- *People resources.* Simply hiring people is not the same as developing capabilities. Here, the focus is on developing employees who are better at selling, customer service, achieving consistency of quality, producing efficiently, developing new services or products, or fulfilling some other business requirement that adds value.
- *Intellectual property resources.* There are creations of the mind that can often receive legal protection that limits the ability of others to copy the creation, giving the entrepreneur a potential advantage. Examples include new product and process inventions, software, databases, symbols, logos, images, and names used in the venture. Protection comes in the form of patents, trademarks, and copyrights. Even without such protection, creations can be treated as trade secrets and can be a source of value.
- *Financial resources.* Finally, money does represent a critical resource, and can include the savings of the entrepreneur, cash that can be obtained through partners or family and friends, and any loan products from banks or financial institutions for which the entrepreneur can qualify. Depending on the nature of the venture and the other types of resources contained in the venture (e.g., intellectual property, people resources), the entrepreneur may also be able to access other sources of finance, such as crowdfunding, angel investors, and venture capitalists (see Chapter 9).

Resources can be further distinguished based on whether they are tangible or intangible. While tangible resources are physical assets such as trucks and equipment, intangible resources include non-physical assets or capabilities controlled by the entrepreneur such as a loyal customer base, a unique company capability such as delivery of superior customer service or better product design skills, and patents or other forms of intellectual property. As a rule, intangible assets contribute to the future value of a company more so than tangible assets, particularly where they result in novel sources of customer value, enable the business to better differentiate itself in the marketplace, and provide a source of competitive advantage.

RESOURCE GAPS OF THE POOR

Payne, DeVol and Dreussi Smith (2009, p. 11) approach poverty as "the extent to which an individual does without resources." In exploring the resource conditions of a person experiencing poverty, they identify resource challenges in eight areas that are relevant for explaining both success in leaving poverty and the reasons many people remain poor over many generations (Box 10.1). While poverty is generally defined in terms of the financial resources one has, these authors argue that positive outcomes are more a function of non-financial (emotional, mental, physical, spiritual, relational, rule-related, and coping) resources.

Sustained conditions of poverty can serve to deplete the individual's pool of resources in all of these categories. Consider the resource implications of a poor education, lack of financial literacy, depleted health, abandonment by a parent, an abusive partner, a criminal record, a network of friends with drug or alcohol abuse problems, constant demands on your time and money from those around you in even more dire circumstances, lack of room for self-improvement because of the need to work three part-time jobs to support four children and cover child care costs while you work, the inability to find or keep a job for a sustained period of time, constant threats to your security or the security of anything you own, and anger over perceived inequities that are regularly experienced. Moreover, with ongoing poverty, the individual is subject to what Paulo Freire (1996) refers to as the "tyranny of the moment." When life is dominated by the need to survive and one is preoccupied with addressing ongoing crisis conditions, planning for the future can become problematic. Such conditions can clearly take away from the individual's ability to save money and build a pool of financial resources. More importantly, though, they can undermine a person's mental, emotional, and spiritual resources.

Specifically, these conditions can make it harder for those in poverty

---

BOX 10.1   RESOURCE GAPS AND THE POOR

While the resource situation will differ significantly among the many who are poor, Payne et al. (2009) conclude that the ability to climb out of poverty depends on an individual's pool of resources in eight general categories:

Financial resources: Lack of savings, little to no collateral, poor credit history, and very limited access to conventional financial sources.

Emotional resources: Ability to find the strength to persist and tenaciously break from old habits, give up certain relationships, learn new ways, and/or develop new values and routines. Critical for maintaining a lifestyle with some sense of order. Can be impacted by role models, family support, self-discipline.

Mental resources: Focus is on ability to process and use information in daily decision-making. Includes literacy, pattern recognition, and sense-making capabilities.

Spiritual resources: The sense of meaning and purpose that a person has about themselves, and the feelings of self-worth and being capable.

Physical resources: A person's health and well-being, and extent to which they are physically capable, mobile, and self-sufficient.

Relationships/role models: The immediate network of people the individual can turn to for assistance in any area (child care, transportation, money, information, advice, help in completing a task or job).

Knowledge of hidden rules: Hidden rules exist within different economic classes. They are unspoken understandings indicating whether a person fits or belongs. They include rules about decorum, language, dress, what is done with extra money, self-reliance, conflict and physical violence, and a host of other variables.

Coping strategies: Mindsets, approaches, and techniques that people use to move issues from the concrete to the abstract, such that they are able to translate from the personal to a particular issue that requires understanding or action.

Source: Based on work by Payne et al. (2009).

---

to abandon old habits, break from established relationships, learn new ways, and process and interpret novel informational inputs. Their lives can lose purpose and meaning, while they develop a lower sense of self-worth and reduced self-efficacy. Support systems can be tenuous and subject to sudden disruption. Separately, we may find the person brings to any new pursuit some of the hidden rules shared by those in poverty, affecting their patterns of thought, cognitive styles, approaches to social interaction and other behaviors. All of this can undermine their ability to be successful at this new pursuit, particularly when that success is tied to interactions and relationships with people who operate based on different rules (e.g., middle class or wealthy class). Payne et al. (2009) conclude that a prime focus of support and intervention programs directed at alleviating poverty must be to help replenish each of these resource pools.

If we consider the types of resources needed to start a venture outlined in the preceding section and compare them to the potential resource shortfalls outlined in Box 10.1, one can appreciate the inherent position of disadvantage from which the low-income entrepreneur operates. The serious shortcomings in money or access to funding sources (see Chapter 9) most directly impacts the ability to acquire physical resources. However, lack of money also hinders development of human resources. The entrepreneur is unable to hire employees with the relevant talents, particularly those that contribute to developing unique organizational capabilities that produce marketplace advantage. Similarly, they cannot adequately invest in technologies, and are unable to create much intellectual property. The latter is additionally constrained by the educational backgrounds and the opportunity horizons of the poor (see Chapter 5). Beyond this, these individuals begin the entrepreneurial journey with small and potentially more unstable networks (i.e., social or relational capital) that have few ties to resources relevant for launching and growing a venture. When their networks include links with greater potential, they may not appreciate the kinds of hidden rules necessary to capitalize on these relationships.

The most important resource in a venture is the entrepreneur. Especially in the early days of a start-up, new ventures succeed based on the passion, optimism, creativity, learning, adaptation, tenacity, and resilience of the founder. When this person has a deficient pool of emotional, spiritual, mental, and/or health-related resources, it becomes extremely difficult to continually learn from both the negative and positive events encountered as a venture unfolds, and then make the appropriate adaptations to various elements of the business model. Further, he or she is held back in terms of his or her ability to change routines, patterns, habits, relationships, and values based on the needs of the venture. In addition, the entrepreneur is less able to recognize and act upon marketplace changes and new, emerging opportunities that could enhance profitability.

These shortfalls explain why many of the poor either do not consider entrepreneurship as an option, or, when they do develop an idea for a business, they fail to launch the venture. For those who do start something, resource constraints often force them to create survival and poorly performing lifestyle ventures. As their opportunity costs and the required rates of return can be quite low, the poor are often able to stretch resources and keep a fairly marginal venture going for a relatively prolonged period. Yet, the entrepreneur and his or her family barely get by, little to no wealth is created, and resources cannot be reinvested in venture growth or enhancement of the equity in the business. A cycle emerges where the initial configuration of resources constrains venture performance as well as the entrepreneur's ability to obtain new resources – such that he or she struggles just to maintain the status quo on an ongoing basis.

At the same time, there are ways to bridge the gap between what the low-income entrepreneur has and what is needed in terms of resources. It is about the application of the entrepreneurial mindset to resource acquisition. This brings us to three critical and highly inter-related principles or concepts: bootstrapping, leveraging and guerrilla behavior.

HOW THE POOR CAN OBTAIN RESOURCES

When it comes to raising money, options and approaches were discussed in Chapter 9. Yet, if we assume that the entrepreneur has very little money and limited access to the money of others, which is typically the case for low-income entrepreneurs, this need not be a reason for not starting a venture.

The Bootstrapping Concept

Bootstrapping refers to using the resources the entrepreneur has at hand to accomplish outcomes. The entrepreneur is starting a venture with very little money, and pulls himself or herself up by the bootstraps. It is a proactive attempt to make the most of things under the entrepreneur's control. Absent any outside funding, the individual instead uses his or her own resources (including credit cards), does as many tasks himself or herself (e.g., figures out how to create their own website or keep their own books), and stretches resources to the limit.

Box 10.2 provides a number of examples of bootstrapping techniques. The low-income entrepreneur is bootstrapping when paying bills as late as possible while collecting from customers as early as possible, using unpaid interns, selling on consignment, using supplier credit, and accelerating receivables (Winborg and Landström, 2001).

A core aspect in many bootstrapping approaches is the concept of resource leveraging. More than just stretching resources, it extends bootstrapping in an attempt to tap a wide variety of resources that can often seem well beyond the entrepreneur's control.

BOX 10.2   SAMPLE BOOTSTRAPPING APPROACHES

- Use of owner's credit cards.
- Loan from relatives/friends.
- Withhold salary for self.
- Assignments in other businesses.
- Relatives working for non-market salary.
- Cease business relations with late payers.
- Use routines for speeding up invoicing.
- Use interest on overdue payments.
- Offer same conditions to all customers.
- Borrow equipment from colleagues.
- Own equipment in common with others.
- Coordinate purchases with other firms.
- Create own website, do own bookkeeping, etc.
- Practice barter instead of buying/ selling.
- Lease equipment instead of buying.
- Delay payment to suppliers.
- Delay payment of tax.
- Use routines in order to minimize inventory or stock.
- Negotiate best conditions possible with suppliers.
- Obtain subsidy from local or state government or agency.
- Offer customers discounts if paying cash.
- Raise money by selling physical assets or accounts receivable.
- Choose customers who pay quickly.
- Use free resources from the Internet.
- Share premises with others.
- Use a cash box instead of a cash register.

The Leveraging Concept

It is normal to assume that if one wants to do something innovative like start a business, it will cost money, and that if one needs a resource, one has to find the money to buy it. Yet, this is a misguided notion, especially for the low-income entrepreneur. Purchasing or owning the resource should more typically be the *last* option considered, not the first.

How does one gain access to a resource without purchasing it? It becomes necessary to rely upon the diverse mix of things that are at hand or readily available, something originally termed bricolage by the famous French anthropologist Claude Levi-Strauss (Baker and Nelson, 2005). In the contemporary environment, the low-income entrepreneur focuses on the concept of resource leveraging and it is core to every resource decision that he or she makes. To leverage is to multiply the outcome of one's efforts without a corresponding increase in the consumption of resources. Consider a man trying to move a large boulder who finds he simply does not have the strength to move it. But by placing a length of pipe or timber (a lever) under the boulder, he is able to move it. So, the low-income entrepreneur must look for levers.

When launching and growing a venture, leveraging can involve:

- using someone else's resources;
- doing more with fewer resources;
- mobilizing a resource that others do not typically recognize as a resource;
- utilizing resources in ways they have not traditionally been used;
- playing resources off of one another to accomplish results;
- combining resources in novel ways to accomplish an outcome.

In practice, leveraging can take a number of forms. Box 10.3 elaborates on 13 specific types of leveraging approaches. Entrepreneurs can borrow, share, or rent the resource. They can outsource, partner, or collaborate with a competitor to get the resource. They can play resources off of one another or capitalize on their personal status.

Consider two examples, the first involving social entrepreneurship. A community soup kitchen leverages relationships with local three- and four-star restaurants to acquire their excess food at the end of each evening. In addition, they enhance cash flow by leveraging the basic soup kitchen facilities to start a professional catering business featuring ex-convicts as the wait staff. Going further, an innovative program is developed with local schools, bartering for use of the school kitchens during the hours they are not used in exchange for teaching culinary skills to students, and in the process producing more meals for disadvantaged members of the community. A second example can be found by considering a young man whose dream is to bring enhanced computer literacy to the inner city. He starts a business that involves computer classes, a low-cost Internet café, and rebuilt computers sold for low prices. He initially offers the classes in local churches, and is able to get free announcements in the church bulletins. He visits a new radio station that is serving this community and barters for a 15-minute radio show on technology topics in exchange for some computers and computer training for the radio station staff. He makes a similar offer to a woman who owns a house on a prominent traffic intersection in exchange for advertising his business on the side of her house. Instead of using an employment agency or help-wanted ads, he hires as employees the best students taking his courses.

When leveraging, there are three questions the low-income entrepreneur continually attempts to address:

1. What internal resources do I have that I am not fully utilizing (e.g., the extent to which I am making full use of my website, packaging,

BOX 10.3 THIRTEEN EXAMPLES OF LEVERAGING STRATEGIES

Borrow: Using a resource owned by someone else on a temporary basis, when they are not using it, such as a vehicle, tool or employee.

Barter: Provide a service or product or give some other asset in exchange for the resource.

Share: Utilize excess capacity, unused space or some other underutilized resource owned by someone else, such as an empty office, a machine when the business is closed, or a prominent area where messages might be posted.

Contract: Sign a contract to use the resource for a fixed term rather than be committed to it indefinitely, such as a temporary employment contract.

Lease or rent: Rather than purchase the resource, attempt to lease or rent it for a defined period of time.

Outsource: Instead of doing a task or function oneself, and having to purchase the necessary equipment, tools and supplies to do so, rely on an outside firm to provide the function or service, thereby lessening one's fixed investment.

License: Use someone else's property (often intellectual property) by paying a licensing fee tied to activity or usage, such as where you are charged per-unit fees for the amount of the item that you make, use or sell.

Partner: Form a business partnership with the resource provider in order to use a resource they control.

Consignment: Rather than purchase the inventory, sell things owned by others on consignment, where you pay them only when an item is sold.

Give equity: Give the resource provider partial ownership in the company in exchange for the resource.

Ham and egg: Use one resource to obtain another, such as where you use the fact that you are doing business with a certain customer in order to get business from another customer, or you are thinking about hiring a particular person because hiring that person might make your business more attractive to someone else you are trying to hire.

Collaborate with other businesses: Rather than simply compete, look for areas where you can collaborate with other firms, such as joint purchasing arrangements to achieve volume discounts.

Exploit personal status: Take advantage of your status as a minority, women, veteran, disabled person, or based on some other personal characteristic in order to win a contract, get a loan, or obtain some other resource.

vehicles, sales and service people, or any other assets under my control)?

2. How well am I leveraging relationships with people or companies in my network (e.g., the extent to which I am capitalizing on relationships with suppliers, vendors, producers of related products or services, financiers, distributors, and customers)?

3. What untapped or underutilized resources exist in the community or marketplace (e.g., the extent to which I have attempted to utilize churches that are not used for many hours of the day, kids who are opinion leaders, houses on prominent corners, walls in restrooms, table tops, car bumpers, abandoned buildings, school kitchens during summer, stay-at-home moms or dads)?

No matter a person's status in life or how limited their financial capital, and regardless of the kind of business they are trying to start, resources are abundant. Realizing this requires that the person does not assume resources have to be purchased or owned. To leverage is to empower the individual by creatively finding ways of accessing what they do not own. In fact, because of technological advances that have seeped into every walk of life, we exist in a time where much more can be accessed by entrepreneurs for much less.

The Guerrilla Concept

Related to bootstrapping and leveraging is the concept of guerrilla behavior. The history of warfare is replete with examples of smaller, weaker, under-resourced combatants who manage to defeat more powerful foes by engaging in clever, unconventional tactics, utilizing the unexpected ambush, taking advantage of surroundings or environmental conditions, employing stealth, and relying on mobility, speed, and the element of surprise (Beckett, 1999; Hutter and Hoffmann, 2011). It goes all the way back to the biblical story of David and Goliath.

Applied in an entrepreneurial context, guerrilla behavior is one of the more prevalent perspectives on how entrepreneurs can pursue opportunity when faced with severe resource constraints (Morris, Schindehutte and LaForge, 2002). In a new venture, guerrilla behavior is most often applied to selling and marketing, an area where the low-income entrepreneur often has no resources (Levinson, 1984). It refers to a novel system of tactics that relies on time, energy, and imagination rather than a large budget. The efforts are creative and unconventional, potentially interactive, and consumers are targeted in unexpected places.

Consider the case of the new pizza restaurant in an urban area that decides to feed and pay homeless people to hold up hand-scrawled messages at locations throughout the city attesting to the fact that they are homeless, have tried every kind of pizza, and believe this restaurant offers the best pizza. Such a tactic is certainly clever, non-conventional, unexpected, and utilizes as a resource something that most others would not view as a resource. Another example is the entrepreneur who starts a restaurant, but runs out of money and so is unable to promote the new business. Undaunted by this obstacle, he or she decides to have a party in the restaurant just before the grand opening. Only one type of person is invited to the party. The entrepreneur invites every hairdresser in the town to a fun, festive and free party. Hairdressers tend to talk all day as part of their jobs, and for many months after the party they are likely to mention this restaurant in very positive terms. This kind of free publicity can produce more powerful results than spending large sums of money (that the low-income person does not have) on conventional advertising on radio or the Internet.

As with leveraging, guerrilla tactics are dependent on the entrepreneur's creativity and resourcefulness. While the possibilities are limitless, Box 10.4 presents some general categories of guerrilla approaches. Examples include co-marketing with other firms, finding opinion leaders and giving them your product, taking advantage of the surroundings such as putting up fliers on backs of restroom doors or putting table top tents on tables in popular areas, creating buzz by making some seemingly outrageous offer to customers, placing products in other people's businesses or ads, doing something provocative that attracts free news coverage, and advertising on grocery carts, floors or ceilings.

By thinking as a guerilla, the low-income entrepreneur finds alternative ways to communicate with customers, create visibility, and build a brand. Guerrilla methods enable the entrepreneur to reach markets and customers that would seem unattainable without large marketing budgets and extensive distribution channels. They can also convey an image of an entrepreneur who is clever, different, fun, and is working hard to get the customer's business.

The Low-income Entrepreneur as Effectuator

One other perspective is useful for understanding how the low-income entrepreneur must approach resources. Saras Sarasvathy (2001) uses the term effectuation to describe a set of mental heuristics used for creatively combining and deploying the entrepreneur's emerging set of means at hand to achieve evolving goals. Consider the scenario where a person is in a kitchen and must prepare a meal. One approach is to find a recipe

BOX 10.4   SOME GENERAL CATEGORIES OF GUERRILLA
MARKETING APPROACHES

Bartering: Trading out goods or services for a marketing resource. Example: printing company gives free services to radio station in exchange for on-air promotions.

Co-marketing and reciprocity: Different companies directly helping one another. Example: two marketers mention one another in their advertising.

Sharing: Different companies going in together to acquire a resource that one could not afford and then share it. Example: two companies share a salesperson.

Using opinion leaders: Placing products with opinion leaders and incentivizing them to use the products in public contexts. Example: fashion clothing company has popular high school students wear their clothing at school.

Taking advantage of surroundings: Turning things surrounding the business into resources. Example: pizza restaurant uses homeless people to market its pizza.

Finding underutilized resources you don't own: Placing promotional messages in public venues where they do not typically appear (e.g., advertising on floors, bathroom stalls or elevator doors as they close).

Making use of underutilized resources you do own: Examining assets or things you own or control that are not being fully utilized. Example: car rental agency at a quiet time uses the cars and employees to deliver donuts to car repair shops to generate referrals; plumber paints toilet on side door of his truck so he looks like he is sitting on it when driving.

Stealth/disguising agents: Having people pretend to not work for you and have them effectively endorse your product. Example: maker of cameras has employees pretend to be tourists asking other tourists to take pictures of them using the company's product.

Placing products: Having products featured in movies, songs, video games or at events. Example: Harley Davidson offers motorcycles at no cost to the organizers of the Super Bowl half-time show.

Creating news: Doing something newsworthy and getting media coverage. Example: local computer store offers free training courses to disadvantaged or at-risk individuals from the inner city and gets local newspaper to publish story on the program.

Creating buzz by being provocative: Engaging in an activity in your business that is highly provocative and gets people talking. Example: Honest Tea runs "The most honest city in America" campaign and sets up unmanned displays with bottles of their tea in city centers to see who pays versus just takes one; or a jewelry store will give back 75 percent of the price of any diamonds purchased during the Christmas season if there is a white Christmas.

Leveraging networks: By belonging to various groups or organizations, the entrepreneur is able to effectively promote his or her business (e.g., membership or sponsorship by an entrepreneur of organization that supports stopping spousal abuse, which results in other supporters using the entrepreneur's services.

Co-creating: Using customers to help produce products or services. Example: YouTube does not create the content that is the essence of its value proposition; Vespa has a contest where customers create videos about why they love their Vespa.

in a cookbook, read it carefully, go out and acquire the items mentioned in the recipe, and then follow a step-by-step approach to producing the meal. This can be considered a planned approach, where the entrepreneur sets a goal, determines and then acquires the needed resources (often the major roadblock for the low-income entrepreneur), and then goes about accomplishing the goal. Alternatively, the effectual approach finds the entrepreneur with no cookbook, and instead looking in the kitchen cupboard, checking the refrigerator, and otherwise determining what resources are at hand, and then creatively putting these items together to make a meal. Low-income entrepreneurs frequently must make maximum use of the resources at hand, or, as Sarasvathy (2001) stresses, start with their means. They learn to see resources that others do not recognize as resources, and realize that they actually have access to more resources than their poverty status would suggest, especially when they are able to leverage their surroundings.

ONGOING RESOURCE CHALLENGES

There is a perceptual dimension to resources (Payne et al., 2009). To someone in poverty, having enough resources to simply get by can seem like a fairly high challenge, while obtaining the resources needed to start a venture can seem overwhelming. Yet, with a mindset that centers on bootstrapping, leveraging and guerrilla tactics, and when taken a step (or resource) at a time, the insurmountable becomes doable.

Ongoing challenges exist, however, when it comes to ventures launched by low-income entrepreneurs. Strategies that center on leveraging and guerrilla tactics can greatly expand the entrepreneur's capacity or capabilities, while accomplishing critical outcomes, but also often provide temporary solutions and ones where the entrepreneur does not have as much control over the resource. While for some resources, he or she may be able to continually bootstrap, leverage and act in guerrilla ways, for certain core resources, the creative tactics represent only a bridge. It becomes important for the low-income entrepreneur to develop longer-term resourcing strategies that build on accumulated savings from leveraging in order to acquire these resources.

A more vexing challenge concerns the types of resources one is able to acquire through these creative tactics. Tangible resources, such as office space, a truck, or prominent places one might place promotional material without paying, are more readily acquired by leveraging and guerrilla approaches. However, the longer-term sustainability and competitive advantage of a business are often dependent on intangible resources such as intellectual property, the application of new technologies in company operations, and development of unique capabilities within the firm. These resources are often more complex and their development can require significant and/or sustained investment over time. As a result, many low-income entrepreneurs struggle to develop such resources, and it becomes much more difficult to grow or scale their enterprises.

REFERENCES

Baker, T. and R.E. Nelson (2005), "Creating something from nothing: Resource construction through entrepreneurial bricolage," *Administrative Science Quarterly*, **50**, 329–66.

Beckett, I.F.W. (1999), *Encyclopedia of Guerrilla Warfare*, Santa Barbara, CA: ABC-CLIO.

Freeman, J., G.R. Carroll and M.T. Hannan (1983), "The liability of newness: Age dependence in organizational death rates," *American Sociological Review*, **48**(4), 692–710.

Freire, P. (1996), *Pedagogy of the Oppressed*, revised edition, New York: Continuum.

Hutter, K. and S. Hoffmann (2011), "Guerilla marketing: The nature of the concept and propositions for further research," *Asian Journal of Marketing*, **5**(2), 39–54.

Levinson, J.C. (1984), *Guerrilla Marketing: Easy and Inexpensive Strategies for Making Big Profits from Your Small Business*, Boston, MA: Houghton Mifflin Harcourt.

Morris, M.H., M. Schindehutte and R.W. LaForge (2002), "Entrepreneurial marketing: A construct for integrating emerging entrepreneurship and marketing perspectives," *Journal of Marketing Theory and Practice*, **10**(4), 1–19.

Payne, R.K., P. DeVol and T. Dreussi Smith (2009), *Bridges Out of Poverty: Strategies for Professionals and Communities*, Highlands, TX: Aha! Process Inc.

Rauch, A., J. Unger and N. Rosenbusch (2007), "Entrepreneurial stress and long term survival: Is there a causal link," *Frontiers of Entrepreneurship Research*, **27**(4), Article 2.

Sarasvathy, S.D. (2001), "Causation and effectuation: Toward a theoretical shift from economic inevitability to entrepreneurial contingency," *Academy of Management Review*, **26**(2), 243–63.

Sirmon, D.G., M.A. Hitt and R.D. Ireland (2007), "Managing firm resources in dynamic environments to create value," *Academy of Management Review*, **32**(1), 273–92.

Stevenson, H.H. and D.E. Gumpert (1985), "The heart of entrepreneurship," *Harvard Business Review*, **85**(2), 85–94.

Winborg, J. and H. Landström (2001), "Financial bootstrapping in small businesses: Examining small business managers' resource acquisition behaviors," *Journal of Business Venturing*, **16**(3), 235–54.

11. From vulnerability to sustainability: The challenges of planning and strategy

> I learned that things are never as complicated as we imagine them to be. It is only our arrogance which seeks to find complicated answers to simple problems.
>
> (Muhammad Yunus)

THE CHALLENGE OF COMPETING

Business is far more simple than complex. And the odds are not inherently against a start-up business. Yet, the journey is never an easy one. Failure rates in the first four years of a venture differ by industry, but are generally between 45 and 60 percent (Statistics Brain Research Institute, 2017). However, there is also a threshold principle that suggests that the entrepreneur who can get past certain thresholds has a much better chance of surviving and growing. Making it beyond two years, then five years, and getting to five and then ten permanent employees, represent sample thresholds. Tenacity and perseverance are important, but so too is good management – which is typically simple, focused and disciplined management. For most low-income entrepreneurs, there is little in their past that prepares them for the everyday rigors of running a small business, and there may be factors from their environments that actually work against good management practice. However, constraining environmental influences can be overcome, while good management practice is learnable.

When a venture is first launched, the entrepreneur almost always makes a number of mistakes and miscalculations. This happens even with a great business plan, something that is often missing with start-ups by low-income entrepreneurs. Price is set too low, the wrong customers are targeted, marketing efforts are misdirected or wasted, the wrong inventory (or not enough of the right inventory) is invested in, the type of employees hired are not what is needed, the location is undesirable, and customer service levels are too inconsistent, among dozens of other possible shortcomings. On top of this, unexpected occurrences, both positive and negative, impact the firm. Success requires that the entrepreneur must continually experiment, learn quickly, make ongoing adaptations in a number of areas of the business, and ultimately uncover a business model that is sustainable.

The challenge of competing is especially formidable when one suffers from severe resource limitations. Interpreting the signals being provided by the marketplace is not easy. Lack of resources, relevant experience, and fear of losing everything can find the entrepreneur hunkering down and resisting change. Further, the low-income entrepreneur typically operates in a highly competitive environment where the margins are low on products and services, and customers do not perceive meaningful differences among the offerings of different providers.

In this chapter, we explore what it takes for those in poverty to start ventures that can be competitive and sustainable. The roles of, and associated difficulties with, planning and goal setting are examined. The need to overcome a proclivity among low-income entrepreneurs to run the venture from a more reactive and tactical rather than strategic vantage point is examined. Methods for transforming what are often perceived commodity businesses into well-differentiated businesses are introduced. Attention is devoted to the central role of price, and the inclination of low-income entrepreneurs to underprice their products and services. Finally, consideration is devoted to the risk orientation of many low-income entrepreneurs, and how it deters the venture from growing.

BAD DECISIONS AND THE DISCIPLINE OF PLANNING

The path to creating a successful venture is uncertain, chaotic, non-linear, and not controllable. These realities make it difficult to plan effectively, as things keep changing. However, they also reinforce the importance of planning.

Planning provides overall direction in terms of the entrepreneur's actions when there is strong pressure to deviate, or go in other directions based on developments or pressures at a moment in time. It requires the entrepreneur to formulate a picture of the future, and set objectives based on what it will take to realize this desired future state. This direction determines priorities within the business and how resources will be allocated. Planning forces a future focus when the entrepreneur tends to be caught in the moment, addressing the immediate demands of customers, suppliers and other stakeholders, dealing with contingencies, and trying to ensure revenue is generated, bills are paid, and the business survives. Ultimately, planning helps reduce the uncertainty surrounding ongoing decision-making. It enables the entrepreneur to anticipate threats and recognize emergent opportunities, build on strengths, and compensate for weaknesses.

For all entrepreneurs, it is difficult to be future focused when the here and now threatens the very survival of the venture. When one comes from poverty, this can be especially daunting. Research on future orientation and planning activity on the part of the poor suggests that planning beyond the moment is a real problem (Banerjee and Duflo, 2011; Shah, Mullainathan and Shafir, 2012).

In attempting to determine whether people in poverty inherently make poor choices or bad decisions, Shah and co-authors (2012) demonstrate through experiments how those with limited resources tend to focus more exclusively on accomplishing the most pressing tasks at hand and ignoring other critical tasks – even where doing so may take away from the ability to accomplish larger goals. Immediate problems loom so large in one's consciousness that they consume a disproportionate amount of one's time, effort and limited financial resources. In the authors' words (p. 682), "people focus on problems where scarcity is most salient." By allocating attention to particular immediate needs, the individual frequently ignores other needs and engages in actions that prove more costly or detrimental in the longer term. They are, in effect borrowing from the future (and will tend to overborrow).

In an entrepreneurial context, this might mean borrowing money (and accumulating debt) at high interest rates to meet some immediate requirement, paying bills that with some effort might have been deferred while then incurring penalties for not addressing other demands, putting off regular maintenance expenditures on facilities or equipment, which subsequently results in major repair projects down the road, or procuring needed goods at retail prices, when better planning over time might have enabled the entrepreneur to buy at wholesale. Shah et al. (2012) conclude that (p. 682) "resource scarcity creates its own mindset, changing how people look at problems and make decisions." The lack of resources produces these attentional shifts and a reliance on locally convenient responses, which for the entrepreneur serves to undermine or constrain the longer-term potential of the business.

This explanation is intriguing, as it suggests that poor or suboptimal decisions can have a certain logic to them. More importantly, such decisions are not inherently attributable to bad traits that some observers attempt to associate with the poor (e.g., weak self-control). Nor are they inherently attributable to environmental factors endemic in low-income neighborhoods and communities. Rather, they stem from simply have less in terms of resources.

As an aside, there can also be a benefit to the poor from these attentional shifts. The research by Shah et al. (2012) found that those with less resources, when compared to those with more resources, were more engaged in the decisions they made, and often realized greater short-term productivity from those decisions – keeping in mind that other decisions were neglected and longer-term costs may well have been higher.

The focusing effect of scarcity can undermine one's ability to plan. Even where the entrepreneur does have a plan for where the venture is going over the next year or two, it affects the ability to stick with and/or achieve the goals of the plan. Planning can be problematic for other reasons as well. Mani et al. (2013) suggest that resource scarcity can impede cognitive function, resulting in poorer decisions. Berkman (2015) cites evidence that scarcity can reduce IQ. He also discusses the difficulties in engaging in the kinds of abstract thought that goes into contemplating how the future could look. He notes how hard this can be when surrounded by highly adverse conditions that threaten many aspects of a person's life. Tirado (2015) emphasizes the sheer lack of time, physical exhaustion from the many demands on the low-income person, and lack of belief or trust in the future.

Planning is also tied to savings. The poor certainly understand the value of saving for the future, and many do manage to put money aside. These savings are usually for some specific purpose, such as a child's education, and not based on some generic sense that one needs to save for the future (Shah et al., 2012). For the entrepreneur, the implication is that business planning can be especially valuable when it targets specific future needs, such as renting a location, acquiring a vehicle, or buying a computer system. There may be a type of mental accounting at work here, where putting money aside for specific purposes serves as a labeling device that encourages commitment and makes the entrepreneur more resistant to spending that particular money to meet ongoing needs or giving it to others. Dupas and Robinson (2013, p. 1163) explain that, "as savings put toward the mental account increase . . . the individual has both greater bargaining power against demands from others, as well as better self-control than in the absence of labeling."

REACTIVE, TACTICAL OR STRATEGIC?

Related to planning is the ability of the low-income entrepreneur to think and act strategically. This means thinking about goals and a vision for where the entrepreneur wants to take the business, and developing enhanced capabilities over time that enable the entrepreneur to move the business forward. It also involves anticipating likely threats and opportunities in the external environment. A strategic approach also emphasizes an understanding of how key decisions impact one another and must be coordinated. For instance, how do the targeted customer audience, products being sold, prices being charged, types of marketing efforts, operating hours, staffing requirements at different times, inventory levels maintained, and cash flow needs all relate to one another? How can these various decision areas be better coordinated in ways that reduce costs, differentiate the business from competitors, and/or increase the amount of value created for customers?

In practice, the low-income entrepreneur is usually scrambling to get by. The managerial approach tends to be more reactive and tactical than strategic. With reactive management the entrepreneur becomes a victim of circumstances, and victimhood is often a prevalent aspect of life in poverty. A disproportionate amount of time is spent on responding to emergencies or critical demands from customers, suppliers, a bank, employees, a partner, or some unforeseen development such as a fire in one's business when the firm carries no insurance. Being reactive suggests a lack of planning or preparation for events. The entrepreneur fails to anticipate developments so that any negative consequences or costs can be minimized (or any benefits can be fully capitalized upon). Moreover, he or she often fails to understand the root cause of the development, which means any solution or response only addresses symptoms. The underlying problem is allowed to fester and will eventually manifest itself again in similar or new ways.

Tactical management finds the low-income entrepreneur not just reacting, but also engaging in a kind of trial-and-error method for employing new or different approaches to some business area. Things are tried on a short-term and seemingly random basis – there is nothing systematic involved. Instead, the entrepreneur attempts to cut prices, run a promotion, add a new product or service, open earlier, change their signage, hire an employee or make some other change just to see if it works. Alternatively, he or she may observe something another business is doing and try to mimic the approach in his or her own business, typically without considering differences in context. Although such tactical moves sometime result in a positive result, they often waste time and money, send mixed or inconsistent messages to customers, confuse employees, and produce other negative outcomes.

Experimentation is the lifeblood of most start-up ventures, but the key is to experiment in ways that reflect particular goals and are consistent with other decision areas in the business (e.g., who is being targeted, how the business is trying to position itself in the market). With purely tactical approaches, there are no clear criteria for determining whether or not the tactic worked.

Finally, all too often tactics are attempted, do not appear to produce results, and are discarded, with no real learning taking place as to why the approach did or did not work. With a more systematic approach, each tactical experiment results in learning and then adjustment, with subsequent tactics designed based on learnings from earlier ones. The learning is designed around questions related to customer behavior, employee motivation, factors influencing costs, and other core business issues.

This brings us back to the need for a more strategic approach to building these ventures. However, operating strategically may be unnatural for entrepreneurs living in poverty. They often have no experience with successful enterprise creation, and experience is a key factor in outcomes. In a major study of African American entrepreneurship, Fairlie and Robb (2007) provide evidence of lower levels of income, start-up capital, and wealth among the Black-owned businesses compared to their White-owned counterparts. Further, they demonstrate how the poorer results (i.e., survival rates, sales, profits, jobs created) produced by these ventures are traceable to lack of exposure to or experience with the workings of a small business. Among other factors, Black-owned business owners are significantly less likely than White business owners to have had a self-employed family member (grandparent, aunt, father, sibling) to which they were meaningfully exposed (i.e., exposed to business-related issues) prior to starting their own business. If there was a business in the family, they are less likely to have actually worked in or assisted with it.

Alternatively, mentors can serve a similar purpose. Consider the case of Daymond John, who arose from poverty to create fashion industry leader FUBU and be a star on *Shark Tank*. He attributes much of his success to mentors ranging from the operator of a corner store near where he grew up, to some of his early customers, to the founder of a leading marketing consultancy.

Finally, being reactive and tactical rather than strategic is tied to micromanagement. Entrepreneurs starting a business when in poverty usually find themselves unable to hire people (and especially qualified people) for some time, and so initially rely on family members and friends to help out. As a result, they have to be able to do everything in the business themselves. So they find themselves involved in negotiation with suppliers, producing the product or service, doing marketing, keeping the books, raising money, cleaning bathrooms, dealing with customer complaints, and begging the landlord for an extension on paying rent. These realities can turn the entrepreneur into a micromanager. Having done all these tasks himself or herself, and having learned how to do them better, the individual struggles to delegate and so does not develop the bandwidth to think and act strategically.

THE SHOTGUN AND RIFLE DILEMMA – AND FINDING WAYS TO FOCUS

All too often, when asked to describe their target audience, the low-income entrepreneur will respond "everyone is a potential customer." Desperate to survive, the entrepreneur who starts from poverty will tend to see anyone and everyone as a potential source of business. This misconception holds many ventures from ever gaining traction in the marketplace. They try to be all things to all people.

In effect, the entrepreneur employs what is termed a shotgun approach to the market, when what is needed is a rifle approach. When firing a shotgun, the shot is sprayed everywhere. Even if the target is hit, typically a lot of other things are also hit. Alternatively, when firing a properly aimed rifle, the target is hit cleanly. There is no waste. The low-income entrepreneur does not have resources to waste, and so must employ rifle approaches when approaching the market. This means breaking the market down into segments, and focusing on particular segments that consist of customers with similar needs and buying behaviors. The entrepreneur specializes in meeting the needs of only these customers.

The segments can be defined by any number of characteristics. With under-resourced start-up ventures, the entrepreneur typically segments based on simple customer descriptors. Examples include, among others, age, gender, employment status, marital status, type and place of residence, usage rates, and the key benefits sought when buying the product or service. Consider the entrepreneur who launches a cleaning company, but segments the market and concentrates efforts on selling to businesses, not households. Further, he emphasizes medical facilities, and further specializes in medical offices where one must regularly deal with biomedical waste. Yet another entrepreneur owns a van and decides to create a transport business. The decision is made to transport people, not goods. This market is further segmented based on the purpose and length of the trip, and the entrepreneur concludes that there is a unique opportunity in transporting people with disabilities who have Medicare coverage and want to visit a doctor located within ten miles.

By engaging in segmentation and then targeting specific types of customers, the entrepreneur is not only more efficient in the use of their resources (i.e., less wastage on people who are unlikely to buy), but they can also be more effective (i.e., produce a bigger response from customers whose needs they are catering to). They can design their product or service offering, prices, staffing, operating hours, and/or marketing approaches in ways that uniquely reflect the needs and buying behaviors of the targeted segments.

Let's use a marketing example involving a low-income entrepreneur with a takeaway food establishment located in a tough inner city community within a mid-sized metropolitan area. Almost all of her customers come from the local area around her establishment. Operating under the misplaced notion that everyone is a potential customer, she decides to run advertisements in the local newspaper, which reaches about 150 000 people. She thinks this broad-based exposure could bring in a variety of new customers, such as local business professionals who work in the central business district, and students from a local university. But this never happens. Even with well-designed ads run a number of times, virtually no increase in customer volume occurs while the ads are running or afterwards. And the entrepreneur has now exhausted her marketing resources for at least the next 12 months.

Alternatively, with some help from a local non-profit that helps small businesses, this same entrepreneur is able to more thoroughly study the market and assess her current customer base. She comes to realize that the inner city community itself has a number of distinct market segments, none of which she is very heavily penetrating. Based on this, she decides to spend her limited marketing funds in a very different way. The marketing effort is now focused on churches attended by people in one or two of these segments. Specifically, she gets her business featured on the backs of the bulletins put out each Sunday by four local churches and sponsors some church events. She subsequently sees a significant increase in revenues and repeat patronage from customers in these segments.

THE COMMODITY TRAP – AND FINDING WAYS TO DIFFERENTIATE

Let's consider another prevalent reason for the poor performance of many of these ventures. Low-income entrepreneurs often fail to build sustainable and profitable businesses because they fall into what we might call "the commodity trap." It starts with having a business that is by and large selling something that is not meaningfully different from what many others in the same market are selling. When customers see no difference among competitors, they buy from whomever has the lowest price or is the most convenient to buy from. They have no loyalties, and effectively see the purchase as a commodity. Firms are forced to compete on price rather than on some other basis. Competing on price is almost always a losing proposition. Margins are squeezed as firms attempt to undercut one another in order to retain or gain customers. Meanwhile, operating costs keep rising, further cutting into margins. The problem is exacerbated when operating in more mature or saturated markets, where there is little to no growth in the size or spending levels of the overall customer base. With smaller margins, the entrepreneur has less to reinvest in the business or take home. Lack of reinvestment means the business only becomes more of a commodity, especially if other firms are trying new and different things.

Consider the kinds of ventures often started by those living in poverty conditions (see also Chapter 4). Painting contractors, child care providers, equipment repair businesses, cleaning services, moving or delivery companies, small restaurants, convenience stores and other small shops, among others, all have one thing in common. They can easily be perceived as commodity businesses by customers, and the entrepreneur is forced to keep prices low no matter what happens to operating costs. Of course, the entrepreneur generally believes their business is different in some way, but this is meaningless if the customer does not see or value the difference.

The goal must be to create meaningful and sustainable differentiation. This means offering something unique that creates real value for enough customers. This can represent a unique challenge for someone who is poor. They first must recognize potential sources of meaningful differentiation, which can require an in-depth understanding of customers, competitors, supplier capabilities, and available technologies. From a more general perspective, new businesses can differentiate themselves from others in many ways, including the quality of their offerings, the kinds of experiences they create for customers, their ability to customize, support after the sale, and value for the money, among others.

A more specific approach to uncovering sources of differentiation can be found in Figure 11.1. This framework, adapted from the work of Levitt (1986), represents a different lens through which to look at the business. It encourages the entrepreneur to look at what they are selling at four levels. The core level involves translating what is being sold into the primary benefit being delivered to customers. An entrepreneur that makes uniforms for local companies is not really selling uniforms, he or she is selling professionalism or image benefits. The tangible level refers to aspects of the basic product or service itself, such as the quality level or the selection available. The augmented level concerns ways in which the basic product or service might be augmented, such as by providing delivery, a warranty, or easy return policy. Last, the communicated level has to do with a unique identity or image the company is trying to convey to customers. A cleaning company might try to project itself as environmentally conscious based on the types of cleaning products and disposal practices it uses, or as a socially concerned business based on employing the disabled or relying on equitable labor practices, or as patriotic based on hiring vets, the colors on its vehicles, and the community events it sponsors.

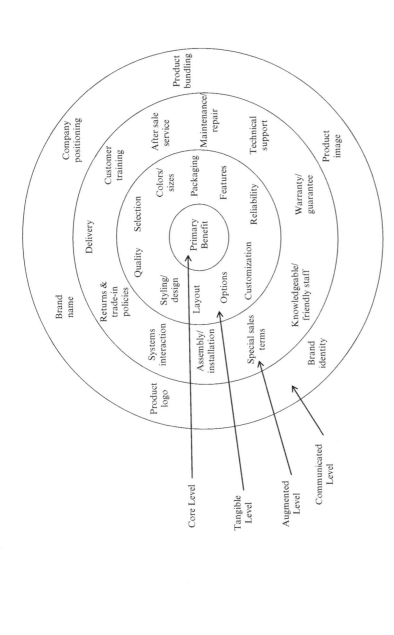

Labels within the figure (from inner to outer):

Primary Benefit

Styling/design, Layout, Options, Customization, Quality, Selection, Colors/sizes, Packaging, Features, Reliability

Assembly/installation, Special sales terms, Knowledgeable/friendly staff, Systems interaction, Returns & trade-in policies, Delivery, Customer training, After sale service, Maintenance/repair, Technical support, Warranty/guarantee, Brand identity

Product logo, Brand name, Company positioning, Product bundling, Product image

Core Level
Tangible Level
Augmented Level
Communicated Level

Source: Adapted from Levitt (1986).

Figure 11.1   A framework for differentiation

Using the framework in Figure 11.1 (and many additional variables can be added at each level depending on the venture in question), the low-income entrepreneur is able to identify variables or combinations of variables that can enable differentiation. This applies to even the most basic of business types. Of particular importance is the need to find sources of difference that are not as easy for competitors to copy given their resource configurations.

Once one or more sources of differentiation are identified, the entrepreneur must build their value offering around this difference. Doing so is not easy for the low-income entrepreneur. Like segmentation and targeting, differentiation requires discipline. The entrepreneur is worried that differentiating in a particular way might alienate other potential customers who are not attracted to this difference. But attracting a number of people who value the source of differentiation will pay off far more than the returns from going after anyone and everyone with a generic approach that is not unlike what various competitors are doing. Further, where customers perceive a difference and it is a difference they value, they are often willing to pay more and demonstrate more loyalty to the business.

Differentiation also requires an investment of time, effort, and money, and has to be continually reinforced in the minds of customers. For someone in poverty, identifying the source of differentiation early on is critical. Once resources are configured in a particularly way, it can be quite costly to change the configuration in ways that create a meaningful difference in terms of how the venture is perceived. This is especially difficult for the entrepreneur caught in the commodity trap, who finds themselves in a continuing downward cycle of lower margins and higher costs. They are unable to find the additional resources and available time needed to break out of this cycle and achieve a sustainable difference in their value propositions and how the firm is perceived.

MISUNDERSTANDING THE ROLE OF PRICE

The discussion above alluded to the fact that those in poverty often start ventures where they seek advantage by offering low prices. One of the biggest errors made by these entrepreneurs is the tendency to underprice. If the venture's only advantage is low price, then it probably has no advantage, as sooner or later someone else will offer an even lower price. In addition, the low price results in low margins, and when combined with low volumes, reinvesting in the business becomes problematic.

A fundamental misunderstanding frequently occurs when it comes to pricing. The assumption is made that prices should be set in a manner that covers costs and produces a margin – such that the key driver of the price is the entrepreneur's costs. Price should not be a statement of costs, but rather, a statement of value. Value is in the mind of the customer. Unfortunately, low-income entrepreneurs will tend to underprice because they undervalue what they are providing to customers.

Howard Schultz, who went from poverty to create the global success story of Starbucks, not only understood the value concept, but made it a core element in the firm's successful strategy. Early on, he priced a cup of coffee at a level more than twice that being charged by many competitors. His price was not driven by his costs, but by the value created through differentiation. And he achieved this differentiation by convincing customers he was not simply selling coffee, but creating a lifestyle experience.

Once prices are set low, or cut, it is hard to raise them. This is one more reason to err on the side of mid-range or higher pricing. With higher prices, it is always possible to temporarily reduce prices to stimulate sales or if circumstances otherwise call for it. The creative entrepreneur looks for ways to do so without permanently cutting price. So the list price remains the same, but what is actually charged is lowered through discounts, coupons, rebates, sales promotions, or special offers.

Low-income entrepreneurs also tend to charge uniform prices to all customers. They can fail to appreciate the idea that customers vary in their price sensitivities and the value they perceive in a given product or service. One only has to consider how an airline may charge different prices to every customer on a given flight, even though it costs no more to fly one customer versus another. The entrepreneur selling lawn and landscaping services may find that simply charging a fixed rate based on the size of the yard or the number of hours involved produces far less revenue than charging different prices to different segments based on their needs and price sensitivities.

A FINAL CONSIDERATION: FEAR OF GROWTH

The strategic approach discussed in this chapter can result in a growing business. However, most new ventures start small and stay small, and this is even more the case for ventures started by those in poverty. Growth is tied to three key factors: (1) the desire for growth; (2) the ability to manage growth; and (3) the upside growth potential of the type of venture one starts. For those in poverty, one might assume the latter two factors play the bigger role. Resource constraints and limited managerial experience can inhibit the entrepreneur's ability to plan, delegate, formalize key aspects of operations, and create the systems and structures needed to enable growth. Further, as we have seen, many of the businesses launched by the poor are commodity ventures, with little differentiation and low margins, and operate in highly competitive markets that are mature or declining. Hence there is little growth potential.

Overcoming these two issues is less relevant, however, if the entrepreneur does not seek growth in the first place. For the poor, once a business is established and appears for the most part to be working, even if only marginally, growth can often be frightening. It implies new risks, where the entrepreneur fears they could lose what they have, while also questioning how much greater the rewards are actually likely to be if they add new products or services, open more locations, and enter new markets. Further, the tough times the low-income entrepreneur goes through, often over an extended period of time, can give rise to a kind of hardened cynicism about the future. This cynicism can reinforce the fears that surround investing in growth.

There is one other factor sometimes at work here. Growth can require a kind of competitive aggressiveness and will to win. Yet, the ethics of competition can be perceived differently by the poor. Harming a competing business, or putting them out of business, means harming a neighbor, often someone else in similar poor circumstances. This reality can lead the entrepreneur to develop a "live and let live" mentality, where growth is only attractive if it does not come at the expense of another low-income entrepreneur.

REFERENCES

Banerjee, A.V. and E. Duflo (2011), *Poor Economics: A Radical Rethinking of the Way to Fight Global Poverty*, New York: Public Affairs Books.

Berkman, E. (2015), "It's not a lack of self-control that keeps people poor," *The Conversation*, September 22, accessed June 14, 2018 at https://theconversation.com/its-not-a-lack-of-self-control-that-keeps-people-poor-47734.

Dupas, P. and J. Robinson (2013), "Why don't the poor save more? Evidence from health savings experiments," *The American Economic Review*, 103(4), 1138–71.

Fairlie, R.W. and A.M. Robb (2007), "Why are black-owned businesses less successful than white-owned businesses? The role of families, inheritances, and business human capital," *Journal of Labor Economics*, 25(2), 289–323.

Levitt, T. (1986), *Marketing Imagination*, New York: Simon and Schuster.

Mani, A., S. Mullainathan, E. Shafir and J. Zhao (2013), "Poverty impedes cognitive function," *Science*, 341(6149), 976–80.

Shah, A.K., S. Mullainathan and E. Shafir (2012), "Some consequences of having too little," *Science*, 338(6107), 682–5.

Statistics Brain Research Institute (2017), "Start-up business failure rate by industry," accessed June 14, 2018 at https://www.statisticbrain.com/start-up-failure-by-industry.

Tirado, L. (2015), *Hand to Mouth: Living in Bootstrap America*, New York: Penguin.

12. Making sense of the economics

> In the United States I saw how the market liberates the individual and allows
> people to be free to make personal choices.
> (Muhammad Yunus)

PROFIT AS A SIGNPOST

The role of profit in a start-up venture is not always well understood by low-income entrepreneurs. People can confuse the profit motive of a business with personal motives for starting a business. As we saw in our discussion in Chapter 3, a number of motives drive people in poverty to start ventures. While some want to make an income or generate wealth, money is not the only driver. There are those who seek independence, want to express themselves through their ventures, are motivated by the challenge, or who want to make a difference in their communities. However, whether driven by money or some other motivator, profit must be a priority if one is to build a sustainable business (Kremer, Rizzuto and Case, 2000). The key is to see profit not as the end, or as the purpose of the venture, but as a means.

Profit is a signpost to guide the entrepreneur along the journey. It is a source of feedback, telling the entrepreneur whether he or she has made the right decisions or needs to make adjustments or corrections. Profit can indicate that the business is focused on the wrong customers, may need to rethink its prices, or is overpaying for rent or labor. It can suggest that the entrepreneur is spending too much time producing and not enough time selling. It can send a signal that the venture is creating real value for customers, and that it is competitive relative to other firms selling the same product or service. Ultimately, without profit, there is no business.

With profit, low-income entrepreneurs can begin to pay themselves. A major issue with many start-ups is the extent to which the business owner extracts all the returns from the business, or reinvests them back into operations and growth. Ongoing personal financial needs and unexpected emergencies experienced by the poor often find that not enough is being reinvested. Profits put into the business are what make it possible for the low-income entrepreneur to hire employees, buy equipment, rent a (bigger) facility, or otherwise expand. Profits allow the entrepreneur to take courses and improve, and invest in the development of employees. As a result, making a real difference in the community is only possible if profits are being realized.

Profit is also not immediate for most start-ups. While not always the case, the bigger the upside potential of the venture, the longer it can take to reach breakeven and see initial profits. One is trying to build a customer base and develop the kind of internal infrastructure that will support growth or the scaling of the business. In high potential ventures, the breakeven point is often not reached until well into year two, three or even later. This creates a distinct problem for the poor. Because they cannot afford to invest in the kinds of equipment, technology and employees that would allow for significant growth, their upfront expenses may be relatively low, as is their overhead. As a result, so long as they do not price their product too low, or pay too much for their cost of goods sold (both of which are common problems for the low-income entrepreneur), then profit could be realized relatively soon. However, what results is a fairly labor-intensive operation that is very difficult to grow (see Chapters 4, 8 and 11 for more discussion on underlying factors explaining why the ventures of the poor do not achieve meaningful growth). Further, as we shall see, whatever profits are realized tend to be small.

In this chapter, we examine the underlying logic of profit in start-up ventures. A simple framework is introduced to capture the entrepreneur's profit model. The model provides an indication of the relative attractiveness of the venture. It helps illustrate why low-income entrepreneurs can struggle to make much money from their ventures, and rarely get rich (e.g., Fairlie and Robb, 2008). The model also serves as a diagnostic tool that the entrepreneur can use to enhance the profit potential of the business.

THE LOGIC OF PROFIT: FOUR KEY VARIABLES

Businesses earn profits in different ways. Even two companies in the same industry may find there are significant differences in the way they are able to make a profit. We will refer to this as the logic of profit – it concerns what has to happen to four key operating variables in order for the company to make money. Many company founders, particularly in the early days of operations, are not consciously aware of their profit model, and this can doom the low-income entrepreneur.

The four variables of interest are margins, volumes, operating leverage (i.e., the cost structure), and revenue capture (Figure 12.1). We start with margins, or the contribution that each product or service makes towards

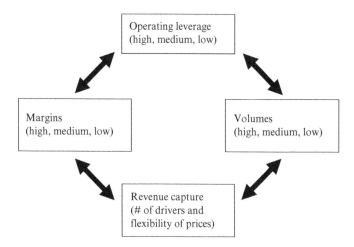

Figure 12.1 The profit model of the entrepreneur

profitability once the direct cost of that service or product has been covered. So margins are the price a customer pays minus the cost to the business of providing that product or service. What affects the margins made on a product or service? Margins can be increased by finding more efficient ways of making or providing the product/service (lowering the unit cost), or by adding value to a product/service so that the entrepreneur can raise the price.

Second, volumes capture the activity levels in the business. Volumes deal with the number transactions the business has over a period of time (e.g., daily, monthly) and the average quantity sold per transaction. A comparison of two types of restaurants will make this clear. A fast food restaurant operates on the premise that it charges low prices for relatively standardized goods produced en masse and will have high volumes or a large number of transactions per day. Conversely, an exotic high-end restaurant will emphasize customized service, a relaxed, luxurious atmosphere, and a talented chef. This high-end restaurant will expect to have much lower volumes than a fast food establishment, but will expect the value of each transaction as reflected in the price (and hence the margins) to be much higher. Expected volumes affect decisions such as staffing needs, equipment purchases, quantities of ingredients and materials to keep in inventory, and space requirements. Once these decisions are made, they limit how much activity the business can handle.

The third variable that determines the firm's profit model is termed operating leverage, or the firm's cost structure. The basic question here is

the extent to which the overall cost structure consists of a higher proportion of fixed costs or of variable costs. Operating leverage is the ratio of
total fixed costs to total variable costs at a given level of volume. A firm
with high fixed costs has high operating leverage, where a firm with costs
that are predominantly variable has low operating leverage. Variable costs
are those that change in direct proportion to the core activity of the firm.
For a factory, the core activity is units produced; for a web-based business, it might be transactions on the website; for a law firm, it might be
billable hours. Examples of variable costs include direct labor hours and
materials used to make a product. Fixed costs are those that remain the
same regardless of activity levels within the firm, such as rent, salaries,
depreciation, and insurance. We can think of them as the firm's overhead.
When starting a venture, having more fixed costs means the entrepreneur
has increased risk. Volumes or margins must be relatively high to offset
high fixed costs. These costs are incurred and have to be paid, regardless
of whether or not sales are being generated. With high fixed costs, it takes
longer to reach breakeven, but once there, the firm makes more profit.
Thus, profits are more volatile when the firm has high operating leverage.
Stated differently, slight changes in revenue lead to much more significant
changes in profitability.

The final question concerns how the firm captures revenue. This includes
how many revenue drivers the firm has, and how flexible the pricing is of
these drivers. Revenue drivers refer to all of the major ways in which the
company makes money, or things it charges for. Consider an automobile
dealership. Money might be generated from car sales, auto leases, repairs,
sales of parts, and warranties. In this instance, the dealer has five revenue
drivers. Revenue drivers include everything that generates revenue, and so
can be thought of as the firm's major product and service lines. Hence, a
restaurant with 150 items on the menu, or a hardware store with thousands
of individual products, organizes these items into a more manageable
set of revenue drivers, such as appetizers versus entrees versus alcoholic
beverages at the restaurant, or hand tools versus lumber versus plumbing
supplies at the hardware store.

Both revenue and profit will likely vary across the different revenue drivers. As a result, the various revenue drivers can play different roles. Some
drivers may be what are called "loss leaders," making little or no profit, but
attracting customers to the business. Some may exist simply to provide a
full line to customers. Others may be critical for how the entrepreneur is
trying to position the firm in the marketplace. One revenue driver may exist
to support sales of other drivers, often because the products are comple-
mentary. For example, our dealership may make relatively little money on
the cars, while earning most of its profits from parts and service. Similarly,

a copier company finds margins are steadily decreasing on their line of copiers as customers begin to view the product as a commodity. However, most of those who buy a copier also buy a service contract, where margins are quite high. So the entrepreneur prices his or her copiers low (perhaps at breakeven), but sells more service contracts as a result, and on balance makes a good profit.

Also important for revenue capture is the flexibility of how these drivers are priced. Pricing can be fixed or flexible. It is fixed when the firm offers its goods at a standard, published price, such as the menu in a restaurant. There is no variation or negotiation. With flexible pricing the entrepreneur is able to modify prices depending on when the product is purchased, who is purchasing it, how much they are purchasing, or what other products they are purchasing (e.g., product bundling). Hence, a restaurant might have a fixed price menu, but when it does catering it negotiates prices. Flexible pricing can give the entrepreneur more creative leeway to capitalize on market opportunities, optimize capacity utilization, and maximize overall revenue. This is why, if a passenger on an airplane flight asked any five of their fellow passengers what price they paid for their ticket, it is likely they will get five different figures.

CONNECTING THE DOTS

The profit model concerns how these four variables, when combined, affect the firm's ability to make money. The interactions among the variables are illustrated in Figure 12.2. The beginning point is the relationship between margins and volumes. Consider a business that sells furniture but has

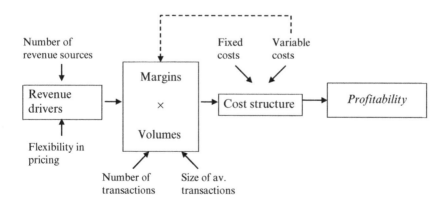

Figure 12.2   Connecting the components of profit

either high (over 100 percent), medium (40–60 percent), or low (10–15 percent or less) margins. Assume the same business has either high (sells 50 pieces of furniture a day, on average), medium (sells 20 pieces of furniture a day), or low (sells four pieces of furniture a day) volumes. A global chain like IKEA makes money with high volumes and medium margins, while a local specialty retailer selling high-end furniture is succeeding based on low volumes but high margins. If the entrepreneur has a high-volume but low-margin business, a decent profit might be earned. The same would be the case for a low-volume but high-margin business. Things look even better with high margins or volumes combined with medium volumes or margins. While it rarely happens, the company that can achieve both high volumes and high margins is going to make huge profits. Apple computers and the iPhone would be an example. The problem with many low-income entrepreneurs, as we shall see, is that they are running ventures with low volumes and margins, which is not sustainable.

Next we factor in the cost structure of the venture. If the business has a lot of fixed costs, again either the margins or the volumes need to be relatively high, and the other should be at least medium. The goal is to spread the fixed costs over as many transactions as possible. A company like Tesla that makes electric cars, which has very high fixed expenses (e.g., salaries, a manufacturing plant, dealerships, and marketing) has relatively high prices, but struggles to turn a profit because it costs a lot to make each car (high variable costs), which means margins are reduced (let's assume they are medium), while volumes are relatively low (Wolters, 2017).

Finally, we factor in the way the firm captures revenue. A business that is experiencing a profit problem in terms of its combination of margins, volumes, and fixed costs is in even worse shape if it only has a single revenue driver. The entrepreneur may be able to improve the picture by adding revenue drivers, or moving to negotiated or flexible prices. Consider a person who owns a small sandwich business located just across the street from a major university. Fixed costs are relative high especially due to rent (based on the desirable location), a manager's salary, insurance and marketing costs. Margins are low as prices are kept down by fairly intense competition. Having a good location is producing decent volumes, but these volumes fall off dramatically during the summer and the Christmas holiday period, when students are gone. This combination has the business barely making any profit. Turning this situation around might involve the addition of a new revenue driver. Perhaps a catering service is added, which serves to offset seasonal fluctuations in sales volume, while also offering higher margins.

THE PROFIT CHALLENGE WITH VENTURES OF THE POOR

The first challenge with low-income entrepreneurs is knowing whether they are actually earning a profit. Poor financial literacy (see Chapter 6) and/or lack of discipline in properly recording revenue as it is received and expenses as they are incurred can lead to uncertainty regarding profit performance. Not having a precise sense of the unit cost of an item, or how much has to be charged to cover the overhead of the business, finds many entrepreneurs charging prices that are below costs for some of their items. It is also important to be able to break profits down by product, customer type, and sales channel. For instance, not knowing which products generate higher profits, or whether more money is made from online versus retail store sales, results in the low-income entrepreneur allocating too much time and money on the wrong things.

While this knowledge is vital, it is just as critical to understand the logic of how the firm makes its money. For the low-income entrepreneur, the profit model serves as a critical indicator of the relative attractiveness of the venture. A model with low volumes, low margins, high operating leverage, and a single revenue driver at a fixed price is going to lose money. A much more attractive economic model would be one where margins are high, volumes are medium to high, operating leverage is medium, and the firm has multiple revenue drivers with considerable price flexibility. As we shall see, the profit model framework can serve as a type of diagnostic tool, where entrepreneurs can identify ways to improve the economic attractiveness of the venture.

We can also see how the profit model helps explain the struggles of many low-income entrepreneurs (see also the discussion of the "commodity trap" in Chapter 11). These ventures tend to experience low margins. Frequently, both prices and unit costs are the culprits. Consider some possible reasons why an entrepreneur who is poor would keep their prices low:

- They think it is only fair to charge an affordable price.
- It is what they and their neighbors can afford.
- They are more worried about covering costs than earning margins.
- They face intense competition.
- They underestimate what the product or service is really worth.
- They assume a low price is their only potential source of advantage.

While the low price will push the margins down, so too will high unit costs. Here, the problem is traceable to three considerations. First, as discussed in Chapters 6 and 7, low-income entrepreneurs tend to create labor-intensive ventures and do not (or are unable to) incorporate technology and advanced equipment into their operating processes. Second, their ventures often produce low volumes, keeping their cost per unit relatively high. Third, they are unable to purchase raw materials, ingredients, or inventory at wholesale prices or in the kinds of quantities that would qualify them for sizable discounts.

Low volumes are attributable to a number of causes, including lack of production capacity within the business, intense competition in the local market, trying to operate in a relatively mature market, and a lack of large buyers. A case in point would be the low-income entrepreneur who establishes a hair salon. It is a labor-intensive business with capacity limited by the number of chairs and the operating hours. The business is trying to earn profits in a fairly saturated market experiencing low growth in overall sales, and the sales volume has to be shared by a large number of competitive players. The entrepreneur might assume that low prices would attract more customers, but this is rarely the case for the ventures of the poor.

Operating leverage tends not to be as much of a problem, as the poor simply cannot afford to pay high rents or salaries, spend a lot on marketing, or buy a lot of equipment. These ventures will be quite lean when it comes to overhead. Of course, not spending money here contributes to low volumes and high unit costs, so it can be a kind of Catch-22. Even here, though, the low-income entrepreneur can find they spend more for a piece of equipment or on other fixed costs because of their low bargaining power, lack of credit history, and with such expenses as insurance, because of the neighborhoods where they operate.

Limitations to revenue capture also affects poverty entrepreneurs. Resource constraints (money, space, time, knowledge) can limit the mix of products and services sold by their ventures. Adding a product can require more investment in inventory and marketing. In our example above involving the restaurant, even adding something like catering can be difficult, as it may require a delivery vehicle, equipment to keep food warm or cold, and more insurance. The skill set to manage a catering business may differ significantly from the entrepreneur's current capabilities. The marketing requirements are also likely to differ. Finally, introducing the new products or services can take a lot of the entrepreneur's time, such that existing parts of the business begin to suffer.

CREATING MORE PROFITABLE AND GROWING VENTURES

The ability of the poor to develop high-earning ventures that have real growth potential can be facilitated in a number of ways. One must apply creativity, imagination, financial insight, resource leveraging and boot-strapping, use of low-cost technologies, and strategic focus when assessing the profit model. Box 12.1 identifies examples of critical questions to guide an entrepreneur's efforts.

Using the profit model as a diagnostic tool, let's examine how the variables might be approached differently by the low-income entrepreneur in order to create a more viable business:

Margins

Increasing margins must be a top priority of the entrepreneur, important in its own right, but in many cases easier to achieve than manipulations of the other three variables. From a pricing vantage point, low-income entrepreneurs need to be willing to price more on the basis of how much value they are providing to different types of customers than based on their estimated unit costs. They must go beyond just focusing on the customers that are most price sensitive (often the people in their neighbor-hoods), or assuming all customers are equally price sensitive. Further, the ability to charge more is tied to differentiation, and examples of sources of differentiation were elaborated upon in Chapter 11. Creative pricing can also improve the picture. Examples include:

- a low base price and selling add-ons at a high margin;
- pricing differently at low or high peak times;
- unlimited use of product or service for a flat fee;
- base price and then variable charges once a threshold is reached;
- different prices for different market segments;
- loyalty schemes for past or heavy users;
- price differences for users who can only buy/use at certain periods;
- prices tied to customer characteristics, such as size of their family, house or car;
- bundled pricing for multiple items;
- cash and quantity discounts;
- trade-in/trade-up schemes.

Margins will differ across the different products or services being sold by the business. Unfortunately, many low-income entrepreneurs do not have a precise knowledge of the margins on each item. This shortcoming can be due to everything from lack of financial literacy or poor book-keeping practices to inconsistencies in pricing and the ways in which the entrepreneur buys materials or inventory. By recognizing these differences, the entrepreneur can utilize tactics that encourage customers to buy the

BOX 12.1   KEY QUESTIONS SURROUNDING THE PROFIT MODEL

As the low-income entrepreneur tries to arrive at a profit model that will sustain the business, he or she should be experimenting with each of the four variables that constitute the model. Here are examples of key questions to be continually addressed:

Margins
Are my margins relatively low (e.g., a grocery store) or high (e.g., a jewelry store)?
Does my business add significant value to the products or services, enhancing the brand?
Might I be able to make higher margins by selling to different kinds of customers?
Could I offer customized services that would allow me to charge significantly higher prices?
Are there ways to cut unit costs by buying in larger quantities, purchasing from lower-cost suppliers, using more equipment, or incorporating technology into my business processes?

Volumes
Do I have significant capacity constraints?
Am I a relatively high-, medium- or low-volume business?
Do I offer highly customized services, which decreases the volumes I can process, or are my goods and services very standardized, allowing me to increase my business's volumes?
How saturated is the overall market?
What quantity of items am I selling relative to the competition over a specific time period?
What is the average value of a transaction in my business and how does that fare against competition? Are there ways to get people to spend more per visit?

Operating leverage
What proportion of my costs are fixed versus variable?
Are there any key fixed costs I can reduce, such as by operating from home, in a smaller facility, or in a borrowed space?
Can I eliminate salaries and just pay people on an hourly basis?
Could I do more to outsource parts of my business so as to convert certain fixed costs into variable costs?

Revenue capture
Do I have a wide variety of revenue drivers or only a few?
Are there other creative ways to capture revenue?
Can I make some of my prices negotiable or subject to a quote?
How often do I change my prices? Is it frequently (hourly, daily, weekly, or biweekly)? Moderately frequently (monthly, bimonthly)? Or rarely (semiannually, annually or longer)?
Might I use product or service bundling, different prices for different market segments, pricing based on customer loyalty, or other creative tactics?

items with higher margins (e.g., by offering deals on things with smaller margins to incentivize the customer to buy the more profitable items, or upselling them with persuasive selling approaches). If the business employs salespeople, commissions might be bigger on the higher compared to the lower margin products or services.

The other side of the equation is finding ways to reduce the variable costs of the goods being sold. The possibilities here are tied to (1) finding ways to produce the product or service in a less labor-intensive manner by using more efficient labor practices, incorporating more or better equipment, or automating tasks (using technology); and (2) reducing costs of materials or goods purchased. The low-income entrepreneur must bring a philosophy of efficiency to every aspect of what they are doing – developing an intimate feel for the flow of how every task is done and how each task contributes to a well-run operation. As outlined in Box 12.2, there are a number of areas that can be focused upon that can significantly bring down costs, from breaking down and systematizing tasks and establishing standard procedures to eliminating clutter and having the right things in the right places. Although buying industrial-grade equipment may be too expensive in the early days of the business, a leveraging strategy (see Chapter 10) can be employed to borrow, share, barter to obtain, or rent the equipment and possibly the technologies belonging to other parties. With procurement, economies can come from negotiating more proactively, shopping around, purchasing in larger lot sizes, buying in tandem with other small businesses, or (if a retailer or wholesaler) buying on consignment.

Volumes

The ability to increase the volume of sales or transactions in the business requires creativity both in defining target markets and in expanding capacity. The core market being served is often too small or being served by too many other firms. The low-income entrepreneur must look for additional niches where, with a little value-added, new sales can be accomplished. For instance, an entrepreneur opens a paintball facility where customers compete on teams to defeat other teams by shooting them with dye-filled gelatin capsules. The target market is teenagers, but this limits volume on the days when school is in session. The entrepreneur recognizes that companies might utilize the facility on school days as an employee team-building exercise, and adapts operations and marketing approaches to attract them. Another entrepreneur has a cake-making business that concentrates on specialty cakes for weddings and formal events. She starts looking for additional niches, and finds sales can be considerably

BOX 12.2   APPROACHES TO LABOR EFFICIENCIES IN LOW-INCOME VENTURES

To make production as efficient as possible while ensuring consistent quality levels, below are sets of steps the entrepreneur can adopt. They reflect an operating philosophy or way of approaching the business on an ongoing basis.

Survey and study (break down the steps involved in producing)
Identify each step in the process of making the product or delivering the service and map out the steps.
Examine the time involved in each step.
Determine if any steps can be eliminated.
Identify ways in which sets of steps might be combined or done in tandem to shorten time required or increase quality and consistency.
Find creative ways to address bottleneck points in the process, where things get backed up.

Sort (determining what is needed and not needed to run the business)
Systematically organize activities beginning with one area of the business and then progressing through the entire operation.
Go through all table/counter tops, drawers, shelves, and storage areas and determine if every item is absolutely essential for operating the business. Dispose of everything not essential.

Systematize (organizing everything, where everything has its place)
Give everything a permanent place.
Label storage areas so that all people in the business can quickly find items as needed.
Clear walkways and floors of clutter for safety and efficiency.
Set up workspaces to be efficient. Place everything needed for a specific task near that workspace.
Designate separate, out-of-the-way areas for personal items. Anything that is going to come in and out of the space should have a designated area.

Keep shipshape (keep things clean and tidy)
Clean the workspaces regularly. Doing this as things are set in order can add efficiencies.

Standardize (set up standard processes)
Create standard operating procedures for key processes.
Make regular maintenance everyone's job.
Implement daily tasks list (cleaning, stocking, etc.) that are checked off.

Sustain (maintain processes and organizing approaches)
Have a procedure to ensure everything is reset and restocked at the end of each day.
Document processes and procedures so employees can adhere to them.
Audit all processes and procedures regularly (monthly, quarterly, annually).

Source: Adapted and modified from Tolino (2015).

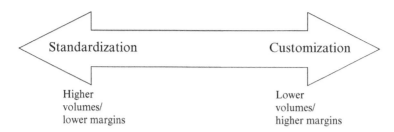

Figure 12.3   Margins, volume and customization

augmented by specializing in church socials, and a monthly program addressing employee birthdays at companies.

Many other approaches can be employed. We might find the entrepreneur attempting to get existing customers to spend more each time they purchase from the entrepreneur (e.g., by bundling items at a combined discounted price, or upselling customers to a better version of a product). Tactics might be used where the goal is to incentivize customers to shop more often (e.g., with loyalty or points programs). Another technique involves customer referral programs, which can take many different forms.

A major issue affecting volumes is the extent to which the entrepreneur is customizing their offering to individual clients. Customization requires time and money and so significantly limits capacity. Anxious to attract and please customers, some business owners will add customized features or provide tailored services such as personal delivery without charging for these things (and when charging a low price to begin with). Figure 12.3 illustrates the basic relationship between degrees of customization and the margin–volume relationship. It is a relationship that low-income entrepreneurs can find themselves on the wrong side of.

Capacity can also be expanded by augmenting one's facilities and equipment. Again, leveraging comes into play, where the entrepreneur seeks to share the facilities or equipment of others. Using another company's machines during down time, sharing space in someone's warehouse, borrowing a truck after hours, or outsourcing parts of the work can enable the entrepreneur to produce more without making big investments.

Operating Leverage (Cost Structure)

Reducing fixed costs can be the most difficult variable to address in the profit model. Most low-income entrepreneurs are operating on a very lean basis to begin with, and simply cannot afford to spend a lot on rent, the purchase of capital equipment, salaries, or marketing. So, there is not much to cut. Again, however, using the assets of others (e.g. facilities, vehicles, equipment, staff) and outsourcing can serve as methods for reducing fixed costs. Similarly, clever guerrilla tactics can bring down marketing costs (see Chapter 10). Taking advantage of the increasing availability of low-cost technology (see Chapter 7) is yet another way to avoid or lessen overhead costs.

Revenue Drivers

Finally, the low-income entrepreneur is continually looking for different ways to capture revenue, both in terms of how the customer is charged, and the different products and services being provided. Making a premium version of one's service available, charging a subscription rate rather than pay-as-you-go, offering an extended warranty, or adding a product that complements or augments the entrepreneur's basic product are a few examples. As adding products or services can be expensive and entails risk, the entrepreneur must have a clear strategy in terms of how these items relate to what is currently being sold, and/or how they will attract customers not currently being served.

In closing, the reality is that the poor need not start marginal businesses that have unattractive profit models and do not grow. The key is continual experimentation with the profit model framework presented here. With insight, ongoing learning, imagination, engagement in different resource-leveraging approaches, clever use of new technologies, and a guerilla mindset, the low-income entrepreneur can produce much more and achieve greater efficiencies, while realizing larger returns on their efforts.

REFERENCES

Fairlie, R.W. and A.M. Robb (2008), *Race and Entrepreneurial Success: Black-, Asian-, and White-owned Businesses in the United States*, Cambridge, MA: MIT Press.

Kremer, C., R. Rizzuto and J. Case (2000), *Managing by the Numbers: A Commonsense Guide to Understanding and Using Your Company's Financials*, New York: Basic Books.

Tolino, L. (2015), "How to set up your business now to save time later," *To BusinessOwners.com*, February 26.

Wolters, V. (2017), "Tesla: A closer look at margins and profitability," *SeekingAlpha. com*, May 23, accessed June 15, 2018 at https://seekingalpha.com/article/4075701-tesla-closer-look-margins-profitability.

13. Policies and programs to support low-income entrepreneurship

> I believe that we can create a poverty-free world because poverty is not created by poor people. It has been created and sustained by the economic and social systems that we have designed for ourselves; the institutions and concepts that make up that system; the policies that we pursue.
>
> (Muhammad Yunus)

PROACTIVELY FOSTERING ENTREPRENEURSHIP

Entrepreneurship may not be the proverbial magic bullet for ending poverty, but its potential to make a dramatic difference has been significantly underestimated by public policy-makers, economic development professionals, educators and others. It is a path that can bring millions of people out of poverty, while improving the lives of millions more. It represents the ultimate source of economic empowerment, as the individual is creating their own future, their own job, their own wealth and their own ability to give back. And when there is more entrepreneurial activity, communities improve.

If we consider the endemic nature of poverty and its many complexities, and then factor in the many obstacles to entrepreneurship described in these chapters – it is amazing that the poor start as many successful ventures as they do. The question becomes, what might be possible if the poor had more help? The issue here is not to give the poor some sort of advantage as entrepreneurs, but to move in the direction of leveling the playing field. It is unlikely the field could ever be completely level, as the poor will always have a struggle that is greater than those with higher income, better education, more extensive networks, fewer health problems, safer surroundings, and more exposure to entrepreneurial ventures, mentors and role models.

Public policy and more institutional support at the local level can make a difference in this regard. Efforts to date have largely been piecemeal and disjointed. They often fail to reflect the context of the person in poverty, or the particular challenges faced by the types of ventures the poor tend to create. Most importantly, they fail to address the changing needs of the entrepreneur depending on the stage of development of a venture. What is required then, is a holistic approach that centers on the entrepreneurial journey as experienced by poor people.

In this chapter, we examine policy recommendations and related initiatives that can foster entrepreneurship among the poor. Ongoing gaps in policies to support low-income entrepreneurs are identified. Attention is devoted to describing the elements of a more holistic policy framework. The SPODER model for facilitating low-income entrepreneurship introduced in Chapter 3 is revisited from a policy perspective.

THE OVERALL POLICY GAP

Addressing poverty has always been a challenging issue for policy-makers. As reflected in Franklin D. Roosevelt's New Deal in the 1930s and the Johnson administration's declaration of an "unconditional war on poverty" in 1964, modern-day governments around the world have made the reduction of poverty a major policy goal. In Europe, poverty alleviation has been a policy priority since the Treaty of Rome in 1957. In 2000, as part of the Lisbon Agenda, the European Council adopted poverty eradication as a primary goal together with economic growth and social cohesion. More recently, the European Commission (2010) established the European Platform against Poverty and Social Exclusion (EPAP) as a broad umbrella, covering a wide range of policies, designed to help reach the target of bringing at least 20 million people out of poverty and social exclusion by 2020. In spite of this visible attention, and many billions of dollars in spending for a wide variety of poverty alleviation initiatives (see Chapter 1), poverty rates in the United States remain pretty much the same today as over 50 years ago (Varghese, 2016). In the European Union, 23.5 percent of the population were at risk of poverty or social exclusion in 2016, a number that has only slightly declined in recent years (Eurostat Newsrelease, 2017). Australia reports a poverty rate of 12 percent, which has held pretty constant for well over a decade (Australian Council of Social Service, 2016), while Japan's rate is 16 percent and has been on the rise (*The Economist*, 2015), and Canada has seen a 20-year decline to a rate of about 5 percent (Lammam and MacIntyre, 2016).

Support for various policies to reduce poverty has been mixed. Proponents suggest these programs are a lifeline for millions of people and are instrumental in helping many of them find a way out, especially those not in extreme or deep poverty. Opponents argue that these programs create welfare dependency, bloated administrative structures, and a misalignment of incentives to find employment and create wealth. Others suggest that the programs are simply ineffective. In a critical study, Ben-Shalom, Moffitt and Scholz (2011) provide evidence that the poverty rate would actually be worse in the US without these programs, while any negative side-effects are marginal in impact. Further, in noting the paternalistic nature of government poverty programs, they find more priority has been given in recent years to the disabled, elderly, and the higher-income range of those in poverty, and produced better results with these groups – perhaps at the cost of those in deep poverty.

What both camps can agree upon is that new and existing policies need to be better aligned with existing poverty conditions, as described in Chapter 3. When it comes to poverty reduction, questions can be raised regarding how strategic the efforts of governments are. While there are programs covering a wide range of basic needs (e.g., housing, food for children, job training, energy) in all developed countries, these efforts would not appear to reflect a well-coordinated, well-integrated, or well-targeted approach, and seem to be more of a hodgepodge of efforts to fill glaring holes. Further, the extent to which programs help people to survive in poverty versus enable them to actually move out of poverty can be debated. In addition, significant time can be required of the poor to learn about, understand, apply for, and qualify for specific benefits, and meet the administrative requirements of different support programs.

As a generalization, governments (at all levels) have no strategy for poverty and entrepreneurship. Rather, a handful of initiatives have been launched at different levels of government. For instance, there is some (passive) recognition of entrepreneurship as a career path. Hence, we see that money historically allocated by governments for job training programs may now be used by training agencies to also help people with basic courses on how to start their own businesses. There are initiatives such as the US Small Business Administration's HUBZone program that helps small businesses in disadvantaged communities get preferential access to federal procurement opportunities, with similar efforts at local government levels. And, as we saw in Chapter 9, there is a growing microcredit movement at local levels in most developed countries, with regional and local governments sometimes providing funds to these loan programs. Further, these microcredit programs increasingly include training in financial literacy and other business basics. Other efforts tend to be more anecdotal. For example, the low-income housing authority in Gainesville, Florida provides residents with a three-track individual development program where a person in poverty can opt for further education, job training, or help in starting their own business. Residents are paid to participate, and they also provide services (cleaning, lawn care) to the housing units. Some ventures have been started around the provision of such services.

If entrepreneurship is to play a bigger role as a pathway out of poverty, it is vital that a more strategic, integrated, and holistic approach be adopted. This approach must be rooted in a much richer understanding of both poverty and the nature of the entrepreneurial journey. Before introducing such an approach, let us consider the kinds of policy tools and programs that can play contributing roles.

PRINCIPAL POLICY LEVERS

Policy development is a complex process that includes a large set of actors such as politicians, lobbyists, domain experts, non-profit organizations, and various interest groups that use a variety of tactics and tools to advance their goals. In the US, policy-makers have several levers they can utilize to effect social and economic outcomes. Let us consider eight of these levers.

Taxation policies provide tax deductions, credits, preferential rates, deferrals, or exclusion of income from taxation. Effective tax rates for the poor in the US and Europe are much lower than for all households. For example, according to recent estimates, low-income households (lowest income quintile) in the US will pay approximately 3.7 percent of their incomes in federal taxes, compared with an average tax rate of 20.1 percent for all households (Congressional Budget Office, 2016). The largest tax burden for the poor comes from paying taxes for goods and services through sales (or value-added) and excise taxes. The poor also receive tax credits. A prominent example is the Earned Income Tax Credit (EITC), which is considered the largest anti-poverty program in the US. The EITC aims at reducing a family's tax liability based on their earnings. Families with one or more children are the main beneficiaries (Lang, 2011). The EITC relies on potential beneficiaries filing their taxes, which can be onerous, especially for the poor. Recent studies showed that less than 50 percent of the eligible EITC beneficiaries claimed the credit (Caputo, 2010). Second, the beneficiaries, usually families with children, receive the credit as a one-time lump-sum payment at the end of the year, thus it is not a favorable safety net mechanism for families that need a more regular inflow of financial resources to manage day-to-day needs. When it comes to entrepreneurship, tax incentives can also be used to encourage people to start particular types of businesses, locate businesses in defined areas, develop innovations and technology, invest in capital equipment, hire employees, improve facilities, and remain in a given locale. The Earned Income Tax Credit is also available for income received through self-employment, which provides poverty entrepreneurs with an opportunity to earn tax credits on their entrepreneurial activities. Another tool is the saver's tax credit, an incentive to help low-income microbusiness owners save for retirement.

Just as relevant is the availability of tax incentives for people and organizations that put money into microlending programs, or invest money, equipment or other resources into the ventures of the poor. As a case in point, the New Markets Tax Credit (NMTC) provides individual and corporate investors with a tax credit for making equity investments in Community Development Entities (CDEs) that can then use the funds to invest in facilities and local businesses led by poverty entrepreneurs. Results from the NMTC Program show that, since 2003, approximately 275 000 jobs were created or retained, 37 million square feet of manufacturing space, 80 million square feet of office space and 61 million square feet of retail space were generated, and the disadvantaged communities became more attractive to investors, creating a ripple effect in terms of further investments (NMTC, 2017).

Our second lever is income subsidy programs. The government provides direct payments to the poor to augment their income. Traditional welfare programs that provide monthly income supplements, such as the Temporary Assistance for Needy Families (TANF) program in the US, would be an example. Technically a block grant to individual states, TANF provides cash assistance for up to 60 months (maximum lifetime benefits), with the explicit goal of incentivizing beneficiaries to find employment. Individual states have a broad mandate and significant latitude in how to distribute the TANF benefits (Coven, 2005). A successful variation of this type of program designed to impact entrepreneurial activity can be found in Germany. The Bridging Allowance was launched as an income-subsidy policy for the unemployed in the mid-1980s with the intention of fostering nascent entrepreneurship. This became the foundation of the Start-up Subsidy program that was active from 2006 to 2011, and its successor, the New Start-Up Subsidy, running from 2012 to the present. The main goal of the program was to provide unemployed people with a monthly subsidy as they made progress with launching a business. The businesses that were subsequently created by the unemployed demonstrated promising survival rates, with 70 percent of male participants in Eastern Germany and 68 percent of those in Western Germany still in business five years after leaving the program. Between 30 percent and 40 percent of business founders created additional jobs beyond their own (OECD/European Union, 2014). There were persistent positive long-run effects of both the Start-Up Subsidy and Bridging Allowance programs, particularly for individuals at high risk of being excluded from the labor market and joining the ranks of the long-term unemployed (Caliendo and Künn, 2011).

A third lever, loan guarantees, represents yet another policy tool. Here, the loan itself is usually made by a commercial bank or other financial institution, but the government is guaranteeing some proportion of the loan (sometimes 75 percent or more) in the instance that the borrower defaults. This enables the lending institution to loan money to those who otherwise might not qualify, and or to provide loans at more attractive interest rates. Key uses of guarantees would include government programs to support the purchase of a home or the development of a business. With regard to the latter, the COSME Program in Europe and the SBA Loan Program in the United States (see Chapter 9) are examples of initiatives that have enabled the development of hundreds of thousands of small businesses over the years. Some programs, such as the 8(a) Business Development Program of the US Small Business Administration, directly serve disadvantaged small business owners with a range of support, including financial assistance, mentoring, business counseling, and collective bidding for government contracts.

In the US, capital access programs (CAPs) are another option in the policy portfolio. CAPs are historically run by the individual states, but are supported by the federal government's State Small Business Credit Initiative (SSBCI). Under these programs, operated by about 27 states, borrowers (small businesses) and lenders (banks) contribute a percentage of the loan or credit (between 2 and 7 percent) into a reserve fund that insures the loan in case of a default. Since 1986, state CAPs have enabled more than $1.5 billion in small business loans to be made at low cost and low risk, benefiting significant numbers of minority entrepreneurs (Barr, 2008). CAPs were built to supply early-stage ventures that do not possess collateral or other resources which are typically needed to receive a conventional loan from a community or private bank. Despite the attractiveness of these loans, borrowers are often unwilling to pay the initial CAP fee, while lenders are reluctant to participate because they need to enroll a large number of loans to build a sufficient loan loss reserve fund.

In a related vein, several European Union countries have introduced policies to support subsidized loan schemes. Italy and France have developed "Honour Loans" (i.e., conceded based on the borrower's word of honor, without requiring collateral or other forms of guarantee), as a combination of grants and interest-free loans, providing loans to several generations of young and female entrepreneurs as a tool to fight against unemployment (OECD/European Union, 2014). The Honour Loan program contributes to formalize hidden economic activities and involves local authorities in incentive schemes to combat unemployment. Moreover, there is a commitment that businesses supported by this program remain located in the disadvantaged part of the community for at least five years after receiving program support (Peer Review Programme for Active Labour Market Policy, 1999).

As government agencies at all levels spend billions each year on purchases of products and services, a high-impact tool involves buying directly from small businesses. With this lever, the government might mandate that a certain percentage of spending must go to small or earlier-stage businesses. So-called set-asides enable small firms to get contracts without competing with larger companies. Preferential procurement gives priority in vendor selection to firms that meet certain criteria, such as being minority owned, woman owned, based in particular areas (e.g., inner city, rural locations), or under a defined size in terms of sales or employees.

Another policy lever available to combat poverty involves voucher programs. Vouchers are subsidies that consumers use to pay for goods or services. Governments at various levels have implemented voucher programs that target child care, food, housing, education, and medical assistance programs (see Steuerle and Twombly, 2002). Vouchers can either be explicit or implicit. They are implicit when beneficiaries use them to access services like housing or school enrollment, without the need to provide a formal voucher document, with essentially the user being the voucher. Vouchers are explicit when the beneficiary provides a formal document such as a food stamp to acquire the good/service. Vouchers shift the provision of public services from the hands of governmental agencies to consumers and private providers, albeit with some restrictions or caps (Colin, 2005). Prominent examples of voucher programs for the poor are the Supplemental Nutrition Assistance Program (SNAP) and the Housing Choice Voucher (HCV) Program. SNAP provides low-income beneficiaries who earn no more than 130 percent of the federal poverty level with financial support for food purchases and is administered through an electronic benefits transfer (EBT) system. The Housing Choice Voucher assists low-income families, the elderly, and the disabled in finding housing in the private market. If we consider venture creation, vouchers could be used to pay for assistance with registering a business, bookkeeping, development of logos and marketing materials, creation of websites, writing a business plan, attending training courses, and paying rent in an incubator, among other business services.

A sixth policy option is to provide grants for particular projects or initiatives (Beam and Conlan, 2002). Grants are effectively free money, although they often come with conditions. They can be made directly to the beneficiary, or to intermediate (public, private or non-profit) agencies who then administer smaller grants to beneficiaries, thereby allowing for more flexibility and tailoring of allocations to reflect local circumstances and needs (ibid.). With regard to entrepreneurship, grants are used to help entrepreneurs develop products or services that address particular problems or needs of the government. They can play a role in seeding microcredit funds administered by local non-profits and other organizations. They can also be designed to support particular actions or behaviors by entrepreneurs, such as retrofitting or upgrading a facility to be used for business purposes, locating in a particular area, investing in technology, or hiring an employee (see also Chapter 9).

Our seventh policy lever is regulatory relief. Early-stage businesses are disproportionately affected by virtually any law or regulation. The costs of compliance are a higher portion of their available resources; it can require a disproportionate amount of their scarce time to understand and then figure out how to comply with a given regulation, and they cannot afford to hire lawyers and other professionals to get them waivers or otherwise find ways around regulations. Beyond making regulations easier to understand and comply with, or hiring government staff to assist small businesses with compliance, regulations can be designed in ways that exempt businesses that are less than three years old, have fewer than five employees, or whose revenues do not exceed $100 000. Similarly, where fees must be paid for a license, permit, variance, or government exemption, these can be waived for those in poverty.

Regulatory relief can also be directed at organizations that form parts of the entrepreneurial ecosystem. Especially important in this regard is the regulation of financing vehicles. Making it easier to create and administer microcredit, peer-to-peer lending, and community-based group lending initiatives could open up large pools of capital to low-income entrepreneurs.

A final lever involves the creation and financial support of government-affiliated or government-run agencies and organizations that directly assist the poor in particular areas. Public health clinics, homeless shelters, community food banks, and housing assistance agencies would be examples. For low-income entrepreneurs, small business development centers, women's business centers, and organizations like the Service Corps of Retired Executives (SCORE) provide free advice and access to other resources. In addition, workforce programs can promote connections between the poor and career opportunities that include self-employment. Here then, existing workforce development programs designed for the unemployed and underemployed can be modified to include delivery of entrepreneurship training and development services. Many other possibilities exist, such as using the postal service as a means of providing low-cost credit to the poor, or using government office space for community incubators (Baradaran, 2016).

OTHER TYPES OF SUPPORT: THE ROLE OF COMMUNITIES

Addressing poverty in a meaningful way is not possible without other players beyond the government. Non-profit organizations (including churches), private companies, financial institutions, and universities work independently and collaboratively with one another and the government on various dimensions of poverty. As we have seen with examples throughout this book, this type of support takes many forms, with particular initiatives created to serve the poor in a particular region or area. Many of these are based on grants from the government, private foundations, or wealthy individuals. Below are some general examples:

- Local functional literacy programs for youth and adults, such as those offered through public libraries, community centers, churches and organizations such as Big Brothers/Big Sisters, the Boys & Girls Clubs, and various other non-profits.
- Financial literacy initiatives launched by schools, banks, financial service firms (e.g., MoneyWi$e offered by Capital One and Consumer Action), and professional associations, and supported by groups like the National Financial Educators Council.
- Entrepreneurship classes offered in middle and high schools attended by the poor, such as those facilitated by the Network for Teaching Entrepreneurship (NFTE).
- Community-oriented training and development programs that focus on entrepreneurship and basic business topics, such as those offered by local workforce development and jobs training agencies, chambers of commerce, and colleges/universities.
- Microcredit schemes and small grants for entrepreneurs offered through community development financial institutions, community banks, credit unions, and other organizations, as well as community-based self-financing groups.
- Availability of alternative debt finance such as overdrafts, factoring, leasing and trade credit, from banks. As poor entrepreneurs face different challenges in accessing bank loans, alternative debt finance is important.
- Supportive physical spaces for low-income entrepreneurs, such as La Cocina food incubator in California, the South Side Innovation Center in Syracuse, New York, the Promálaga retail incubator in Spain, and FabLab Lisboa in Portugal.
- Mentoring and advice from business professionals and small business assistance centers, including online resources such as

Meetup.com, Small-Business-Forum.net, and informative small business blogs.

- Company procurement programs that commit to make a percentage of product and service purchases from small and early-stage businesses, and associated mentor–protégé initiatives to help small businesses learn how to get and retain business from larger companies.
- Internship programs in local small businesses and new start-ups that emphasize assisting minorities, the poor, and other disadvantaged individuals.
- In-kind services and free products provided to low-income entrepreneurs by existing businesses (e.g., law firms, advertising agencies, printing services, accounting firms, website and app developers).
- Free or very low-cost broadband access subsidized by local utilities and other community partners.
- Access to free or very low-cost online products and services, such as the Wave, PostBooks, and GnuCash accounting software packages, logo design services from FreeLogoDesign.org or Tailor Brands, or social media services from providers like Hootsuite and Buffer.
- Broader access to the sharing or collaborative economy, where the entrepreneur, typically through online platforms, is able to take advantage of resource gifting, sharing, renting, selling, and other forms of collaboration.

This is but a partial listing of the kinds of elements that must come together with the earlier-mentioned policy levers if the poor are to be systematically assisted in recognizing, developing, and capitalizing upon their entrepreneurial potential. Especially critical is the need for creativity in leveraging different types of resources in ways that support poor entrepreneurs. For instance, the Boston University Business Accelerator offers programs where college students offer training in financial and economic literacy to low-income individuals. The University of Florida leverages the small business community to augment its training of low-income entrepreneurs with mentors and in-kind services, while giving students credit and experience as consultants as they work on registering businesses, creating marketing materials, helping entrepreneurs institute better pricing approaches and get better vendor terms, and otherwise develop their ventures, and collaborating with city government and local financial institutions to offer a microcredit program.

TOWARD A MORE HOLISTIC APPROACH: THREE GENERAL LEVELS OF FOCUS

Although a number of high-impact programs for fostering entrepreneurial activity by the poor can be found in developed economies, what is lacking is any sort of holistic approach to elevating entrepreneurship as a path out of poverty. The beginning point is to recognize the need for integration of efforts at different levels of development. For simplicity (given the many stakeholders involved and the complexities that can lie behind the design, approval, funding, and execution of some program elements), we propose three core developmental levels. Policies and programs at each level will reflect different goals and objectives.

As illustrated in Figure 13.1, the most basic level is termed Basic Survival, and here the priority is the infrastructure shortcomings, discussed

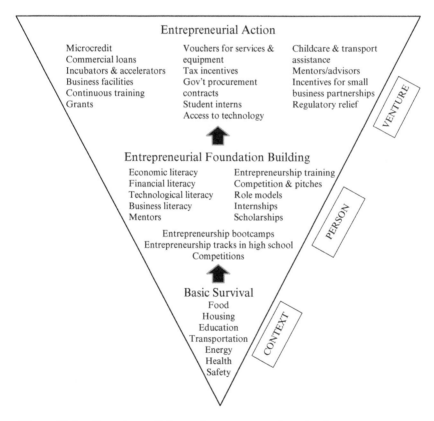

Figure 13.1   Focusing policies and programs at three levels

in Chapter 8, to ensure the basic physical, cognitive, and emotional well-being of the individual. Coordinated programs must address fundamental housing, energy, education, safety, health, nutrition, and transportation needs. From an entrepreneurial perspective, the primary concern at this level is with a sound education and good functional literacy. As we move to the second level, which is labeled Entrepreneurial Foundation Building, the emphasis must be on providing the individual with an understanding of entrepreneurship as an option and preparing him or her for the entrepreneurial journey. Now the concern becomes developing the other four literacies (financial, economic, business, and technological), providing entrepreneurship-related education, training and internships, enabling the poor to compete in business plan competitions and pitches, promoting entrepreneurial role models, and augmenting their networks with mentors and others from the entrepreneurial community. Finally, in the Entrepreneurial Action stage, policies should center on facilitating the launch of ventures by the poor, enabling them to stabilize, and helping them grow. Here, the focus is on the development of microcredit programs and grants, incentives for bank credit, the provision of space in incubators and accelerators and other buildings, awarding of procurement contracts to ventures of the poor, and vouchers to use for training and professional service providers, as well as child care and transportation, mentors, and tax incentives.

Each level in this framework is dependent upon the one below it. A poor person who has not resolved the problems of housing, transportation, energy, or nutrition, while struggling with functional literacy, will find it much more difficult to develop a strong entrepreneurial foundation. Without this foundation, either no venture will be launched, or it is much more likely to be a survival or marginal lifestyle venture that suffers from the commodity trap (see Chapter 11) with an inability to make much money (see Chapter 12). Yet, for many poor people, particularly adults who have launched or are about to launch a business, they are trying to address issues at all three levels simultaneously.

TOWARD A MORE HOLISTIC APPROACH: THE SPODER FRAMEWORK

When attempting to coordinate and integrate various policies and support programs, it is also necessary to consider specific steps in the entrepreneurial journey of a person in poverty. A useful tool in this regard is the SPODER framework introduced in Chapter 3 and elaborated upon throughout this book. Table 13.1 presents a summary of public sector and

Table 13.1   *Designing entrepreneurship support efforts using the SPODER framework*

	Public Sector Initiatives	Community-based Initiatives
(S) Supportive infrastructure	Housing allowances & energy assistance Improved schools, incentives to stay in school – priority on functional literacy Vouchers for transportation, child care Improve child & health care facilities Low-cost broadband & telecommunications Tax incentives for private investors to invest in low-income communities and CDEs Enhanced Earned Income Tax Credits for low-income entrepreneurs	Create bridges between the poor and actors of the entrepreneurial ecosystem Expand/refine entrepreneurial ecosystem to address low-income needs Low-cost space for ventures of the poor Banking and financial community that prioritizes investments in the poor Small business assistance centers targeting the disadvantaged
(P) Preparation of the entrepreneur	Prioritization of school curriculum and programming that develop functional, technological, financial, business and economic literacies Facilitate access to books, manuals, software, online databases, websites, hardware, machinery Entrepreneurship tracks in high schools Supplemental income assistance tied to progress in pursuing a venture Vouchers/scholarships for training	Local training bootcamps on entrepreneurship-related topics Small business internships for the poor Entrepreneurial advisory boards for schools Creation of resource compendiums of tools, resources and infrastructure components available to the poor Multi-stakeholder networks to support low-income entrepreneurs, including mentors and small business sponsors Business plan/pitch competitions for the poor
(O) Expanded opportunity horizon	Housing relocation opportunities Access to knowledge resources Broadband/Internet access	Access to incubators and accelerators Technology literacy programs Company internships Entrepreneurial mentor programs

Table 13.1   (continued)

	Public Sector Initiatives	Community-based Initiatives
	Vouchers to attend conferences, trade shows, fairs, workshops High school exchange programs Enhanced transportation options	Small business counselors and advisors Community events to connect the poor to local company founders
(D) Finding sources of differentiation	Easy access to industry and company databases Vouchers for assistance with branding, marketing, and intellectual property Support for small business development centers with priority on the poor	Specialized training programs Access to mentorship, coaching, consultancy Support development of intellectual property, including fablabs and makerspaces Partnerships with local small businesses to enhance capabilities of ventures of the poor
(E) Well-designed economic model	Tax incentives tied to start-up activity Tax incentives to others for sharing facilities, equipment Government procurement contracts directed at ventures of the poor	Access to mentorship, coaching, consultancy Buying cooperatives Access to low-cost technologies to reduce costs Company procurement contracts Local financial literacy programs
(R) Leveraging community resources	Support for small business development centers with priority on the poor Vouchers to use local service providers Loan guarantees and microcredit grants Regulatory relief and simplification Fiscal incentives for investors and platforms to promote participation in peer-to-peer lending to poor entrepreneurs, Legislation making microcredit programs easier to create & administer Co-investment with private investors	Cooperative networks that encourage gifting, sharing, renting, selling, and other forms of collaboration – to include businesses, non-profits, churches, others University engagement with the poor Creative microcredit and other lending programs Entrepreneurial mentors and advisors Peer-to-peer lending networks and community-based self-financing groups Matchmaking angels and poor entrepreneurs

community-related policies and programs relevant to the six components of the SPODER framework.

Orchestrated policies, initiatives and actions begin with supportive infrastructure (S). Here, on the government side, the enabling of affordable housing, quality schools that produce highly literate graduates, and access to broadband must be combined with changes to local entrepreneurial ecosystems so that they embrace and can better address the needs of low-income entrepreneurs, and a financial community that prioritizes investments in the poor.

Preparation of low-income entrepreneurs (P) requires much more emphasis in public and charter schools on the five literacies discussed in Chapter 6, the creation of entrepreneurship tracks within high school curricula, and vouchers to support training and development of adults. Supplemental income assistance can be tied to meeting benchmarks in terms of preparation and then launch of a venture. These are efforts on the public sector side. The corollary community-based efforts can include local entrepreneurship bootcamps, internships in small businesses, local competitions for the ventures of the poor, mentors and small business sponsors, and local clearinghouses of tools and resources to help poor entrepreneurs.

Policy efforts should also enable the low-income individuals to discover new contexts, get out of the neighborhood, explore other worlds, or, as we define in Chapter 5, enlarge their opportunity horizons (O). Here, policy priorities should include housing relocation opportunities, high school exchange programs, enhanced transportation options, vouchers for attendance at conferences, trade shows, fairs and workshops, and Internet access, among others. From the community side, enabling the poor to access incubators, participate in technology literacy courses, pursue company internships, use mentors, counselors and advisors, and attend events that connect the poor to local company founders can all contribute to helping the poor recognize opportunities they otherwise might be unaware of.

Escaping the commodity trap (see Chapter 11) means developing businesses with a unique value proposition and a meaningful source of differentiation (D) in the marketplace. Government bodies can help here by providing vouchers for use in acquiring the services of professional service providers, including marketing and branding companies, as well as law firms and others who can assist with intellectual property. They can enable the poor to gain easier access to industry and company databases. Small business development centers can also assist here. These efforts can then be coupled with community support for specialized training courses, access to mentoring, coaching and consultants, and partnerships with local small businesses to enhance the capabilities of the ventures of the poor.

Profit or economic models (E) that feature low volumes and margins, and limited revenue capture can be improved by government policies that highlight creative tax incentives like the Earned Income Tax Credit tied to venture launch, and incentives to other organizations who share facilities, equipment or personnel with low-income entrepreneurs. Another key is preferential government procurement efforts targeting poor entrepreneurs. The community can help again with mentoring, coaching and consultancies, but also with financial literacy training, buying cooperatives that bring down costs of materials and goods, and access to low-cost technologies that also reduce costs.

Finally, as ventures get launched and attempt to grow, there is an ongoing need for assistance in leveraging resources (R) from the community (see also Chapter 10). The public sector can help with loan guarantee programs and funding for microcredit schemes, relief from onerous regulatory requirements, tax incentives for investors, legislation making microcredit and other non-traditional forms of financing easier to establish and administer, support for small business development centers, and vouchers for use with local service providers. From the community must come cooperative networks that encourage gifting, sharing, renting, selling, and other forms of collaboration, creative microcredit programs and other lending programs, and novel types of university/college engagement efforts with the poor, among many other possibilities.

CONCLUSION

Stevenson (2000, p. 1) notes that entrepreneurship flourishes in communities where (1) resources are mobile; (2) successful members of a community reinvest excess capital in the projects of other community members; (3) success of other community members is celebrated rather than derided; and (4) change is seen as positive rather than negative. By and large, these conditions do not describe low-income neighborhoods and communities. Even when they do describe the larger metropolitan area or region, the poor and their neighborhoods are generally excluded.

But this state of affairs need not continue. A more holistic approach to the components of entrepreneurial development can produce a ladder that individuals in low-income conditions can use to climb out of poverty. Such an approach to venture creation by the poor is built around inclusion rather than marginalization, around a developmental process over time rather than momentary interventions, and around collaboration among multiple stakeholders rather than a complex array of unconnected elements and participants that do not always understand the needs of the poor. In the end, it comes down to the poor themselves, and their ability to imagine, persevere, adapt, leverage, and sustain. But we can move towards leveling the playing field by creatively pursuing the kinds of public and community-based initiatives described herein – and in a cohesive manner. The alternative is a society that fails to capitalize on the incredible entrepreneurial potential of millions of its citizens, in the process reinforcing the status quo in terms of lack of opportunity, compromised quality of life, and the continued expenditure of billions of dollars each year on poverty programs.

REFERENCES

Australian Council of Social Service (2016), *Poverty in Australia*, Social Policy Research Centre, accessed June 15, 2018 at http://www.acoss.org.au/wp-content/uploads/2016/10/Poverty-in-Australia-2016.pdf.

Baradaran, M. (2016), *How the Other Half Banks: Exclusion, Exploitation, and the Threat to Democracy*, Cambridge, MA: Harvard University Press.

Barr, M.S. (2008), "Policies to expand minority entrepreneurship: Closing comment," in G. Yago, J.R. Barth and B. Zeidman (eds), *Entrepreneurship in Emerging Domestic Markets: Barriers and Innovation*, The Milken Institute Series on Financial Innovation and Economic Growth, Vol. 7, New York: Springer, pp. 141–50.

Beam, D.R. and T.J. Conlan (2002), "Grants," in L. Salamon (ed.), *The Tools of Government: A Guide to the New Governance*, New York: Oxford University Press.

Ben-Shalom, Y., R.A. Moffitt and J.K. Scholz (2011), "An assessment of the effectiveness of anti-poverty programs in the United States," *NBER Working Paper No. 17042*.

Caliendo, M. and S. Künn (2011), "Start-up subsidies for the unemployed: Long-term evidence and effect heterogeneity," *Journal of Public Economics*, **95**(3–4), 311–31.

Caputo, R. (2010), "Prevalence and patterns of Earned Income Tax Credit use among eligible tax-filing families: A panel study, 1999–2005," *Families in Society: The Journal of Contemporary Social Services*, **91**(1), 8–15.

Colin, F. (2005), "Public service vouchers," *International Review of Administrative Sciences*, **71**(1), 19–34.

Congressional Budget Office (2016), *The Distribution of Household Income and Federal Taxes, 2013*, Washington, DC: Congressional Budget Office.

Coven, M. (2005), *An Introduction to TANF*, Washington, DC: Center on Budget and Policy Priorities.

European Commission (2010), *Communication from the Commission to the European Parliament, the Council, the European Economic and Social Committee and the Committee of the Regions. The European Platform against Poverty and Social Exclusion: A European Framework for Social and Territorial Cohesion*, accessed June 15, 2018 at http://eur-lex.europa.eu/legal-content/EN/TXT/?uri=celex:52010DC0758.

Eurostat Newsrelease (2017), "Downward trend in the share of persons at risk of poverty or social exclusion in the EU," October 16, accessed June 15, 2018 at http://ec.europa.eu/eurostat/documents/2995521/8314163/3-16102017-BP-EN.pd f/d31fadc6-a284-47f3-ae1c-8212a581b0c1.

Lammam, C. and H. MacIntyre (2016), *An Introduction to the State of Poverty in Canada*, Vancouver: Fraser Institute.

Lang, K. (2011), *Poverty and Discrimination*, Princeton, NJ: Princeton University Press.

NMTC (2017), "Community revitalization by rewarding private investment," *NMTC Program Fact Sheet*, US Department of the Treasury, CDFI Fund, accessed June 15, 2018 at https://www.cdfifund.gov/programs-training/ Programs/new-markets-tax-credit/Pages/default.aspx.

OECD/European Union (2014), *Policy Brief on Access to Business Start-Up Finance for Inclusive Entrepreneurship: Entrepreneurial Activities in Europe*, Luxembourg: Publications Office of the European Union.

Steuerle, C.E. and E.C. Twombly (2002), "Vouchers," in L. Salamon (ed.), *The Tools of Government: A Guide to the New Governance*, New York: Oxford University Press, pp. 445–65.

Stevenson, H. (2000), "Why entrepreneurship has won," in *Proceedings, Annual Meetings, United States Association for Small Business & Entrepreneurship*, pp. 1–8.

The Economist (2015), "Struggling: Japan's working poor," April 4, accessed June 15, 2018 at https://www.economist.com/news/asia/21647676-poverty-worsens-more-japanese-work-non-permanent-contracts-struggling.

Varghese, S.A. (2016), "Poverty in the United States: A review of relevant programs," *Poverty & Public Policy*, **8**, 228–47.

Index

Printed and bound by CPI Group (UK) Ltd, Croydon, CR0 4YY

23/04/2025

14660965-0002